Carnegie Treasures Cookbook

Mary Cassatt
(American, 1845-1926)
Young Women Picking Fruit, 1891
Oil on canvas
51⅜ × 35¾ in.
(130.5 × 90.8 cm.)
Patrons Art Fund, 1922

Carnegie Treasures Cookbook

Women's Committee, Museum of Art
Carnegie Institute
Pittsburgh, Pennsylvania

Foreword by
James Beard

Introduction by
James M. Walton and John R. Lane

Atheneum   New York   1984

Edited by
Edith H. Fisher

Designed by
Frank Garrity
Frank Garrity Graphic Design

Written by
The Cookbook Committee

Food and settings photographed by
Tom Barr

Photographic styling and design by
George A. Griffith and
Thomas J. O'Brien

Food Consultant
Dana Kline

First published 1984
First printing, June 1984
Second printing, August 1984
Third printing, December 1984

Library of Congress Cataloging in Publication Data
Main entry under title:
The Carnegie treasures cookbook.
   1. Cookery. 2. Menus. I. Carnegie Institute.
Museum of Art. Women's Committee.
TX715.M96 1984 641.5 83-15037
ISBN 0-689-11428-1

Printed in Japan

Andy Warhol
(American, b. 1928)
Andrew Carnegie, 1981
Acrylic and silkscreen on canvas

98 × 79 in. (248.9 × 200.7 cm.)
Richard M. Scaife American
Paintings Fund, 1981

Contents

The Cookbook Committee
is indebted to all the cooks
who have inspired the
recipes in this book.

Abbreviations for metric
measurements used in this
book are in accordance
with current National
Bureau of Standards
guidelines:
mL — milliliter
L   — liter
kg — kilogram
g   — gram

Milton Avery
(American, 1885-1965)
Dunes and Sea I, 1958
Oil on canvas
54 × 72 in. (137.2 × 182.9 cm.)

Museum Purchase: Gift of
Kaufmann's and the Women's
Committee of the Museum of
Art, Edith H. Fisher Fund,
Fellows of the Museum of Art
Fund, James A. Fisher, The
Henry L. Hillman Fund,

Mr. and Mrs. Leon D. Black,
Mr. and Mrs. Robert H. Falk,
Mrs. Grace Borgenicht Brandt,
The Jeanette and Samuel Lubell
Foundation, and The Morton
Foundation, 1983

Foreword

Our thinking about what used to be called the arts has been revolutionized to such an extent in the past few decades that it is hard to remember that we once meant "the fine arts"—painting, sculpture, music. Perhaps it was Gilbert Seldes who started the new era when he wrote *The Seven Lively Arts* back in the 1930s. Heaven knows, since then the arts have all become livelier, more a part of our working lives than ever before. Paintings sell at premium prices. Sculpture has become an important part of architecture. Jazz is honored as much as the classics. Design is visible in practically everything, from buildings to kitchen utensils.

Not the least commendable of these developments has been the acceptance, finally, of gastronomy into the sacred precincts of the arts. It has taken centuries of eating, experimenting, and refining—for the pleasure of the eye as well as of the palate—to accomplish this. The Chinese and Japanese, particularly, with their genius for design and arrangement, have become a major influence on cuisines of the West. The French, the Italians, the Scandinavians, the British, and the Americans are all sold on the idea that food should be beautifully arranged, not merely served up, and that even everyday cooking can be creative.

Several years ago Janet Wurtzberger, who was on the boards of the Walters Art Gallery and the Baltimore Museum of Art, became interested in doing a book for the benefit of the Walters. It would combine the arts of painting, decorating, eating, and drinking in a way that had not been done before in other museum books of the kind. Since I was a close associate of Mrs. Wurtzberger and eventually contributed an introduction to the book, I was able to participate in the food testing and observe the choosing of artifacts that were to be reproduced. It was a meticulously executed project, and the resulting book, which proved to be the final task of Mrs. Wurtzberger's life, gave her the satisfaction of knowing she had achieved something distinguished and unique. It was the first truly great museum cookbook, and I still treasure it.

This was followed by a flow of other museum cookbooks, very elaborate ones in a few cases, such as that produced by the women of the San Francisco Museum of Modern Art about two years ago, a splendid volume, more intimate than its predecessors, presenting contemporary artists who were also cooks. As a watcher of museum cookbooks, therefore, I cheered no end when I was given the galleys of the cookbook of Carnegie Institute's Museum of Art, because along with glorifying the museum itself, it does service to the artists and designers included in it, and it heaps encomiums on the donors of recipes. It is a brilliantly planned, highly diverting book.

I know the museum well, because I was a student at nearby Carnegie Tech for a year of my life. It was a refuge for me. I found a certain warmth and sense of peace whenever I went there to see an exhibit or simply to get away from the hurly-burly, and it has remained a tender memory for me. I have gone back from time to time since that period, and I always feel that the museum is very much alive and part of the present while it continues to be a guardian of the past. Its embrace of some of the more lively arts—music, dance, drama, the creativity of the city of Pittsburgh itself—has added to its stature.

I do not know who chose the recipes for this volume, but I can say that they had an almost uncanny sense of what food fitted what picture. This was only one of the things that intrigued me as I considered the various components of the book—food against painting against text against design. Naturally I have not tried every recipe in the book, but most of them appear to have that precious quality of being the expression of someone's creativity, someone's pattern of living. This is not merely a showpiece.

If you have a palate and imagination, a reading of the recipes will send you to the range, saying to yourself, "Now that sounds rather wonderful." And after you have carefully prepared one of the dishes and handsomely arranged it for serving, remember: It's not just something to eat. It's art.

James Beard

Introduction

Taste. It is a word that finds ready associations not only with eating but also with looking at art with discrimination. Frequently the two activities are wedded. Artists have historically shown an uncommon sensitivity to good food and appealing settings both in the depiction of these subjects in paintings and sculpture and in the making of decorative arts objects and furniture to enrich the visual experience of table service. What a happy occasion it is to have this traditional conjunction of fine food and fine art so conspicuously reaffirmed by the Women's Committee's *Carnegie Treasures Cookbook*. This book features masterworks from the museum's collection joined with the culinary creations and decorative inventions of Pittsburgh and western Pennsylvania's accomplished cooks and hosts and their friends in this country and abroad.

Since its founding in 1957 the Women's Committee has assumed responsibility for the Museum of Art's entertaining and in so doing has established an international reputation for the warmth of the hospitality and the festiveness and beauty of the receptions and dinners arranged on the museum's behalf. This, however, has been but one of the important roles of the Women's Committee since its members have also committed themselves with the greatest dedication to the prospect of enriching the museum's collection through the purchase of highly significant works of art. This book is one in a history of notable projects undertaken to benefit museum activities, particularly art acquisitions. The number of works in the collection purchased through the Women's Committee Acquisition Fund (a selection of which are to be found in this book) is a testament to the success of these projects and to the generosity of the Women's Committee.

A grant from the H. J. Heinz Company Foundation contributed very substantially to the costs of production of the cookbook. The support of this Pittsburgh corporation, famous around the world for its high-quality food products, has provided special encouragement, as has the enthusiasm of Anthony J. F. O'Reilly, Heinz's president and chief executive officer.

No publication as handsome and ambitious as this book appears without an extraordinary amount of thought and effort. Edith H. Fisher, with the exceptional dedication of the Cookbook Committee and an abundance of support from numerous other volunteers, guided this project from beginning to end with vision and determination.

James M. Walton
President
Carnegie Institute

John R. Lane
Director
Museum of Art,
Carnegie Institute

Albert F. King   16 × 22 in. (40.6 × 59.0 cm.)
(American, 1854-1945)   R. K. Mellon Family
Late Night Snack, c. 1900   Foundation Fund, 1983
Oil on canvas

Menus

Levi Wells Prentice
(American, 1851-1935)
Still Life with Strawberries,
c. 1890
Oil on canvas

16⅛ × 20 in. (40.9 × 50.8 cm.)
Mary Oliver Robinson Fund,
Bequest to the Women's
Committee, Museum of Art;
and Women's Committee
Acquisition Fund, 1981

Levi Wells Prentice, 1851–1935
Still Life with Strawberries, circa 1890

Every spring New York's Adirondack region trades one blanket of white for another. Between receding snows and the first warm breezes, tiny blossoms of *Fragaria virginiana*, fragrant wild strawberries, cover the hills and fill the air with their heady sweetness. These delicate woodland berries have delighted all who ever lived there, including Levi Prentice, a still life painter, born in Lewis County, New York.

In the latter half of the nineteenth century, the still life became a popular American subject. With photographic precision Prentice devoted himself almost exclusively to portraying berries and other fruit, with attention to bruises and blemishes as well as to nature's perfection.

His settings are rustic and unpretentious. The smooth, rounded forms of his fruit contrast with rough woven baskets and wooden tabletops. In a setting more elegant than most, Prentice's *Still Life with Strawberries* crisply defines this "wonder of all fruits."

Doubtless God could have made a better berry, but doubtless God never did.
William Butler, circa 1600
Physician

Aurora

Menu

Romaine Soufflé

Marinated Rock Cornish Game Hens

Watercress and Belgian Endive

Lemon Popovers

Fresh Strawberries

Mint Meringue Mushrooms and Chocolate Truffles

Serves Four

Wine

French Beaujolais or

Pink Champagne or

California Blanc de Noirs Sparkling Wine

Although at first this menu may appear more appropriate for later in the day, it is all the more satisfying as a breakfast for its bold, nontraditional content. To accommodate the early hour, Mint Meringue Mushrooms and Chocolate Truffles can be made and frozen well in advance. The marinade may be mixed and the game hens split the night before to simplify the morning's tasks.

The focus of the meal is its edible centerpiece, a luscious cascade of unhulled berries which exaggerates the aroma of the fruit and heightens the excitement of the season they herald. Wrapping a fern leaf or ivy strand around each napkin brings a touch of spring to each place.

Romaine Soufflé

About ½ cup (120 mL/62 g) Parmesan cheese

1 medium head romaine lettuce, chopped into coarse pieces

4 tablespoons (60 mL/57 g) butter

3 scallions, chopped

3 tablespoons (45 mL/25 g) all-purpose flour

1 cup (240 mL) light cream

4 eggs, separated

1 cup (240 mL/114 g) shredded Cheddar cheese

⅓ teaspoon (1.7 mL) Worcestershire sauce

Salt to taste

4 drops of Tabasco sauce

Preheat oven to 400°F (205°C).

Grease a 1½-quart (1.44 L) soufflé dish. Sprinkle it with grated Parmesan cheese, reserving some for topping. Turn the dish to coat the bottom and sides, shake out the excess. With tape or string, attach a foil collar to the dish. The collar should reach about 3 inches (8 cm) above the rim.

In a heavy saucepan, cook the lettuce in a little water until wilted. Drain well, and chop fine.

In a skillet, melt 1 tablespoon (15 mL/14 g) of the butter. Add the scallions, and cook until soft. Add the lettuce, and cook, stirring, until the moisture evaporates.

In a saucepan, melt the remaining butter over medium heat. Stir in the flour. Cook for 3 minutes, stirring occasionally. Add the cream slowly. Cook until thickened, stirring occasionally. Beat in the yolks, one at a time. Stir in the Cheddar cheese, and cook until smooth.

Add the lettuce mixture, Worcestershire, salt, and Tabasco. Mix together. Remove from the heat.

Beat the egg whites until stiff. Fold them into the egg yolk-Cheddar mixture. Pour into the soufflé dish. Sprinkle with the reserved grated Parmesan cheese.

Place in the oven. Immediately reduce the heat to 375°F (190°C). Bake for 25 to 30 minutes, or until puffed and browned. Serve at once.

Serves 4 to 6.

Singer Euwer

Marinated Rock Cornish Game Hens

Marinade:
¼ pound (115 g) unsalted butter

¼ cup (60 mL) lemon juice

¼ teaspoon (1.3 mL/1.5 g) salt (optional)

¼ teaspoon (1.3 mL/0.7 g) freshly ground pepper

¼ teaspoon (1.3 mL/0.2 g) oregano

¼ cup (60 mL) white wine vinegar

¼ cup (60 mL) vegetable oil

2 Rock Cornish game hens, split

The hens may be roasted or grilled. If they are roasted, preheat oven to 325°F (165°C).

Combine and heat all the marinade ingredients until the butter is melted. Pour the marinade over the hens. Marinate for 2 to 4 hours, turning once.

To roast:
Place the hens, uncovered, in a shallow baking pan. Baste frequently with the marinade. Turn the hens once. Roast for 1 to 1¼ hours, depending upon the size of the hens.

To grill:
Place hens, skin side up, on the grill. Baste frequently. Turn several times. Grill for approximately 45 minutes, depending upon the size of the hens.

Note:
Hens may also be served, cut side up, with peas in the cavity.

Serves 4.

Sybil P. Veeder

Watercress and Belgian Endive

Walnut Vinaigrette:
⅓ cup (80 mL/39 g) walnuts

2 tablespoons (30 mL) red wine vinegar

½ teaspoon (2.5 mL/ 2.8 g) Dijon mustard

½ teaspoon (2.5 mL/3 g) salt

⅓ cup (80 mL) olive oil

¼ teaspoon (1.3 mL/ 0.7 g) freshly ground pepper

Salad:
2 to 3 bunches watercress

2 Belgian endives

Vinaigrette:
Chop the walnuts into coarse pieces, by hand—do not use food processor. Combine all the ingredients and blend well.

Salad:
Toss the watercress and endives with enough walnut vinaigrette to coat lightly. Divide the endive and watercress among 4 salad plates. Top each with remaining vinaigrette.

Serves 4.

The Cookbook Committee

Lemon Popovers

1 cup (240 mL/120 g) sifted all-purpose flour

½ teaspoon (2.5 mL/3 g) salt

1 tablespoon (15 mL/14 g) sugar

1 teaspoon (5 mL) lemon extract

1 cup (240 mL) milk

2 eggs

Preheat oven to 425°F (220° C). Use a popover pan with 4-ounce (120 mL) cups; grease the cups well.

With a rotary beater, beat all the ingredients together just until smooth (overbeating will reduce volume). Fill the cups three-fourths full. Bake for 40 to 45 minutes, or until golden brown (popovers will collapse if they are not baked long enough).

Makes 6.

Edith H. Fisher

Fresh Strawberries

2 quarts (1.92 L/920 g) strawberries with hulls rinsed thoroughly in cold water and dried on paper towels

Arrange a cascade of strawberries on a serving platter, and garnish with mint meringue mushrooms (below) and chocolate truffles (below). These are to be picked up with the fingers.

Serves 4.

The Cookbook Committee

Mint Meringue Mushrooms

4 egg whites, at room temperature (reserve eggshells)

⅛ teaspoon (0.6 mL/0.8 g) salt

⅛ teaspoon (0.6 mL/0.3 g) cream of tartar

1 cup (240 mL/225 g) sugar

⅜ teaspoon (1.9 mL) mint, lemon, or almond extract, **or** ¾ teaspoon (3.8 mL) vanilla extract

1 teaspoon (5 mL/2.4 g) cocoa

4 ounces (115 g) semisweet chocolate chips

2 tablespoons (30 mL) heavy cream

Preheat oven to 225°F (105°C). Cover 3 baking sheets with parchment or wax paper.

In a large bowl, beat the egg whites, salt, and cream of tartar. When the egg whites begin to stiffen, add the sugar slowly, and continue to beat until very stiff and shiny. Add the mint or other flavoring.

Because meringue becomes limp with humidity, prepare mushrooms in a dry place. To form mushrooms, use a pastry bag with a large, plain round opening on the nozzle. Make the stems and caps while the meringue is very stiff. Make the stems first. These should measure about 1¾ inches by ¾ inches (4.4 cm by 1.9 cm). The caps should measure about 1¾ inches (4.4 cm) in diameter. When squeezed out, caps and stems will be pointed like chocolate chips. To eliminate the point, dip your finger in the egg white still clinging to the shells and gently smooth the meringue to the desired shape. Meringue mushrooms should resemble fresh mushrooms' natural shapes.

For variety, about 1 teaspoon (5 mL/2.4 g) cocoa may be shaken through a very fine strainer over the caps and stems before they are baked to give them the appearance of wild mushrooms.

Bake for about 1 hour, or until firm and dry. If they are not firm, leave the mushrooms in the oven 1 hour longer with the heat off. They should not change color.

In a saucepan, melt the chocolate with the cream. When the chocolate mixture is cool, use it to attach the caps to the flat ends of the stems.

Note:
Mushrooms should be stored in airtight containers.

Makes 3 to 4 dozen.

Margaret F. McKean

Chocolate Truffles

6 ounces (170 g) semi-sweet (preferably Swiss bittersweet) chocolate

4 tablespoons (60 mL/ 57 g) unsalted butter

2 egg yolks, slightly beaten

3 tablespoons (45 mL) bourbon or cognac, **or** ½ teaspoon (2.5 mL) mint, coffee, or other extract

½ cup (120 mL/57 g) unsweetened Dutch-process cocoa

3 tablespoons (45 mL/ 13 g) powdered instant, not freeze dried, coffee

Ground nuts, shaved chocolate, chopped coconut (optional)

Break the chocolate into small pieces. Place in the top of a double boiler over barely simmering water. Cover, and let stand until the chocolate is partially melted. Then stir until it is completely melted. Remove the top of the double boiler, keeping the water in the bottom heated. Add the butter to the chocolate, a few small pieces at a time, stirring until smooth after each addition. Stir the egg yolks into the chocolate, and place the mixture over the simmering water. Stir slowly for 2 to 3 minutes. Remove from the heat. Add the desired amount of liqueur by tablespoons (15 mL) or the extract by ½ teaspoons (2.5 mL), stirring after each addition. Taste to determine the desired amount of flavoring.

Set the pan in a large bowl of ice water. Stir constantly until the mixture forms a firm, nonsticky ball. Place slightly rounded teaspoonfuls on a sheet of wax paper. The truffles should now be ready to shape; if they are still sticky, let them dry for about 20 minutes, or until firm enough to handle.

Combine the cocoa and coffee on a sheet of wax paper. Coat your hands with the mixture, and gently roll each truffle into a round shape—they need not be perfect. Then roll the truffle in the cocoa mixture to coat. Dry the truffles, uncovered, overnight.

If you wish to roll the truffles in the optional nuts, chocolate, or coconut, allow the cocoa-covered truffles to dry for 1 to 2 hours, tap off the excess cocoa, and roll in the desired combination.

Truffles will keep for 2 or 3 days at room temperature, but they are best fresh. They may be refrigerated but should be served at room temperature.

Makes 2 dozen.

Nina Humphrey

Frans Hals (Dutch, 1580-1666)
Man with a Herring, 1616
Oil on panel transferred to canvas
34⅝ × 27⅜ in. (88 × 69.5 cm.)
Presented through the generosity
of Mrs. Alan M. Scaife, 1961

Frans Hals, 1580–1666
Man with a Herring, 1616

Frans Hals lived among the prosperous burghers of Haarlem, a member of the society he painted. The world belonged to these Dutch men in black who built it, ran its businesses, signed its contracts, and came to Hals to certify their triumphs. Their success was Hals's own.

Hals's best portraits, like *Man with a Herring*, catch a fleeting expression, usually the flicker of a smile or a laugh, and his paintings sparkle with the vitality of the captured instant.

Pieter Cornelisz van der Morsch, the painting's subject, was actually a minor town official. He was also a member of the Leiden Chamber of Rhetoricians, a troupe of would-be actors. Van der Morsch chose to have himself immortalized not as a town bailiff but as Piero, the wag he often played in the group's amateur presentations. His posing with a basket of fish does not reflect his occupation so much as his theatrical wit. In Dutch, "iemand een bokking geven (to give someone a smoked herring)" means to tease him with a pointed and clever remark.

*. . . a trout especially, if he
is not eaten within four or
five hours after he is taken,
is worth nothing.*
Izaak Walton
Author and fisherman

Forel

Menu

Trout Meunière

Parsleyed Potato Cake

Mushroom-Stuffed Tomatoes

Orange Marmalade Soufflé

Serves Six

Wine

German Riesling Spätlese or

California Riesling

The cook's demand for absolutely fresh fish is a long-standing one. Amelia Simmons's 1796 *American Cookery* counsels that "fresh gills, full bright eyes, moist fins and tails are denotements of their being freshly caught."

Serving the silver-skinned trout on a bed of white pine boughs invokes the outdoor intimacy of a cool woodland bower. A fresh and natural tablescape can be used to suggest the icy habitat of the trout. Mounds of crushed or chopped ice make a beautiful and practical base for clusters of early spring flowers: tulips, blooming cyclamens, daffodils, and paper-whites. And a scattering of smooth, rounded stones furthers the illusion of a swift-running brook.

Glory be to God
for dappled things. . .
For rose-moles all in stipple
upon trout that swim.
Gerard Manley Hopkins
Poet

Trout Meunière

9 tablespoons (135 mL/30 g) chopped parsley

1 tablespoon (15 mL) Worcestershire sauce

Salt and pepper to taste

6 trout, cleaned, heads removed

½ cup (120 mL/66 g) all-purpose flour

12 tablespoons (180 mL/ 170 g) Clarified Butter (see below)

1 tablespoon (15 mL) lemon juice

12 slices lemon, peeled

Parsley sprigs for garnish

6 wedges each of lemon and lime, for garnish

Combine 6 tablespoons (90 mL/20 g) of the chopped parsley, Worcestershire sauce, salt, and pepper, and spread inside the trout. Flour the trout lightly, and sauté them in 8 tablespoons (120 mL/115 g) of the butter for 10 to 15 minutes, or until done. Remove the trout to individual plates, and keep warm.

In the same pan, combine the remaining butter, the lemon juice, and chopped parsley. Heat through. Top each trout with 2 lemon slices and the hot butter sauce. Serve with a sprig of parsley and wedges of lemon and lime.

Clarified Butter:
Cut unsalted butter into small pieces. Melt slowly over low heat. Skim off the foam from the top, and strain the clear yellow liquid into a container. Discard the milky residue. Clarified butter will keep for several months in the refrigerator.

Serves 6.

Willi Daffinger
Rolling Rock Club

Parsleyed Potato Cake

2 pounds (905 g) potatoes

¼ pound (115 g) butter

1 large clove garlic, minced

½ cup (120 mL/27 g) chopped parsley

6 tablespoons (90 mL) vegetable oil

Chopped parsley, for garnish

Boil the potatoes until cooked but still firm in the center. Cool, peel, and grate them into coarse pieces.

In a heavy skillet, melt 4 tablespoons (60 mL/ 57 g) of the butter over low heat. Sauté the garlic, but do not let it brown. Add the garlic butter and ½ cup (120 mL/27 g) parsley to the potatoes. Mix gently. Heat 2 tablespoons (30 mL/28 g) butter and 3 tablespoons (45 mL) of oil in the heavy skillet. Add the potatoes, and pat them down gently. Cook over medium-high heat until the bottom is crisp

and brown. Invert the potatoes onto a plate. Add the remaining butter and the oil to the skillet. Slide the potatoes back in, and cook until the other side is crisp and browned.

Garnish the top with chopped parsley.

Serves 6.

Mrs. J. Todd Simonds

Mushroom-stuffed Tomatoes

6 medium tomatoes

1 pound (455 g) mushrooms

4 tablespoons (60 mL/ 57 g) unsalted butter

1 medium onion, chopped into fine pieces

½ teaspoon (2.5 mL/3 g) salt

4 tablespoons (60 mL/ 67 g) tomato paste

2 tablespoons (30 mL/7 g) chopped parsley

2 tablespoons (30 mL/ 14 g) chopped black olives

Buttered bread crumbs

Sliced black olives and parsley sprigs, for garnish

Preheat oven to 400°F (205°C). Grease a shallow baking dish.

Slice and remove the tops from the tomatoes. Remove the pulp, seeds, and juice.

Wash and dry the mushrooms. Chop them into fine pieces. In a skillet, melt the butter. Add the mushrooms and onion. Cook, uncovered, until the moisture has evaporated. Mix in the salt, tomato paste, chopped parsley, and chopped olives. Spoon the mixture into the tomatoes. Place the tomatoes in a baking dish. Top with the bread crumbs. Bake for 15 minutes. Garnish each tomato with 3 thin slices of black olive and a small sprig of parsley.

Note:
This also makes a fine accompaniment for steak.

Serves 6.

Edith H. Fisher

Orange Marmalade Soufflé

Soufflé:
3 egg whites

¼ cup (60 mL/57 g) granulated sugar

1 teaspoon (5 mL) orange extract **or** 1 tablespoon (15 mL) Cointreau or other orange liqueur

2 tablespoons (30 mL/ 41 g) orange marmalade

Sauce:
1 cup (240 mL) heavy cream

3 eggs yolks

¾ cup (180 mL/88 g) confectioners' sugar

½ teaspoon (2.5 mL) vanilla

A dash of salt

Candied violets **or** fresh orange peels, for garnish

Soufflé:
Beat the egg whites until stiff but not dry. In the top of a double boiler, combine the egg whites with the granulated sugar, orange extract or Cointreau, and marmalade. Cook the mixture, uncovered, over simmering water for 1 hour.

Sauce:
Whip the cream. With a fork, beat the egg yolks lightly. Combine them with the confectioners' sugar, vanilla, salt, and whipped cream. Refrigerate until ready to serve.

To serve:
Scoop a spoonful of the soufflé onto a dessert plate. Spoon the sauce on top, or, for variation, sauce may be put on the plate and topped with the soufflé. Garnish with the violets or orange peels. Serve immediately.

Serves 6.

Sibby McCrady

Hilaire-Germain-Edgar Degas
(French, 1834-1917)
Chevaux de courses, 1885
Pastel on paper

15¼ × 34¾ in. (38.7 × 88.3 cm.)
Acquired through the generosity
of the Sarah Mellon Scaife
family, 1968

Edgar Degas, 1834–1917
Chevaux de courses, 1885

Chevaux de courses is more than a moment caught in time. It is
a meticulous study of motion. Sir Kenneth Clark called Edgar
Degas the greatest draftsman since the Renaissance. Though Degas
was a master of classical linear style, we are always struck by the
immediacy of his paintings of working girls, women bathing, ballet
dancers, and racehorses.

From the time he visited a Normandy breeding farm in 1861, Edgar
Degas was fascinated with the horse as subject. He followed with
great interest the early locomotion photographs of Eadweard
Muybridge, who demonstrated that, at a gallop, a horse is actually
completely off the ground for part of its stride. Horses figured
prominently in Degas's early paintings, a theme to which he
returned again and again.

This pastel reflects another of the artist's fascinations, Japanese
prints, in which subject matter is frequently arranged diagonally.
Chevaux de courses is read from left to right, along a line of
intensifying action. Although the picture conveys the feeling of
spontaneous movement, it is the result of a deliberate selection
of detail.

*No art was ever less
spontaneous than mine.
What I do is the result of
reflection and study of the
great masters; of inspiration,
spontaneity, temperament I
know nothing.*
Edgar Degas

A Deux

Menu

Oysters and Artichokes

Chèvre with Assorted Fruits

French Bread

Nectarine Tarts

Serves Two

Wine

French Premier Cru Chablis (first course)

Italian Asti Spumante (main course and dessert)

A morning spent in quiet company is a luxury to be savored. This leisurely breakfast for two is elegant and easy to manage.

Chèvre's slightly salty taste provides the right counterpoint to fresh figs, seedless grapes, and mild melons. In addition to familiar Montrachet, with its coating of white or black ash, there are other goat cheeses worth sampling: Cendre Rouergue, Chabis, Cornilly, and Boucheron.

Oysters and Artichokes

1⅓ cups (320 mL/335 g) oysters with liquor

½ cup (120 mL) half-and-half

2 artichokes, boiled or steamed

2⅔ tablespoons (40 mL/38 g) unsalted butter

2 tablespoons (30 mL/ 17 g) all-purpose flour

⅔ cup (160 mL/77 g) minced onion

1 tablespoon (15 mL/8 g) minced garlic

½ teaspoon (2.5 mL/0.7 g) thyme

⅓ teaspoon (1.7 mL/2 g) salt

Pepper to taste

⅓ teaspoon (1.7 mL) lemon juice

1⅓ tablespoons (20 mL/ 4 g) minced parsley

Buttered bread crumbs

Lemon slices

Drain the oysters. Reserve ⅓ cup (80 mL) of the oyster liquor. Soak the oysters in the half-and-half for 30 minutes. Drain, and add this liquid to the reserved oyster liquor. Set aside both oysters and liquid.

Grease individual ramekins. Remove the artichoke leaves, and scrape the underlying meat; reserve the scrapings. Save 16 unscraped leaves for garnish. Remove the choke, and discard. Quarter the artichoke hearts and bottoms, and place in the ramekins.

Combine the butter and flour over low heat. Add the onion and garlic. Cook until tender. Add the thyme, salt, pepper, lemon juice, and reserved artichoke leaf scrapings.

Heat for 1 minute, stirring. Gradually add the oyster liquor mixture; the sauce should be thick. Reduce the heat, and simmer for 30 to 45 minutes.

Preheat oven to 350°F (175°C).

Add the oysters and half of the parsley. Simmer for an additional 5 to 10 minutes. Remove from the heat. Pour into the ramekins.

Sprinkle with the bread crumbs, and heat thoroughly in oven for 15 to 20 minutes. Garnish with lemon slices and the remaining minced parsley. Surround with the reserved artichoke leaves.

Note:
Recipe may be made a day ahead to the point at which it is to be heated in the oven.

The recipe may be tripled to serve 6.

Serves 2.

Mrs. Anthony J. A. Bryan

Nectarine Tarts

Apricot Glaze:
½ cup (120 mL/160 g) apricot preserves, strained

2 tablespoons (30 mL/28 g) granulated sugar

⅓ recipe Pâte Sucrée (Sweet Pastry Dough) (see page 270)

2 tablespoons (30 mL/ 14 g) crushed vanilla wafers

2 teaspoons (10 mL/6 g) slivered blanched almonds

1¼ cups (300 mL/160 g) peeled, pitted, and halved ripe nectarines

Confectioners' sugar (optional)

Apricot Glaze:
Combine the apricot preserves and granulated sugar. Cook over moderately high heat for 2 to 3 minutes, or until thick enough to coat a spoon. Reheat before using. Makes about ½ cup (120 mL).

Preheat oven to 400°F (205°C).

Place the dough in 2 4-inch (10 cm) tart pans with removable bottoms. Spread the wafer crumbs and almonds evenly over the dough. Arrange the nectarines, flat sides down, on top of the crumbs.

Bake for about 30 minutes, or until the nectarines are soft and the crust is baked through and browned around the edges. Remove from the oven. Brush the fruit with warm apricot glaze. Cool.

Confectioners' sugar may be sprinkled over the tarts before they are served, if desired.

Note:
Leftover apricot glaze will keep indefinitely in the refrigerator.

Serves 2.

John Cheek

27

Claude Monet
(French, 1840-1926)
Nymphéas (Water Lilies), 1920-21
Oil on canvas

78 × 235 in. (198 × 597 cm.)
Purchased through the
generosity of Mrs. Alan M.
Scaife, 1962

Claude Monet, 1840–1926
Nymphéas (Water Lilies), 1920–1921

Claude Monet's paintings of water lilies have been called the most aesthetically perfect paintings of the century.

From 1874, the year he exhibited *Impression, Sunrise*—the painting which led an outraged critic to give the Impressionist movement its name—Monet never stopped pursuing the perfect fusion of light and subject. As paints became available in ready-to-use tubes and painting was no longer bound to the studio, Monet moved outdoors, where he would chart the course of light on the landscape around him and the course of modern painting as well.

At Giverny, a small village fifty miles northwest of Paris, he cultivated the garden that was to dominate his work for forty years. Zinnias, fuchsias, hollyhocks, and Michaelmas daisies flourished under his painstaking attention. He employed several full-time gardeners, one of whom was assigned the sole task of picking off blooms which had passed their prime.

The water lilies, however, were Monet's greatest prize. He recorded their limpid beauty in every season on more than 200 canvases. Nineteen were commissioned for the great elliptical rooms of the Orangerie in Paris and were presented there in a 1927 celebration of the World War I armistice.

Light is the most important
person in the picture.
Claude Monet

Au Jardin

Menu

Scallops and Kiwi Mousseline

Sautéed Frogs' Legs

New Potatoes

Belgian Endive with Cognac Dressing

Gougère

Lemon Mousse in Cookie Baskets

Serves Six

Wine

Alsatian or

Gewürztraminer

This combination of tastes and flavors beautifully reflects the subtle harmonies of Monet's canvases. The luncheon is meant for a sun-dappled conservatory, a poolside terrace, or a garden through which guests may make their way as leisurely as the sun overhead.

Kiwis, now New Zealand's most popular export, were once known as Chinese gooseberries until the name was changed for political reasons. Brilliant sea green in color, they seem to marry the flavor of ripe bananas and raspberries.

Decidedly not seafood, frogs' legs are nevertheless catalogued among fish recipes in most cookbooks and satisfy the requirements of a meatless meal. Besides, they are satisfying without being heavy, an important consideration for a fanciful meal served this early in the day.

. . . not how to depict things, but how to manifest them as part of a field of energy.
Robert Hughes
Art critic

Scallops and Kiwi Mousseline

1 cup (240 mL) dry white wine

1 shallot, minced

1 sprig parsley

1½ pounds (680 g) uniformly sized sea scallops or lobster medallions

Mousseline Sauce:
  ¼ pound (115 g) butter, clarified (see page 20)

  ¼ cup (60 mL) reserved poaching liquid

  2 to 3 egg yolks

  ¼ teaspoon (1.3 mL/0.6 g) white pepper

  ½ teaspoon (2.5 mL) lemon juice

  2 to 3 tablespoons (30 to 45 mL) heavy cream

  Salt to taste

3 to 6 kiwi fruits

In a skillet, bring to a boil the wine, shallot, and parsley. Reduce the heat to a medium simmer. Add the scallops. Cover, and poach for 5 to 7 minutes, or until opaque and firm. Remove the scallops with a slotted spoon. Cool; then chill. Strain the poaching liquid; reduce to ¼ cup (60 mL); reserve for sauce.

Mousseline Sauce:
Melt the clarified butter. In a separate pan, bring to a boil the reserved poaching liquid.

In a blender or food processor, combine the egg yolks, pepper, and lemon juice. Process for 3 seconds. Add the butter in a thin stream, processing until incorporated. Add the poaching liquid in a thin stream, processing until incorporated. Add the cream. Process for an additional 1½ to 2 minutes. Add salt.

Assembly:
Slice the scallops into uniformly thick medallions. Peel the kiwis, and slice them in the same manner. On chilled plates, arrange alternate slices of scallops and kiwis, slightly overlapping. Use approximately 5 slices of each per serving. Pipe the sauce in the center and in a thin border around the edges. Serve at once.

Serves 6.

John Cheek

Sautéed Frogs' Legs

18 pairs (about 3 pounds) (1.36 kg) frogs' legs

1 tablespoon (15 mL/8 g) all-purpose flour

Salt and pepper to taste

6 tablespoons (90 mL/ 86 g) unsalted butter

6 tablespoons (90 mL) lemon juice

½ cup (120 mL/27 g) chopped parsley

1 tablespoon (15 mL/8 g) fine-chopped garlic

6 lemon wedges

Clean the frogs' legs, and soak them in cold water for 2 hours. Dry well, and dust with the flour. Season with salt and pepper. Melt 3 tablespoons (45 mL/43 g) of the butter, and sauté the legs until browned on both sides and cooked thoroughly.

Arrange the legs on a platter. Sprinkle with the lemon juice and some of the parsley. Add the remaining butter and the chopped garlic to the cooking pan. Scrape the pan while lightly browning the butter and garlic. Pour over the frogs' legs, garnish with the remaining parsley, and serve with the lemon wedges.

Note:
Frogs' legs should be served with new potatoes (below).

Serves 6.

The Cookbook Committee

New Potatoes

18 to 24 new potatoes

¼ pound (115 g) unsalted butter

¼ to ½ cup (60 mL/13 g to 120 mL/27 g) chopped parsley

Cook the potatoes in boiling salted water for 10 to 15 minutes, or until fork-tender. Drain, cut into halves and quarters, and toss in the butter and parsley.

Note:
Allow 3 or 4 potatoes per person, depending upon the size of the potatoes— the smaller the better. Serve with the sautéed frogs' legs.

Serves 6.

The Cookbook Committee

Belgian Endive with Cognac Dressing

Cognac Dressing:
2 tablespoons (30 mL) horseradish juice

Juice of ½ lemon

A few drops of Worcestershire sauce

½ cup (120 mL/135 g) ketchup

A drop of Tabasco sauce

1 cup (240 mL/230 g) mayonnaise

2 ounces (60 mL) cognac

Salt and white pepper to taste

4–5 Belgian endives (large leaves only)

Cognac Dressing:
Combine the horseradish juice, lemon juice, Worcestershire, ketchup, and Tabasco. Gradually add the mayonnaise, and mix thoroughly. Stir in the cognac, and season with salt and pepper. Makes about 2 cups (480 mL).

Separate the endive leaves. Cut the leaves into 4-inch (10 cm) lengths. In each of 6 individual ramekins, place 8 endive leaves on end around the ramekin, forming a crown. Then place 1 tablespoon (15 mL) of the cognac dressing in the center, so that the leaves may be dipped in it.

Note:
Remaining cognac dressing may be kept for several days in the refrigerator. It is also delicious with cold shrimp, lobster, crabmeat, or other seafood.

Serves 6.

Willi Daffinger
Rolling Rock Club

Gougère

5 ounces (140 g) Swiss cheese

1 cup (240 mL) milk

4 tablespoons (60 mL/ 57 g) unsalted butter

A dash of salt and pepper

⅞ cup (1 cup less 2 tablespoons) (210 mL/ 115 g) all-purpose flour

5 eggs

1 tablespoon (15 mL) heavy cream, whipped

Preheat oven to 325°F (165°C). Grease and flour a 10-inch (25 cm) pie plate.

Grate 4 ounces (115 g) of the Swiss cheese. Cut the remaining cheese into cubes.

In a saucepan, bring to a boil the milk, butter, salt, and pepper. Remove from the heat. Add the flour, and mix well. Return to the heat. Cook for 2 minutes, stirring. Remove from the heat. Add 4 of the eggs, one at a time, stirring vigorously after each addition. Add the grated cheese and whipped cream.

Turn into the pie plate. Press the cheese cubes into the dough. Lightly beat the remaining egg, and brush it on the top of the gougère. Bake the gougère on the lowest shelf of the oven for 50 minutes. Do not open the door for the first 30 minutes.

Serves 6.

Mrs. Brittan C. MacIsaac

Lemon Mousse in Cookie Baskets

Baskets:
4 tablespoons (60 mL/ 57 g) unsalted butter

¼ cup (60 mL/44 g) brown sugar

¼ cup (60 mL) light corn syrup

3½ tablespoons (53 mL/29 g) all-purpose flour

½ cup (120 mL/58 g) fine-chopped walnuts

1 teaspoon (5 mL) vanilla

Mousse:
Juice and rind of 3 large lemons

7 eggs, separated

1 cup (240 mL/225 g) granulated sugar

1 envelope (¼ ounce/ 7 g) unflavored gelatin

¼ cup (60 mL) water

Lemon slices, mint leaves, and strawberries, for garnish (optional)

Baskets:
Preheat oven to 325°F (165°C). Grease and flour 2 or 3 baking sheets.

In a saucepan, melt the butter over low heat. Add the brown sugar and syrup. Cook over high heat, stirring constantly, until the liquid boils. Remove from the heat. Stir in the flour and nuts. Add the vanilla.

For each basket, place 2 to 3 tablespoons (30 to 45 mL) of batter about 8 inches (20 cm) apart on the baking sheets. Bake for 10 to 12 minutes, or until golden brown. Place the baking sheets on wire racks. Let the cookies stand for about 1 minute, or until slightly firm.

Using a wide spatula, loosen the edges of each cookie; remove it; and turn and drape it over the bottom of an upturned glass that measures 2 inches (5 cm) across. Gently cup the cookie around the glass. Flatten the bottom, and flare out at the sides. Cool for about 2 minutes. Remove carefully.

Repeat the entire process with the remaining batter. Grease and flour the baking sheets each time.

Mousse:
In the top of a double boiler, combine and cook the lemon juice and rind, egg yolks, and ½ cup (120 mL/115 g) of the granulated sugar over low heat until thickened.

Dissolve the gelatin in the water, and add to the yolk mixture. Cook until slightly thickened.

Beat the egg whites until soft peaks form, gradually adding the remaining sugar. Fold into the yolk mixture. refrigerate until ready to serve.

Assembly:
Spoon the mousse into the cookie baskets. Decorate them with lemon slices, mint leaves, and strawberries, if desired.

Note:
Baskets may be stored in an airtight container for up to 1 week; for longer storage, freeze them.

Baskets may also be filled with fresh fruits.

Serves 6 to 8.

Sibby McCrady

Pierre Bonnard
(French, 1867-1947)
Nude in Bathtub, 1941-46
Oil on canvas

48 × 59½ in. (122 × 151 cm.)
Acquired through the generosity
of the Sarah Mellon Scaife
family, 1970

Pierre Bonnard, 1867–1947
Nude in Bathtub, 1941–1946

Pierre Bonnard found beauty in the commonplace. Filtered through his imagination, the ordinary details of French domestic life take on exquisite color and form.

Although he was known for his spontaneity, Bonnard was nevertheless painstakingly slow at his craft. He laid on color a daub at a time, taking months or years to finish a single work. Even when a painting was sold or exhibited, he often considered it unfinished, and with color tubes and brushes hidden in his coat, he would visit the exhibition and furtively add a touch of color here and there.

In 1894 Bonnard met Marthe de Meligny (the name preferred by Maria Boursin), who became his model and later his wife. At that time he abandoned a somber palette in favor of the bright, vibrant colors for which he is known. His figures became more solid, and his brushstrokes loose and energetic.

Although Bonnard prized the faithful rendering of subject, he seldom painted from life. Many of his best works were executed entirely from memory, which he exercised without constraints. *Nude in Bathtub* shows Marthe as a young woman, although she was well past seventy when the painting was begun.

A painting is a series of spots which are joined together and ultimately form the object, the unit over which the eye wanders without obstruction.
Pierre Bonnard

Mélange

Menu

Chilled Cream of Spinach Soup

Lobster Salad with Avocados, Mangoes, and Oranges

Roquefort Bread Sticks

Raspberries Among Roses

Serves Eight

Wine

French White Burgundy or

California Chardonnay

This luncheon was prepared from a palette as vital as Bonnard's own. It features a green soup, stripes of oranges, mangoes, and avocados alternating with white lobster meat, and a dessert of bright pink and raspberry reds.

The secret of the exceptionally refreshing summer soup is peppery watercress. Cooked ever so briefly with the spinach, a large shiny bunch of watercress adds a delicious, cooling flavor.

The main course salad could stand on the merits of its color alone, and the mélange of flavors is equally striking. It can be assembled as much as four hours in advance.

The dessert may be served in oversize red wineglasses lined with edible rose petals.

Chilled Cream of Spinach Soup

1 pound (455 g) spinach, washed

1 bunch scallions, minced

1 to 2 bunches watercress, washed

1 medium onion, minced

1 clove garlic, minced

1½ cups (360 mL/215 g) cooked and diced potatoes, **or** 1½ cups (360 mL/200 g) cooked and fine-puréed lima beans

A pinch of nutmeg

2½ tablespoon (38 mL/8 g) chopped parsley

½ tablespoon (8 mL/2 g) tarragon

3 cups (720 mL) veal **or** chicken stock

Juice of ½ lemon

Salt and pepper to taste

1 cup (240 mL) light cream

In a heavy skillet, place the spinach, scallions, watercress, onion, and garlic. Cook, covered, over high heat until the spinach is wilted but retains its form and color. Drain, cool, and purée or chop into coarse pieces. Mix in all the remaining ingredients except the cream. Stir in the cream. Chill for 4 to 8 hours before serving.

Serves 8.

John Cheek

Lobster Salad with Avocados, Mangoes, and Oranges

Salad:
4 12-ounce (340 g) frozen lobster tails, defrosted

3 oranges

4 avocados

4 mangoes

½ cup (120 mL) lemon juice

Mayonnaise:
4 eggs

1 teaspoon (5 mL/2.3 g) dry mustard

2 teaspoons (10 mL/12 g) salt

¼ cup (60 mL) lemon juice

4 teaspoons (20 mL) wine vinegar

4 cups (960 mL) olive oil

A pinch of thyme

3 scant tablespoons (45 mL) Grand Marnier

4 heads Boston lettuce, separated

Salad:
Skewer each lobster tail lengthwise, and poach in simmering water: allow 10 minutes per inch of thickness. Remove, and cool. Remove the shell, and slice the lobster into approximately ¼-inch (0.6 cm) pieces, straight through the tail, leaving the orange markings.

Peel the oranges, and cut into sections, removing all pith. Peel the avocados and mangoes, and cut them into wedges. Brush with the ½ cup (120 mL) lemon juice.

Mayonnaise:
Break the eggs into a food processor. Add the mustard and salt. Process slowly, adding the ¼ cup (60 mL) of lemon juice and the vinegar. Add the oil, by drops, until the sauce begins to thicken. Blend in the thyme to taste. Add the Grand Marnier.

Assembly:
Form lettuce beds on 8 plates. Stand 1 slice of lobster, red-orange side up, on edge; follow with 1 slice of avocado, 1 slice of orange, and 1 slice of mango. Continue the sequence around the plate until the lettuce bed is covered.

Serve the mayonnaise separately.

Serves 8.

Dana Kline

Roquefort Bread Sticks

2 envelopes (½ ounce/ 14 g) dry yeast

1 tablespoon (15 mL/14 g) sugar

1 tablespoon (15 mL/18 g) salt

⅓ cup (80 mL/28 g) powdered milk

2 cups (480 mL) hot water

5 to 6 cups (1.2 L/660 g to 1.44 L/790 g) all-purpose flour

Unsalted butter, for bowl, plastic wrap, and baking sheets

8 tablespoons (120 mL/ 115 g) unsalted butter, melted

½ cup (120 mL/60 g) Roquefort cheese, crumbled

In a large bowl, combine the yeast, sugar, salt, and powdered milk. Add the hot water all at once, and stir to dissolve the yeast. Slowly stir in 1 cup (240 mL/130 g) of the flour. Gradually add the remaining flour until the dough becomes too stiff to work with a spoon. Place the dough on a work surface, and knead in the remaining flour. Continue to knead for about 6 minutes, or until the dough forms a smooth, elastic ball.

Place the dough in a clean, well-buttered bowl, and roll the dough to coat it with butter. Cover it with buttered plastic wrap. Allow the dough to rise in a warm, draft-free place for about 2 hours.

Preheat oven to 350°F (175°C). Butter 4 baking sheets.

Punch the dough down once. On a lightly floured surface, roll half the dough at a time into a 12- by 10-inch (30 cm by 25 cm) rectangle. Brush the surface with some of the melted butter. Sprinkle generously with half the Roquefort cheese.

Cut the rectangle into strips about 1 by 12 inches (2.5 by 30 cm). Pick up each strip, and twist it. Place on a baking sheet, and press down the ends to prevent shrinking. When the sheet is full, brush the sticks again with melted butter, and sprinkle with the remaining cheese.

Bake for 10 minutes; reverse the baking sheets if necessary. Continue baking for 10 minutes longer, or until bread sticks are golden brown; be careful not to overbrown. When the bread sticks are done, turn the heat off, and leave them in the oven to dry (this helps preserve the sticks).

Note:
Roquefort cheese may be stored at room temperature in an airtight container; it will keep up to 1 month in dry weather.

To make Parmesan sticks, substitute ½ cup (120 mL/54 g) grated Parmesan cheese, crumbled, for the Roquefort.

Serves 8.

Dana Kline

Raspberries Among Roses

⅔ cup (3 to 5) (160 mL) egg whites

2 cups (480 mL/235 g) confectioners' sugar

2 teaspoons (10 mL) rose water*

1½ cups (360 mL) heavy cream

Rose petals

1 quart (960 mL/460 g) raspberries

1 tablespoon (15 mL) Framboise **or** other raspberry brandy (optional)

Place the egg whites and 1½ cups (360 mL) of the sugar in the top of a double boiler. Place over boiling water, making sure that the water does not touch the top of the double boiler. With a wire whisk, beat gently until the mixture is moderately hot, about 120°F (49°C).

*Rose water may be purchased at a pharmacy.

Pour into a mixing bowl. Beat at high speed for 3 to 8 minutes, or until the mixture more than doubles in volume. Reduce the speed. Continue beating until the mixture is cool to the touch. Fold in the rose water, and place the mixture in the freezer to cool.

Whip the cream until soft peaks form. Sift in the remaining sugar. Continue beating until stiff. Fold into the chilled egg white mixture. Return to the freezer for 4 to 8 hours, or until lightly frozen. Fold the mixture every 20 to 30 minutes.

To serve:
Line berry (or other) plates with rose petals; top with berries; sprinkle with liqueur, if desired, and cover with the frozen mixture. Or fold the berries into the mixture, reserving some for garnish; spoon into iced coupes or other stemmed dessert dishes; top with the reserved berries.

Note:
This dish may be altered dramatically by substituting peaches, violets, and violet water or blueberries, myrtle water, and apple blossoms. For subtle results, fragrant waters and liqueurs should be used sparingly.

Serves 8.

John Cheek

George Segal
(American, b. 1924)
The Tightrope Walker, 1969
Plaster

65 × 60 in., rope 204 in.
(165.1 × 152.4 cm.,
rope 518.2 cm.)
National Endowment for the
Arts Matching Grant and
Fellows of the Museum Art
Fund, 1970

George Segal, 1924–
The Tightrope Walker, 1969

Balanced fifteen feet above the entranceway to the Scaife Gallery,
George Segal's *The Tightrope Walker* has become an unofficial symbol
of the Museum of Art, Carnegie Institute. It is cast from life, a
process the artist started to explore as early as 1958.

To create one of his distinctive figures, Segal directs his model
through a series of movements and postures. He studies the resulting
tableaux for the ideal pose. Then Segal wraps his subject from head
to toe in bandages soaked in plaster. When hardened, the plaster
cast is carefully removed and reassembled.

The Tightrope Walker is a perennial delight to museum visitors. Its
frozen moment on the wire is a triumphant one, purposeful and
confident.

*The human body is an
infinite armature for saying
anything.*
George Segal

Carnival

Menu

Hot Olive Cheese Puffs

Herbed Shrimp

Carnival Delight

Teriyaki Grilled Chicken Wings

Pickled Mushrooms

Spicy Peanuts

Serves Twenty

Wine

California Jug Wine—

Red and White

Limited space is no impediment to a rollicking good time. Carefully proportioned for an apartment or a small home, this cocktail party features a circus motif, suggested by *The Tightrope Walker.* Bright helium-filled balloons tied with colorful streamers fill the room. The menu, too, was selected for its brilliant carnival colors.

The standout is Carnival Delight, a five-layer hors d'oeuvre "cake" of brown jalapeño beans, green avocado, red chili-speckled mayonnaise, and cream-colored Monterey Jack, topped with red and green tomatoes and scallions.

Everything is finger food, an eclectic selection of tasty tidbits easily passed. The plan is totally casual, permitting gracious entertaining on a modest scale.

Hot Olive Cheese Puffs

3 cups (720 mL/220 g) grated Swiss cheese

1½ cups (360 mL/200 g) all-purpose flour

¾ teaspoon (3.8 mL/4.5 g) salt

1½ teaspoons (8 mL/ 3.8 g) paprika

9 tablespoons (135 mL/ 130 g) unsalted butter

90 medium stuffed green olives

Preheat oven to 400°F (205°C).

In a bowl, combine by hand the cheese, flour, salt, paprika, and butter into a dough. Tear off a small piece of the dough, approximately the size of an olive. Make an indentation, insert an olive, and wrap it completely in the dough. Repeat for each puff.

Place puffs on an ungreased baking sheet. Bake for 10 minutes.

Note:
The puffs may be made ahead and frozen. Reheat them before they are served.

Makes 90.

Mrs. Edward T. Brennan

Herbed Shrimp

8 pounds (3.63 kg) shelled and deveined shrimp

4 medium red onions, sliced

4 lemons, sliced

2 cups (480 mL/225 g) pitted black olives

4 cups (960 mL/670 g) artichoke hearts, halved

8 tablespoons (120 mL/ 90 g) chopped pimiento

1 cup (240 mL) vegetable oil

2 cups (480 mL) lemon juice

4 tablespoons (60 mL) wine vinegar

4 cloves garlic, crushed

2 bay leaves, broken

4 tablespoons (60 mL/ 27 g) dry mustard

1 teaspoon (5 mL/2.3 g) cayenne pepper

4 teaspoons (20 mL/24 g) salt

Freshly ground pepper to taste

Bring a large pot of water to a boil. Drop in the shrimp, and return the water to a boil. Cook for 1 minute. Drain.

Place the shrimp in a serving bowl. Add the onions, lemons, olives, artichoke hearts, and pimiento. Combine the remaining ingredients. Pour over the shrimp, and toss. Cover the bowl. Refrigerate for several hours before serving.

Serves 20.

Mrs. Brittan C. MacIsaac

Carnival Delight

10½ ounces (300 g) prepared jalapeño bean dip

3 avocados, peeled

3 tablespoons (45 mL) lemon juice

6 tablespoons (90 mL/ 87 g) mayonnaise

2 tablespoons (30 mL/ 17 g) dry taco mix

4 tablespoons (60 mL/ 63 g) sour cream

4 ounces (115 g) Monterey Jack cheese, shredded

4 ounces (115 g) Cheddar cheese, shredded

3 scallions, sliced

3 tomatoes, peeled and chopped

2 4¼ ounce cans (238 g) chopped black olives (optional)

Thin tortilla chips

Spread the bean dip on a serving plate.

Mash together the avocados, lemon juice, and 1 tablespoon (15 mL/ 15 g) of mayonnaise.

Combine the taco mix, the remaining mayonnaise, and sour cream.

Mix together the Monterey Jack and Cheddar cheeses.

Layer the ingredients in this order: avocados, taco mix, cheeses, scallions, tomatoes, and olives. Serve with thin tortilla chips.

Note:
If recipe is doubled, make two hors d'oeuvre cakes.

Serves 12.

Mrs. Robert G. Runnette

Teriyaki Grilled Chicken Wings

40 chicken wings

36 ounces (1.08 L) teriyaki sauce

1 cup (240 mL/135 g) sesame seeds

Preheat charcoal grill.

Trim and discard the wing tips. Cut the wings in half. Cover them with the teriyaki sauce, and sprinkle with the sesame seeds. Marinate for at least 4 hours. Grill over charcoal until crisp and browned.

Serves 20.

Singer Euwer

Pickled Mushrooms

⅔ cup (160 mL) lemon juice

1⅓ cups (320 mL) olive oil

2 cloves garlic, minced

2 4-ounce (115 g) cans anchovies, drained and mashed

2 teaspoons (10 mL/8 g) MSG (optional)

4 strips pimientos, chopped

Salt and pepper to taste

4 pounds (1.81 kg) medium-size mushrooms

Pimientos, for garnish (optional)

The day before, combine the lemon juice, oil, garlic, anchovies, MSG, chopped pimientos, salt, and pepper to make a marinade. Set aside.

Cook the mushrooms in salted water for 10 minutes. Drain. Add the mushrooms to the marinade, mixing thoroughly. Refrigerate overnight. Garnish with additional pimientos if desired.

Serves 20.

Mrs. David M. Davis

Spicy Peanuts

10 cups (2.40 L/1.44 kg) salted peanuts

½ teaspoon (2.5 mL/1.1 g) powdered cumin

½ teaspoon (2.5 mL/1.2 g) chili powder

½ teaspoon (2.5 mL/1.7 g) garlic powder

½ teaspoon (2.5 mL/1.2 g) cayenne pepper

Grease an iron skillet with nonstick spray. Combine all the ingredients, and stir in batches over medium heat until thoroughly mixed and hot. Be careful that the peanuts do not burn. Serve warm or at room temperature.

Makes 10 cups (2.40 liters).

The Cookbook Committee

William Merritt Chase
(American, 1849-1916)
The Tenth Street Studio, c. 1905-6
Oil on canvas

47 × 66 in. (119.4 × 167.6 cm.)
Museum Purchase, 1917

William Merritt Chase, 1849–1916
The Tenth Street Studio, circa 1905–1906

William Merritt Chase was the *bon vivant* of American art for thirty years following his return to the United States in 1879. He first became acquainted with European-style studios during his studies at the Royal Academy in Munich and, upon his return to New York City, announced that he would soon have the finest salon in America.

He took a small room on fashionable Tenth Street and later added a larger room for exhibitions. Walls, floors, and tables were covered with European objets d'art which Chase had collected during his student days.

The New York art world had never seen anything like the Tenth Street studio. It quickly became a center of artistic life, where painters, sculptors, dancers, musicians, and patrons were entertained at a series of extravagant soirées.

Although he was successful as a portraitist and recognized as a master, Chase's flamboyant tastes rapidly overtook his ability to support them, and in 1889 he was forced to vacate the fabulous salon. *The Tenth Street Studio*, begun in 1889, remained unfinished until 1905 or 1906, long after Chase had abandoned his showplace. It reflects the artist's grand style.

Salon

Menu

Liver Pâté with Apple Slices

Roasted Pecans

Bleu Cheese Mousse with Crudités

Oysters on the Half Shell

New Potatoes with Sour Cream and Caviar

Baked Crabmeat

Old-Fashioned Biscuits with Smithfield Ham

Serves Twenty-five

Wine

Kir Royal* and

Champagne

The drama of the party is heightened by an irreverent assemblage of elegant candlesticks, candelabra, and vases, in both silver and crystal, combined with a silvery mound of fresh oysters.

The leafy cloth required several hundred fiddle-leaf fig leaves, hand-stitched on burlap by three people sewing for three hours. It is perishable but will stay fresh for about a day.

Tiny new potatoes are served in their jackets with sour cream and caviar. Vegetables overflow a basket beside the mousse. Radishes are served with leaves intact. Zucchini and summer squash, thin-sliced beets (hard-to-find orange ones are most interesting), and fennel bulbs may be offered along with the more familiar cherry tomatoes, romaine leaves, and carrots. Beans, broccoli, and cauliflower are better slightly cooked and then chilled before they are added to the colorful array.

*Champagne and Cassis;
 use French or domestic Champagne.

Liver Pâté with Apple Slices

1 pound (455 g) chicken livers

4 tablespoons (60 mL/ 29 g) chopped onion

1 teaspoon (5 mL/0.9 g) rosemary

About 1 cup (240 mL) chicken stock

4 slices bacon, cooked crisp

½ pound (225 g) unsalted butter, melted

2 teaspoons (10 mL/4.5 g) dry mustard

1 teaspoon (5 mL/6 g) salt

A pinch of cayenne pepper

½ teaspoon (2.5 mL/1.2 g) ground cloves

½ teaspoon(2.5 mL/1.2 g) nutmeg

2 teaspoons (10 mL/ 12 g) anchovy paste

2 cloves garlic, peeled

2 tablespoons (30 mL) cognac

Parsley, watercress, or cherry tomatoes, for garnish

3 or 4 large apples, unpeeled

In a saucepan, bring to a boil the chicken livers, onion, rosemary, and stock. Cover, and simmer for 15 minutes. Cool in the broth. Drain, reserving the broth.

In a blender or food processor, combine the chicken liver mixture, ½ cup (120 mL) reserved broth, and the remaining ingredients except for the garnish. Blend at high speed until smooth.

Pour into a crock. Refrigerate for 6 hours or longer. To serve, garnish with parsley, watercress, or cherry tomatoes.

Slice the apples very thin—you should have about 75 slices in all—and set them around the pâté as a tasty alternative to crackers.

Makes 4 cups (960 milliliters).

William P. Hackney

Roasted Pecans

5 pounds (2.27 kg) pecan halves

15 ounces (425 g) unsalted butter, melted

5 tablespoons (75 mL/ 90 g) coarse salt, or to taste

Preheat oven to 350°F (175°C).

Spread the pecans in a single layer on flat, ungreased pans. Dribble butter over them, and stir to coat. Bake for 10 minutes. Mix the nuts, and sprinkle them sparingly with the salt. Bake for another 10 minutes. Serve warm.

Makes 5 pounds (2.27 kilograms).

Dana Kline

Bleu Cheese Mousse with Crudités

6 egg yolks

2 cups less 2 tablespoons (450 mL) heavy cream

1½ tablespoons (⅜ ounce/ 10.5 g) gelatin

4 tablespoons (60 mL) cold water

¾ pound (340 g) bleu cheese

3 egg whites

Watercress

Crackers **or** Melba toast

Cucumber, zucchini, and carrot slices and romaine lettuce leaves, for garnish (optional)

Oil a 4-cup (960 mL) mold.

Beat the egg yolks and 6 tablespoons (90 mL) of the cream until well mixed. In a saucepan, cook over low heat until creamy.

Soften the gelatin in the cold water. Add it to the egg yolk mixture.

Push the bleu cheese through a sieve. Add it to the egg yolk mixture. Cool.

Whip 1½ cups (360 mL) of the cream. Beat the egg whites until stiff. Fold the whipped cream and egg whites into the egg yolk mixture. Pour the mousse into the mold. Chill for 2 hours.

Serve on a bed of fresh watercress with crackers or Melba toast. If desired, garnish with cucumber, zucchini, carrot, and romaine.

Note:
May be made ahead and kept refrigerated for 1 day or frozen.

Serves 25.

The Cookbook Committee

Oysters on the Half Shell

9 dozen oysters, shucked

5 lemons, cut into wedges and seeded

Scrub the oysters. Open them just before serving. Loosen them from the shell with a sharp knife, but do not remove from the shell. Chill them well. Arrange them over cracked ice on serving platters.

Garnish with lemon wedges.

Serves 25.

The Cookbook Committee

New Potatoes with Sour Cream and Caviar

20 small halved, cooked new potatoes

3½-ounce (43 g) jar red salmon roe caviar

½ pint (240 mL/255 g) sour cream

Dill or parsley sprigs, for garnish

Prepare the potatoes as described on page 33, but omit the butter and parsley. Arrange on a serving platter. Put a small dollop of sour cream in the center of each. Top with caviar. Garnish with a sprig of dill or parsley.

Serves 25.

The Cookbook Committee

Baked Crabmeat

2½ pounds (1.13 kg) crabmeat, back fin if possible

5 cups (1.2 L/1.16 kg) mayonnaise

2½ tablespoons (38 mL/ 45 g) horseradish

7½ tablespoons (115 mL/ 77 g) capers

2½ teaspoons (13 mL/ 3.3 g) grated lemon rind

1 to 2½ tablespoons (15 mL to 38 mL) Tabasco sauce, or to taste

2½ tablespoons (38 mL/ 38 g) grated onion

2½ tablespoons (38 mL) Worcestershire sauce

About 2 cups (480 mL/ 240 g) grated Cheddar cheese

Melba toast

Preheat oven to 350°F (175°C).

Combine all the ingredients except the Cheddar cheese. Pour into a baking dish, and sprinkle the grated cheese over the top.

Bake for about 20 minutes, or until bubbly. Place under the broiler for 1 or 2 minutes, or until the top becomes crusty.

Spread on homemade Melba toast, if desired. Serve immediately.

Serves 25.

James B. Stevenson

Old-Fashioned Biscuits with Smithfield Ham

3 cups (720 mL/395 g) all-purpose flour

1½ teaspoons (8mL/5 g) baking powder

1 tablespoon (15 mL/14 g) sugar

1 cup (240 mL/230 g) vegetable shortening

½ cup (120 mL) milk

2 tablespoons (30 mL/ 29 g) melted, unsalted butter

Preheat oven to 450°F (230°C). Grease a baking sheet.

Sift together the dry ingredients. With a fork, cut in the shortening until it is well incorporated. Add just enough milk to moisten. Knead for a minute to improve consistency.

Dust a work surface with flour. Roll out the dough ¼ inch (0.6 cm) thick for tiny biscuits suitable for hors d'oeuvres. Cut out with a round cutter approximately 1¼ inches (3.2 cm) in diameter. Place on the baking sheet. Brush with the melted butter. Bake for 8 to 10 minutes.

Note:
The dough may also be rolled ½ inch (1.3 cm) thick to make standard biscuits. The baking time is the same: 8 to 10 minutes. Serve with thin-sliced precooked Smithfield ham.

Makes 100.

The Cookbook Committee

Jean-Baptiste-Siméon Chardin
(French, 1699-1779)
*La Bouillotte (The Hot Water
Jug), 1728-31*
Oil on canvas

12¾ × 16⅛ in. (32.4 × 41 cm.)
Purchase with funds received
from estate of Howard A.
Noble, 1966

Jean-Baptiste Chardin, 1699–1779
La Bouillotte (The Hot Water Jug), 1728–1731

He painted during the reign of Louis XV in the Age of Enlightenment. His contemporaries were Voltaire, Goethe, Boucher, Fragonard, and Mozart. Yet in those dazzling times Jean-Baptiste Chardin painted still lifes and humble interiors.

Chardin treats everyday subjects with reverence but without affectation. His ability to evoke the textures of plain brown crockery, wooden objects, and common vegetables is extraordinary.

The lucidity and unwavering calm of his little masterpieces attracted Cézanne and Matisse. In his own time Chardin won the admiration of many, including the critic and encyclopedist Diderot, who, in describing the function of art, might have spoken Chardin's own words. "It is the chief business of art," Diderot wrote in 1765, "to touch and to move and to do this by getting close to nature."

The pheasant is a bird
which inspires fantasies
in the kitchen.
Elizabeth David
Writer on food

Winterset

Menu

Avocado with Golden Caviar

Pheasant Stew with Wild Rice

Bundled Vegetables

Chocolate Mousse Soufflé

Serves Eight

Wine

French or
Domestic Champagne (first course)

French Châteauneuf-du-Pape or
California Petite Sirah (main course)

A Chardin evening radiates the warmth of good company gathered on a snowy night.

The dinner begins with golden caviar, once the exclusive province of the czars. Although it may sometimes be difficult to locate the honey-hued delicacy, it is well worth the search. Salmon caviar, however, is an adequate substitute.

Pheasant is the most popular of the game birds. It makes a full-bodied stew, best accompanied by a simply prepared green vegetable and the nutty flavor of wild rice.

The sweet dessert is spiked with freshly ground pepper and warmed with a hint of apricot. Its success depends on choosing the finest chocolate.

Avocado with Golden Caviar

4 medium avocados

About ¾ cup (180 mL) lemon juice

1 cup (240 mL/255 g) sour cream

¼ cup (60 mL/71 g) golden caviar **or** red caviar

2 bunches watercress

8 thin slices lemon

With a vegetable peeler, peel the avocados. Slice into rings, approximately 1 inch (2.5 cm) thick, and carefully ease them away from the pit to prevent breaking. Immediately place the rings in lemon juice to prevent discoloring.

Arrange the avocado rings on 8 plates. Spoon over each serving in the following order: 1 teaspoon (5 mL) lemon juice, 2 tablespoons (30 mL/32 g) sour cream, and 1½ teaspoons (8 mL/9 g) caviar.

Garnish with sprigs of watercress and a thin slice of lemon.

Serves 8.

The Cookbook Committee

Pheasant Stew with Wild Rice

Stock:

Backs, necks, and wings from 2 pheasants, about 3 pounds (1.36 kg) each, cut into serving pieces

2 medium onions, chopped into coarse pieces

2 medium carrots, chopped into coarse pieces

4 celery stalks, chopped into coarse pieces

Stew:

4 tablespoons (60 mL/ 57 g) Clarified Butter (see page 20)

3 tablespoons (45 mL) vegetable oil

6 to 8 shallots, minced

2 bay leaves

Salt and freshly ground pepper to taste

16 dried apricots

32 prunes, pitted

½ cup (120 mL) water

2 cups (480 mL/400 g) wild rice

2 cups (480 mL) heavy cream

Stock:

The day before, place the pheasant backs, necks, and wings in a large saucepan. Cover them with water, and bring to a boil. Skim the surface. Add the onions, carrots, and celery. Return to a boil, reduce the heat, cover, and simmer for 1 to 2 hours. Strain, and set aside.

Stew:

In a large saucepan or Dutch oven, brown the remaining pheasant pieces in 3 tablespoons (45 mL/ 43 g) of the clarified butter and the oil. Remove from the pan.

In the same pan, heat the remaining butter, and lightly sauté the shallots. Return the pheasants to the pan with enough stock to cover. Add the bay leaves, salt, and pepper. Simmer for 40 minutes; do not boil. Add the apricots and half the prunes. Simmer for 20 to 30 minutes, or until the meat falls off the bones; do not boil. Remove pheasants

from the pan, cool, and debone. Cut into bite-size pieces, and return to the pan.

In a separate saucepan, cook the remaining prunes in the water until very soft. Purée in a blender. Stir the purée into the pheasant mixture. Refrigerate overnight.

The next day, cook the wild rice, according to package directions.

Before serving, reheat the pheasant stew slowly, and stir in the cream. Reduce over medium heat for about 20 minutes, or until the sauce is thickened. Adjust the seasonings to taste. Serve with the wild rice.

Note:
The flavor improves if the stew is prepared a day in advance.

Serves 8.

Les Parisiennes
Toronto, Ontario

Bundled Vegetables

½ pound (225 g) green beans

6 bunches scallions

6 stalks celery

½ pound (225 g) carrots

1 to 2 sweet red peppers

1 to 2 green peppers

Juice of 1 lemon

4 tablespoons (60 mL/ 57 g) unsalted butter, melted **or** 1 cup (240 mL) Sauce Vinaigrette (see page 125)

Rinse all the vegetables in cold water. Trim the beans to 5-inch (13 cm) lengths. Remove the root and dry layer from the scallions, and cut them to 5-inch (13 cm) lengths. Cut the celery stalks and the carrots into julienne strips, 5 inches by ¼ inch (13 cm by 0.6 cm). Cut the red and green peppers crosswise into ¼-inch (0.6 cm) round slices; cut away the seeds and membranes. Cook each group of vegetables separately in boiling water, as follows:

green beans	10 to 15 minutes
scallions	6 minutes
celery	6 minutes
carrots	6 minutes
peppers	20 minutes

Drain the vegetables. On a greased, ovenproof serving platter, arrange all but the peppers in bundles. Wrap each bundle with a strip of red or green pepper.

To serve hot:
Dribble the lemon juice and melted butter over each bundle. Bake at 400° F (205° C) for about 5 minutes or until hot.

To serve cold:
Arrange the bundles on an ungreased platter, and top with vinaigrette sauce.

Serves 8.

Makes 24 bundles.

The Cookbook Committee

Chocolate Mousse Soufflé

4 ounces (115 g) unsweetened chocolate

2 ounces (57 g) semisweet chocolate

7 egg whites

½ teaspoon (2.5 mL/1.1 g) cream of tartar

1 cup (240 mL/225 g) sugar

1 cup (240 mL) heavy cream

1 tablespoon (15 mL) dark rum

2 tablespoons (30 mL/ 15 g) grated orange peel

2 tablespoons (30 mL/ 16 g) julienne dried apricots

1 teaspoon (5 mL/1.5 g) instant coffee powder

¼ teaspoon (1.3 mL/0.7 g) black pepper

Shaved chocolate, for garnish (optional)

With wax paper, make a collar for a 6-cup (1.44 L) soufflé mold. The collar should reach about 3 inches (8 cm) above the top of the mold. Attach it with tape or string.

In the top of a double boiler, melt the chocolates together over hot, not boiling, water.

In a large mixing bowl, beat the egg whites and cream of tartar until frothy. Add the sugar by spoonfuls. Beat until the meringue is stiff but not dry.

In a smaller bowl, whip the cream and rum until firm peaks are formed. Set aside.

To the melted chocolates, add the orange peel, apricots, coffee, and pepper. Stir until mixed. Quickly fold the chocolate mixture into the whipped cream. Using a large spatula, fold the chocolate cream into the meringue only until combined.

Turn the mousse into the prepared soufflé dish. Smooth the top. Cover it with wax paper. Freeze. Defrost in the refrigerator 1 to 1½ hours before serving. Remove the collar. Decorate with shaved chocolate, if desired.

Note:
This very rich dessert may be made up to a week ahead.

Serves 8.

Fred Anderson

John Kane
(American, 1860-1934)
Highland Hollow, c. 1927
Oil on canvas

26½ × 36½ in.
(67.3 × 92.7 cm.)
Gift of Mr. and Mrs. Leland
Hazard, 1961

John Kane, 1860–1934
Highland Hollow, circa 1927

John Kane saw beauty in the smokestacks of Pittsburgh's mills, in trains chugging beneath its bridges, and in the forthright faces of his relatives and friends. Self-taught, with no formal training, Kane recorded in marvelous detail the countryside around him. *Highland Hollow* reflects his love of the Scotland he knew as a boy as well as the affection he felt for his adopted country. It records the exuberance of Scottish Americans at the annual Scots' Day in Pittsburgh's Kennywood Park.

Kane lived a hard life as an itinerant laborer and in his spare time loved to make sketches of the streets, buildings, and bridges he had helped construct. However, as he committed the sketches to canvas, he often changed the positions of familiar landmarks and buildings to where they suited him better in the composition.

When he first received public recognition, Kane was sixty-seven years old. The jury of the 1927 Carnegie International in Pittsburgh chose the work of this Sunday painter to hang alongside that of Munch and Matisse. Of the fame that followed during the last few years of his life, Kane said, "I have lived too long the life of the poor to attach undue importance to the honors of the art world or any honors that come from man and not from God."

For subjects to paint, I can
honestly say I have found
none too lowly.
John Kane

Ardsheal House

Menu

Stilton Soup

Rack of Lamb

Lima Bean Purée

Beets Julienne

Brown Bread Ice Cream

Serves Eight

Wine

French Red Burgundy or

California Pinot Noir

The Scotland of John Kane owes much of its charm to green countryside and comfortable inns. Adapted from the menu of a rural Highland inn, this stalwart dinner is built around rack of lamb, for which the region is justly famous. The lamb is most flavorful simply seasoned with garlic and roasted medium rare.

The unusual soup is made of blue-veined Stilton and full-bodied Cheddar cheeses. A julienne of beets and a purée of lima beans are offered with the roast instead of the usual potatoes, rice, or barley. The intriguing surprise of this meal is the delicious Brown Bread Ice Cream.

I am certain of nothing but the holiness of the heart's affection and the truth of the imagination.
John Kane

Stilton Soup

2 tablespoons (30 mL/ 29 g) unsalted butter

1 medium onion, minced

2 cloves garlic, minced

½ pound (225 g) Stilton cheese, crumbled

½ pound (225 g) Cheddar cheese, grated

¼ cup (60 mL/33 g) all-purpose flour

3½ cups (840 mL) chicken stock, all fat removed

½ cup (120 mL) dry white wine, or more, if required

1 bay leaf

1 cup (240 mL) heavy cream

Milk, if required

In a large saucepan, melt the butter. Add the onion and garlic. Cook until tender. Add the cheeses and flour. Continue to cook for 2 to 3 minutes, stirring constantly.

Remove from the heat. Gradually add the stock and wine. Add the bay leaf. Return to the heat. Whisk vigorously until the mixture just comes to a boil. Lower the heat, add the cream, and simmer for 5 to 10 minutes. Remove the bay leaf.

If the soup is too thick, add milk or white wine to the desired consistency.

Note:
Stilton soup may be made ahead and reheated.

Serves 8 to 10.

Ardsheal House
Kentallen of Appin, Scotland

Rack of Lamb

2 8-rib racks of lamb, chine bones removed

Salt and pepper to taste

1 to 2 tablespoons (15 to 30 mL) vegetable oil

1 cup (240 mL/53 g) minced parsley

1 cup (240 mL/115 g) bread crumbs

6 to 8 cloves garlic, minced

Preheat oven to 450° F (230° C).

Remove any small bones. Trim the excess fat, leaving a thin layer. Trim fat and meat from ends of bones, about ½ inch (1.3 cm). Season with salt and pepper. In a skillet, heat the oil, and brown the racks lightly.

Combine the parsley, bread crumbs, and garlic, and press firmly on top of the racks. Place them in a roasting pan, and bake them for 45 minutes for medium. Adjust cooking time if you prefer lamb rare or well done.

Note:
Grilled tomatoes and buttered barley also are nice accompaniments.

Serves 8.

Ardsheal House
Kentallen of Appin, Scotland

Lima Bean Purée

1 small onion

1 bay leaf

3 10-ounce (285 g) packages frozen baby lima beans

4 tablespoons (60 mL/ 57 g) unsalted butter

4 tablespoons (60 mL) light cream

1 teaspoon (5 mL/1.8 g) savory

Freshly ground pepper to taste

Salt to taste

Chopped parsley

Slice the onion and cook it and the bay leaf with the beans until tender. Drain, reserving the liquid. Remove the bay leaf. In a food processor or blender, purée the mixture, adding small amounts of reserved liquid as necessary.

Transfer the purée to the top of a double boiler and add the butter, cream, savory, salt, and pepper, and heat through.

Serve garnished with parsley.

Serves 8.

Mrs. Brittan C. MacIsaac

Beets Julienne

1½ pounds (680 g) beets, peeled

3 tablespoons (45 mL/ 43 g) unsalted butter

Salt and pepper to taste

Cut each beet into ⅛-inch (0.3 cm) -thick julienne slices of equal length. Steam the beets over boiling water for 2 to 3 minutes, or until just tender. Toss with the butter, season lightly with salt and pepper, and serve hot.

Serves 8.

The Cookbook Committee

Brown Bread Ice Cream

1 cup (240 mL/90 g) crumbs made from about 3 slices of a good coarse brown bread

¾ cup (180 mL/130 g) light brown sugar

4 eggs, separated

¼ cup plus 2 tablespoons (90 mL/44 g) sifted confectioners' sugar

1 cup (240 mL) heavy cream

Spread the bread crumbs on an ungreased baking sheet. Sprinkle evenly with half of the brown sugar. Place under the broiler until the sugar caramelizes. With a spatula, carefully turn the crumbs, and sprinkle with the remaining sugar. Broil again until caramelized. (Watch carefully so that the mixture does not burn.)

Beat the egg whites until stiff. Continue beating, adding confectioners' sugar, a tablespoon at a time.

Beat the egg yolks. Fold into the egg white mixture.

Whip the cream until soft peaks form. Fold the cream and crumbs into the egg mixture. Pour into an enameled pan or ice trays, and place, uncovered, on the bottom of the freezer for several hours, or until frozen. Stir once after 2 hours.

Note:
This recipe may be doubled.

Serves 8.

Ardsheal House
Kentallen of Appin, Scotland

Stuart Davis
(American, 1894-1964)
Composition Concrete, 1957
Oil on canvas
203 in. × 96 in.
(515.6 × 243.8 cm.)
Gift of the H. J. Heinz
Company, 1979

Stuart Davis, 1894–1964
Composition Concrete, 1957

When New York swayed to the rhythm of ragtime, a young painter named Stuart Davis went out into the streets to absorb the stuff of America. Davis found himself drawn to the dance halls, honky-tonks, and back alleys.

The music of the streets became for him the art of the city; his own work became visual music. Using line, form, and color, he explored tone, syncopation, even improvisation.

Composition Concrete was commissioned for the lobby of the Heinz Research Center. The number 57, inscribed in the painting's lower left, represents not only the year in which the picture was painted but the famous food manufacturer's 57 varieties. Never one to lull his viewers with the obvious, Davis inverted the "5" and the "7" and distilled them into pure form. It was, he explained, a warning not to look too hard for meaning.

An artist without his mystery is a bum.
Stuart Davis

Fourth of July

Menu

Popcorn Soup

Grilled Steak

Frybakers

Friggione

Meringue Shells with Blueberries

Serves Twelve

Wine

French Red Bordeaux or

California Pinot Noir

*He is in a very real way,
the quintessential American
artist.*
Michael Botwinick
Director
Corcoran Gallery of Art

Nothing is more American than the barbecue. Whether a makeshift wood fire or a stationary gas grill, the cooking process is the same: quick searing over high heat to seal in natural juices.

Cherry or other fruitwood fires add a delicious flavor to grilled meat, fish, or poultry. A handful of hickory chips can impart a hint of smoky taste when added to hot coals just before grilling. To enliven the flavor still further, dried herbs may be sprinkled on the fire a minute or two before the steaks are done. Rosemary or thyme is recommended, especially when these herbs are repeated in the potatoes.

The keynote here is simplicity. Except for the steaks, everything is served chilled or at room temperature. Set the table with soup and vegetables, and guests can help themselves to a complete meal when their steaks are ready.

Brimming bowls of popcorn do double duty as a garnish for the soup and as a convenient nibble for the guests. Friggione, a colorful medley of summer vegetables, is a delicious variation on the tossed salad. Dessert is a mixture of creamy ice cream and tart, juicy blueberries nestled in a "plate" of meringue. It is a finale calculated to go off like a firecracker.

Popcorn Soup

8 ears of corn

2 medium onions, sliced

3 bay leaves

8 cups (1.92 L) chicken stock

¼ pound (115 g) unsalted butter

6 egg yolks

4 quarts (3.84 L) freshly popped popcorn

Pepper to taste

Remove the corn from the cob to make 3 cups (720 mL). Cook it in a small amount of water for about 5 minutes or until tender. Drain and rinse in a sieve.

Cook the onions and bay leaves in 2 cups (480 mL) of the stock for about 15 minutes, or until tender. Remove the bay leaves.

In a blender, purée the corn and the onion mixture with 2 cups (480 mL) of the stock. Pour into a saucepan.

Melt the butter until bubbly. Place the egg yolks in a blender. Slowly add the butter, then 2 cups (480 mL) of the corn mixture, blending at high speed. In a saucepan, combine both corn mixtures.

In a blender, purée 2 quarts (1.92 L) of the popcorn with the remaining stock. Strain the mixture through a sieve to remove coarse hulls. Combine with the corn mixture, stirring until thoroughly mixed. Add pepper to taste. Chill.

Sprinkle each portion with about ½ cup (120 mL) of the popcorn just before serving. Some of the popcorn will sink.

Note:
Popcorn soup may also be served hot.

Serves 12.

Edith H. Fisher

Grilled Steak

12 10-ounce (285 g) 1¼-inch (3 cm) -thick New York strip steaks
or
12 8-ounce (225 g) 2-inch (5 cm) -thick filets
or
7 or 8 pounds (3.18 or 3.63 kg) 3-inch (8 cm) -thick boneless sirloins

Grill steaks over a hot charcoal fire. If large sirloins are used, they should be sliced on the diagonal before being served.

Serves 12.

The Cookbook Committee

Frybakers

¼ cup (60 mL) vegetable oil

Salt and pepper to taste

1 onion, minced (optional)

½ teaspoon (2.5 mL/ 0.4 g) rosemary, or to taste

½ teaspoon (2.5 mL/ 0.7 g) thyme, or to taste

1 teaspoon (5 mL/0.3 g) dill, or to taste

6 large baking potatoes, halved lengthwise

Preheat oven to 350° F (175° C). Coat the bottom of a baking pan with the oil. Sprinkle with the seasonings.

Place the potatoes, cut sides down, in the pan. Bake for 45 to 60 minutes, depending on the size of the potatoes. The surface should be crusty; the inside, soft.

Serves 12.

Mrs. John T. Morris

Friggione
(Pepper, Tomato, and Onion Stew)

4 pounds (1.81 kg) tomatoes, peeled, halved, and seeded

2 teaspoons (10 mL/12 g) salt

4 tablespoons (60 mL/ 57 g) unsalted butter

½ cup (120 mL) olive oil

4 pounds (1.81 kg) green and red peppers, ribs and seeds removed, chopped into coarse pieces

4 garlic bulbs, separated into cloves, blanched, peeled, and minced

2 pounds (905 g) small white pearl onions, cut into thin slices

1 cup (240 mL/50 g) chopped fresh basil **or** 2 tablespoons (30 mL/ 5 g) dried basil

½ teaspoon (2.5 mL/ 1.4 g) freshly ground black pepper

Lightly sprinkle the insides of the tomatoes with 1 teaspoon (5 mL/6 g) of the salt. Place them upside down in a colander for ½ hour to drain. Chop into coarse pieces.

In a large skillet, heat the butter and oil. Add the peppers, garlic, and onions. Cook, stirring, until the onions are soft and translucent. Add the tomatoes and basil. Cover, reduce the heat, and cook for about 10 minutes. Add the remaining salt and the black pepper. Remove the lid, increase the heat, and cook, stirring, until almost all the liquid has evaporated.

Serve hot or cold.

Serves 12.

The Cookbook Committee

Meringue Shells
with Blueberries

6 egg whites, at room temperature

2 teaspoons (10 mL) vanilla

½ teaspoon (2.5 mL/ 1.1 g) cream of tartar

A dash of salt

2 cups (480 mL/455 g) sugar

Fruit Filling:
   2 cups (480 mL) heavy cream

   4 cups (960 mL/460 g) blueberries

   1 cup (240 mL) orange juice concentrate

   2 teaspoons (10 mL/ 2.6 g) grated orange rind

Preheat oven to 275°F (135° C). Cover 2 baking sheets with ungreased brown paper. Using a 9-inch (23 cm) round cake pan as a guide, draw a circle on each baking sheet.

In a large bowl, combine the egg whites, vanilla, cream of tartar, and salt. Gradually add the sugar, beating until soft peaks form and the meringue is glossy. Spread the meringue over each circle. Shape into 2 shells with the back of a spoon, making the bottoms ½ inch (1.3 cm) thick and the sides about 1¾ inches (4.4 cm) high. Bake for 1 hour. Turn off the heat. Let the meringues dry in the oven with the door closed for at least 2 hours.

Fruit Filling:
Whip the cream. Combine with the other ingredients, and mix well.

Assembly:
Fill the meringues with the fresh fruit filling.

Note:
To make ahead, freeze the fruit mixture. Keep the shells, uncovered, on brown paper.

Meringue shells may also be filled with 2 cups (480 mL) French vanilla ice cream and chocolate or another sauce.

Serves 12.

Pat Barnett

John Singer Sargent
(American, 1856-1925)
Venetian Interior, c. 1882
Oil on canvas

27 × 34 in. (68.6 × 86.4 cm.)
Museum Purchase, 1920

John Singer Sargent, 1856–1925
Venetian Interior, circa 1882

John Singer Sargent was born in Italy, the son of an enlightened Philadelphia physician and a mother who insisted on all the advantages for her children. His childhood was a perpetual grand tour. At the age of eighteen he entered the Academy of Fine Arts of Florence and then moved to Paris, where he studied with Carolus-Duran, the most successful and popular portraitist in Europe.

"Velázquez, Velázquez, Velázquez. Ceaselessly study Velázquez," advised his teacher, and the young student learned his lessons well. Sargent loved the Spaniard's fluidity of line and treatment of space. Sargent owes much to the seventeenth-century master's work, particularly *Las Meninas*, which, like *Venetian Interior*, is a study of figures carefully placed in receding space. Although Sargent painted street scenes, landscapes, and interiors, he is known chiefly for his portraits. Like his close friend Henry James, Sargent was fascinated by social nuance. His paintings invariably give the viewer a sense of underlying psychological drama.

A portrait is a painting with
a little something wrong
about the mouth.
John Singer Sargent

Bravissimo

Menu

Curried Mussel and Broccoli Soup

Veal Stuffed with Pesto

Eggplant Timbale

Champagne Zabaglione with Berries

Serves Sixteen

Wine

Italian Soave (first course)

Italian Barolo (main course)

If he painted only what he saw, he painted with a firm belief in the truth of his vision.
Donelson Hoopes
Art historian

No city was ever more celebrated for its opulence than Venice, Queen of the Adriatic. Initially much of its fabled wealth came from the spice market, which Venetian traders dominated from the Middle Ages until the fifteenth century. To protect their monopoly, the merchants of Venice bribed the masters of the treasury with an annual pound of pepper. That royal spice, freshly ground, makes an essential contribution to this meal's first course and entrée.

The veal is flavored with basil, a seasonal herb, so prized by the Greeks that its very name means "kingly." Fortunately for pesto lovers, the basil leaves may be frozen, or the pesto may be preserved with a light coating of olive oil and stored in the refrigerator or freezer.

Prodigious quantities of egg yolks and heavy cream, plus a main course worth a king's ransom, make this dinner rich in every detail.

Curried Mussel and Broccoli Soup

9 quarts (8.64 L/5 kg) small mussels, scrubbed

3 cups (720 mL) white wine **or** water

6 bay leaves, crumbled

6 tablespoons (90 mL/ 20 g) minced parsley

¾ teaspoon (3.8 mL/1.1 g) thyme

¾ teaspoon (3.8 mL/0.3 g) tarragon

3 cloves garlic, chopped into coarse pieces

6 shallots, chopped into coarse pieces

9 tablespoons (135 mL/ 130 g) unsalted butter **or** vegetable oil

12 shallots, minced

3 pounds (1.36 kg) broccoli, separated into florets and stems peeled and diced

3 teaspoons (15 mL/7 g) curry powder

Chicken stock

6 egg yolks

1½ cups (360 mL) Crème Fraîche (see page 119)

Juice of 1½ lemons

Salt and pepper to taste

Combine the mussels, wine or water, bay leaves, parsley, thyme, tarragon, garlic, and chopped shallots. Cover, and steam for 5 to 10 minutes, or until the mussel shells open. Discard any mussels that do not open. Drain the liquid, and set it aside.

In a saucepan, heat the butter or oil. Sauté the minced shallots and broccoli stems until the shallots are transparent and the broccoli is partially cooked. Add the broccoli florets, and sauté for 2 minutes more. Add the curry powder.

Measure the reserved mussel liquid, and add enough stock to make 18 cups (4.32 L). Add to the saucepan, and simmer for about 15 minutes, or until the broccoli is cooked but still crisp.

In a bowl, whisk the egg yolks and crème fraîche. Slowly add one-third of the hot liquid, stirring constantly. Return the mixture to the saucepan, stirring constantly. Heat, but do not boil. Add the mussels, lemon juice, salt, and pepper.

Serve hot or cold.

Serves 16.

Mrs. Anthony J. A. Bryan

Veal Stuffed with Pesto

Pesto:
2 cups (480 mL/100 g) fresh or frozen basil leaves

5 cloves garlic, minced

¼ cup (60 mL/34 g) pine nuts (pignoli)

½ cup (120 mL) olive oil

2 tablespoons (30 mL/ 29 g) unsalted butter, at room temperature

3 tablespoons (45 mL) vegetable oil

3 tablespoons (45 mL/ 43 g) unsalted butter

4 carrots, sliced

4 medium onions, sliced

4 sprigs parsley

2 bay leaves, crumbled

1 tablespoon (15 mL/4 g) thyme

Veal:

9- to 10-pound (4.08 to 4.54 kg) veal roast or butterflied leg of veal

1 tablespoon (15 mL/ 18 g) salt

1/4 teaspoon (1.3 mL/ 0.7 g) freshly ground pepper

8 slices bacon

2 cups (480 mL) chicken stock

1/2 cup (120 mL) dry white wine

Pesto:

Using a food processor with a steel blade, process the basil for 1/2 minute. Add the garlic, and process for 20 seconds. Add the pine nuts, oil, and butter, and process for 20 seconds.

Preheat oven to 350° F (175° C).

In a large ovenproof pan, heat the oil and butter. Add the carrots and onions, and sauté over moderately high heat for about 15 minutes. Add the parsley, bay leaves, and thyme. Cover with foil, and continue cooking for 10 minutes. Set aside.

Veal:

Rinse the roast in cold water, and dry with paper towels. On a work surface, open the roast flat, and spread the top with the pesto mixture. Roll the roast, and secure it with string at four equally spaced intervals. Sprinkle with the salt and pepper. Drape with the uncooked bacon. Insert a meat thermometer in the thickest part.

Place the roast on top of the sautéed vegetables. Spoon some vegetables over the top. Add the stock, cover with foil, and place in the oven. Baste frequently with pan juices during roasting. Roast for about 2 hours, or until the meat thermometer registers 160° F (71° C). Place on a hot platter, remove the strings, and carve.

Heat the pan juices, skimming off the fat. Stir in the wine. Spoon over the roast. Serve immediately.

Serves 16.

The Cookbook Committee

Eggplant Timbale

Tomato Sauce:

½ cup (120 mL) olive oil

2 large onions, minced

2 cloves garlic, minced

6 pounds (2.72 kg) tomatoes, peeled, seeded, and chopped into coarse pieces

2 pinches of sugar

1⅓ teaspoons (7 mL/ 8 g) salt

¼ cup (60 mL/11 g) fine-chopped fresh rosemary

¼ cup (60 mL) Crème Fraîche (see page 119) **or** sour cream

Timbale:

4 pounds (1.81 kg) eggplant, peeled (reserve skins) and sliced about ¼ inch (0.6 cm) thick

2 tablespoons (30 mL/ 36 g) salt

About 2½ cups (600 mL) olive oil

2 medium onions, minced

8 cloves garlic, minced

12 eggs

2 cups (480 mL) heavy cream

Salt and pepper to taste

Tomato Sauce:
In a large, heavy skillet, heat the oil, and saute the onions and garlic until soft and translucent. Add the tomatoes, and cook for 20 minutes. Add the sugar, salt, and rosemary, and cook for 5 minutes longer. Add the creme fraiche or sour cream.

Timbale:
Preheat oven to 350° F (175° C). Grease 16 custard cups or ramekins with nonstick spray.

Cut the reserved eggplant skins into 32 leaf-shaped pieces. Blanch for 2 minutes, and place 2 pieces, purple side down, in the bottom of each cup.

Using a sharp knife, score both sides of the eggplant slices. Salt, and let stand for 10 minutes. Drain on paper towels.

In a heavy skillet, heat 2 tablespoons (30 mL) of the oil, and sauté the onions and garlic until soft and translucent. Remove from the skillet. Add about ¼ cup (60 mL) of oil to the skillet, and sauté the eggplant for about 5 minutes on each side, or until golden brown and soft. Add oil to the pan as needed. Drain each slice in a colander. Reserve excess oil.

Combine the eggplant, onions, garlic, eggs, and cream. In a food processor, purée until smooth (this may have to be done in batches). Season with salt and pepper. Ladle the eggplant custard into each cup, filling it almost to the top. Set the cups in 2 baking pans. Pour boiling water into the pans to reach halfway up the cups. Bake for 30 minutes. Remove from the oven, but leave in the water for 15 minutes.

To serve:
Unmold the cups, and surround with the tomato sauce. Serve warm, at room temperature, or chilled.

Note:
Oil used to sauté the eggplant may be used to make the tomato sauce if the sauce is made while the eggplant is being baked.

Serves 16.

Dana Kline

Champagne Zabaglione with Berries

24 egg yolks*

6 cups (1.44 L) dry champagne

1½ cups (360 mL/340 g) sugar

4 quarts (3.84 L/1.84 kg) strawberries **or** raspberries

Place the egg yolks, champagne, and sugar in the top of a double boiler. Whisk over low heat for 5 to 10 minutes, or until thick and smooth. Do not overcook or sauce will curdle. Serve over strawberries or raspberries.

Serves 16.

The Cookbook Committee

*The egg whites may be frozen for another use.

Chinese, Mi-shien kiln,
Northern Sung Dynasty,
960-1126
Vase, early 11th century
Stoneware, white slipped and
glazed (Tz'u-chou ware)
H. 15½ in. (39.4 cm)
Gift of Walter Read Hovey,
1973

Chinese, Northern Sung Dynasty, 960–1126
Vase, early eleventh century

In China and other Asian countries tea is more than a national drink. A symbol of welcome, the benchmark of hospitality, the hot, fragrant beverage is given special honor by the Japanese, who call it *o-cha*, meaning "respected tea."

By the time this stoneware vase was made the Chinese had been enjoying the pale green brew for 500 years. Part of the joy of tea was, and continues to be, taking it in surroundings contrived to enhance the experience.

Vases such as this were frequently placed in tearooms to be admired at leisure as much for their decoration as for their contents. Known in Chinese as *mei-p'ing*, these narrow-necked oval vases were designed to hold a single flowering branch of plum blossoms.

This piece dates from the Northern Sung dynasty (960–1126), a period of unprecedented peace and harmony. Known as the golden age of Chinese landscape painting, the era is remembered here in leafy scrollwork at the top of the vase, a series of lotus petals at the base, and a garden setting for its three figures, one of whom seems to be proffering a steaming cup of tea.

In art, the Sung dynasty . . .
saw the potters' art brought
to a perfection which has
never been surpassed.
William Watson
Professor of Chinese art
and archaeology
London University

Mei-p'ing

Menu

Four Happiness Dumplings

Tomato Flower Soup

Ivory Noodles with Chicken

Peking Duck with Mandarin Pancakes

Kung Pao Shrimp

Steamed Fish with Black Bean Sauce

Almond Float

Serves Eight

Wine

Alsatian or

California Gewürztraminer

Exotic names, unfamiliar flavors, and combinations that seem unlikely make Chinese foods fun to prepare and an unusual treat for all who share them.

The cornerstone of Chinese food is the bite-size morsel. Anxiety about the elaborate preparations can be relieved by careful planning and choreography. All ingredients should be cut and chopped and arranged in cooking sequence beforehand. The filling for the dumplings, all the sauces, the mandarin pancakes, and the scallion brushes may be made the day before. The inevitable last-minute steps are quickly performed. With a little practice, even a confirmed Western cook can soon be steaming Chinese dumplings with ease.

Four Happiness Dumplings

Cornstarch

4 teaspoons (20 mL/11 g) Sechuan peppercorns*

1 large clove garlic, minced

8 scallions (bulbs and stems), minced

1-inch (2.5 cm) -slice ginger root, peeled and minced

1⅓ pounds (605 g) ground pork

2 eggs, unbeaten

5 tablespoons (75 mL) soy sauce

3 tablespoons (45 mL) sesame oil*

70 won ton wrappers*

2 eggs, slightly beaten

1 large carrot, cut on the diagonal into thin slices

3 Chinese black mushrooms*, soaked and cut into thin slices

1 large scallion (stem only), sliced on the diagonal

Dipping Sauce:
   3 tablespoons (45 mL) soy sauce

   5 tablespoons (75 mL) red wine vinegar

   1 tablespoon (15 mL) sesame oil

Cut parchment paper to fit, and place in the trays of a Chinese steamer. Cover a baking sheet with parchment paper. Dust lightly with cornstarch.

Heat an ungreased small heavy pan, and cook the peppercorns until they begin to smoke. Place peppercorns in a mortar, and grind slightly to release the flavor.

In a small bowl, mix together the garlic, minced scallions, ginger, and pork. Stir in the 2 unbeaten eggs, the soy sauce, and sesame oil.

Place a won ton wrapper on a work surface. Dab each corner of the wrapper with beaten egg. Place 1 teaspoon (5 mL) of pork filling in the center. Take a pair of opposite corners, and pinch them together over the center. In each of the four pockets formed, insert a single slice of carrot, mushroom, and scallion. Place the dumplings on the prepared baking sheet, and cover them with damp paper towels until ready to steam.

Heat the steamer to a rolling steam. Place the dumplings on the parchment-covered steamer trays. Steam for 20 minutes.

Dipping Sauce:
Combine the soy sauce, vinegar, and oil. Serve with the hot dumplings.

Makes 65 to 70.

Dana Kline

*May be purchased in Asian food stores.

88

Tomato Flower Soup

1¼ pounds (565 g) tomatoes

3¾ teaspoons (19 mL) peanut **or** other vegetable oil

1 large scallion (bulb and stem), chopped

6¼ cups (1.5 L) chicken or beef stock

2 teaspoons (10 mL/12 g) salt

3 eggs, slightly beaten

A dash of freshly ground pepper

Peel the tomatoes, cut them into wedges, and remove the seeds.

In a saucepan over high heat, heat the oil. Add the tomatoes and scallions, and stir-fry for 1 minute. Add the stock and salt, bring to a boil, and slowly stir in the eggs. Cook for about ½ minute, or until the eggs are lightly set. Sprinkle with the pepper, and serve immediately.

Note:
Tomatoes and scallions may be prepared earlier.

Serves 6 to 8.

Anna Kao

Kung Pao Shrimp

2 teaspoons (10 mL/5 g) cornstarch

6 tablespoons (90 mL) cold water

½ cup (120 mL) vinegar

Salt to taste

4 tablespoons (60 mL) light soy sauce

3 tablespoons (45 mL/ 43 g) sugar

8 cloves garlic, minced

4 tablespoons (60 mL/ 29 g) chopped scallions (bulb only)

3 tablespoons (45 mL/ 25 g) chopped fresh ginger

½ cup (120 mL) peanut **or** vegetable oil

2 pounds (905 g) large shrimp, shelled and deveined—about 32 shrimp

Snow peas, for garnish (optional)

Dissolve the cornstarch in the cold water. Set aside.

In a small bowl, combine the vinegar, salt, soy sauce, and sugar. Set aside.

Combine the garlic, scallions, and ginger.

In a wok or skillet, heat the oil. Add the garlic mixture. Stir-fry for 30 seconds. Remove. Add the shrimp, and stir-fry vigorously for 1½ to 2 minutes, or until pink. Add the vinegar and garlic mixtures. Bring to a boil, and cook for about 1 minute. Add the cornstarch, stirring quickly to combine all the ingredients. Serve immediately. Garnish with snow peas, if desired.

Note:
Serve the shrimp with rice.

Serves 8.

The Cookbook Committee

Ivory Noodles with Chicken

1 tablespoon (15 mL) dry sherry

5 tablespoons (75 mL) soy sauce

2 teaspoons (10 mL) water

4½ teaspoons (23 mL) sesame oil

½ teaspoon (2.5 mL/3 g) salt

1 pound (455 g) chicken breasts, boned and cut into ⅛-inch (0.3 cm) shreds

12 ounces (340 g) thin Chinese egg noodles or spaghettini

About 4½ tablespoons (70 mL) peanut oil

2 eggs

6 tablespoons (90 mL) chicken stock

¼ cup (60 mL/65 g) smooth peanut butter

1 tablespoon (15 mL/14 g) sugar

1 tablespoon (15 mL/8 g) minced garlic

2 teaspoons (10 mL/6 g) peeled and minced ginger root

2 teaspoons (10 mL) Chinese black vinegar **or** Worcestershire sauce

2 teaspoons (10 mL) hot chili oil

2 cups (480 mL/180 g) fresh bean sprouts

1 cup (240 mL/115 g) shredded scallions

In a bowl, combine the sherry, 2 teaspoons (10 mL) of the soy sauce, the water, 1 teaspoon (5 mL) of the sesame oil, and the salt. Add the shredded chicken. Toss to coat. Marinate for at least 20 minutes.

In a large pot, cook the noodles according to package instructions, adding 1 tablespoon (15 mL) of the peanut oil to the cooking water. Cook for 3 to 5 minutes, or until they are *al dente*. Rinse and drain in a colander. Transfer to a large bowl. Toss with 1 tablespoon (15 mL) of the peanut oil and 2 teaspoons (10 mL) of the sesame oil.

In a small bowl, beat the eggs lightly. Brush a 7-inch (18 cm) skillet with peanut oil, and heat over high heat until very hot. Remove the skillet from the heat for 1 minute. Add half the eggs, tilting and rotating the skillet to make a thin layer. Cook the egg sheet until it is just set. Turn, and cook the other side briefly. Transfer it to a plate. Make another sheet in the same manner. Cool, stack, and shred the egg sheets into fine pieces. Combine with the noodles.

In a small bowl, combine the stock, the remaining soy sauce, peanut butter, the remaining sesame oil, sugar, garlic, ginger root, vinegar or Worcestershire, and hot chili oil.

In a saucepan, cover the bean sprouts with boiling water. Blanch them for 30 seconds, and drain. Refresh them under cold water, and dry them in paper towels. Add the bean sprouts and scallions to the noodle mixture.

Heat a wok or skillet until it is very hot. Add 2 tablespoons (30 mL) of the peanut oil, and heat until very hot. Add the chicken, and stir-fry for 2 minutes, or until the shreds separate and change color. Transfer the chicken to a plate. When it is cool, combine it with the stock and noodle mixtures. Toss lightly but thoroughly to combine all the ingredients.

Serve at room temperature.

Serves 8.

Audrey and David Alpern

Steamed Fish with Black Bean Sauce

1 4-pound (1.81 kg) black bass or sea trout, cleaned

Sauce:
4 teaspoons (20 mL/22 g) fermented black beans*

2 cloves garlic, crushed

4 thin slices fresh ginger root, peeled and minced

4 tablespoons (60 mL) imported soy sauce

2 tablespoons (30 mL) medium dry sherry

2 tablespoons (30 mL) peanut oil

1 teaspoon (5 mL/4.7 g) sugar

Salt

Shredded scallions, for garnish

In a small bowl, cover the fermented beans with cold water, and soak for about 10 minutes. Drain.

Squeeze out the excess moisture. Mash the beans with the garlic. Add the ginger root, soy sauce, sherry, oil, and sugar. Combine well.

Rinse the fish under cold running water. Pat it dry with paper towels. Lightly score the fish on both sides. Sprinkle inside and out with salt. Place it in a shallow, greased, heat-proof dish.

Spread the bean sauce over the fish. In a steamer or on a rack over boiling water in a covered pan, steam the fish for 20 minutes, or until the flesh near the back of the head is white and opaque.

Garnish with shredded scallions. Serve immediately.

Serves 8.

The Cookbook Committee

*May be purchased in Asian food stores.

Peking Duck with Mandarin Pancakes

Ducks:
1 cup (240 mL) honey

1 cup (240 mL) soy sauce

1 cup (240 mL) molasses

2 3½- to 4-pound (1.59 kg to 1.81 kg) ducklings

Pancakes:
¾ cup (180 mL) boiling water

2 cups (480 mL/265 g) all-purpose flour

½ cup (120 mL) sesame oil*

Sauce:
1½ cups (360 mL) hoisin sauce*

½ cup (120 mL/130 g) peanut butter

Scallion Brushes:
2 bunches scallions

Ducks:
In a bowl, combine the honey, soy sauce, and molasses. Set aside.

*May be purchased in Asian food stores.

Bring a kettle of water to a boil. Wash the ducklings thoroughly (reserve giblets for some other purpose). With heavy twine, hang or hold the ducks by the neck over the sink. Slowly pour the boiling water over the ducks. Drain, and dry thoroughly with paper towels.

Now hang the ducks over the sink, and brush them with the honey-soy mixture. Repeat 1 hour later. Dry for 8 hours with an electric fan placed 1 foot from the ducks.

Preheat oven to 450° F (230° C).

Place the ducks, breast sides up, on a rack in a roasting pan. Prick the ducks all over. Roast for ½ hour. Reduce heat to 350° F (175° C). Cover the ducks, and continue roasting for 1 hour longer.

Pancakes:
Slowly stir the boiling water into the flour, using a fork to blend (the dough will be very stiff). Wrap the dough in plastic wrap, and let it rest for ½ hour.

Dust a work surface with flour. Roll out the dough to ¼-inch (0.6 cm) thickness. Using a 2-inch (5 cm) round cutter, stamp out rounds. Spread each with sesame oil, and place two together, oiled sides facing. Repeat until all rounds are oiled and stacked.

Heat a 7-inch (18 cm) crêpe pan (oil, if required). Roll each double round into a thin pancake, 4 to 6 inches (10 to 15 cm) in diameter, maintaining a circular shape. In the heated pan, lightly brown the pancakes, one at a time (the pancake should hiss when placed in the pan). Cook for about 2 minutes on one side, for 1 minute on the other side. Stack the cooked pancakes on a plate. When half the recipe is cooked, gently separate the double pancakes by pulling them apart at the center. Repeat the process for the remaining half of the recipe.

Wrap the pancakes in plastic wrap, and refrigerate. Just before serving, remove the plastic wrap, wrap the pancakes in a damp towel, and steam in a Chinese or other steamer for 8 minutes. (To steam, the wrapped pancakes are placed on a rack over boiling water.)

Sauce:
Combine the hoisin sauce and peanut butter. Spoon into 8 small dishes.

Scallion Brushes:
Trim the scallions to 5½-inch (14 cm) lengths. Make several lengthwise cuts approximately ¾ inch (1.9 cm) in each end. Place in ice water to curl the cut ends.

Assembly:
Remove the legs and wings from the ducks, leaving them whole. Using poultry shears, cut the ducks into bite-size pieces. Discard any fat. Cut the skin into 1½-inch (4 cm) squares.

Reassemble the meat in the shape of ducks on two platters. Mound the meat to form the bodies. Cover with squares of skin. Place the wings and legs in their original positions. Garnish with the scallion brushes.

Each guest spreads a pancake with the sauce, using a scallion brush. Pieces of duck and a scallion brush are then placed on the pancake, which is rolled like a crêpe. Pancakes are eaten with the fingers.

Note:
Pancakes may be made several days ahead; refrigerate for one day ahead; freeze for a longer period of time.

Serves 8.

Dana Kline

Almond Float

4 cups (960 mL) water

½ cup (120 mL) evaporated milk

9 tablespoons (135 mL/ 130 g) sugar

3 envelopes (¾ ounce/ 21 g) unflavored gelatin

2 tablespoons (30 mL) almond extract

Ice cubes

1 13-ounce (370 g) can mandarin oranges, drained (reserve juice)

In a saucepan, combine the water, milk, and sugar. Sprinkle the gelatin on top. Heat to dissolve the gelatin, stirring constantly. Do not boil.

Cool slightly. Add the almond extract.

Pour into a shallow 1-quart (960 mL) glass pan. Cool. Refrigerate for at least 1 hour, or until gelled. Cut into 1-inch (2.5 cm) squares.

Combine the reserved mandarin orange juice with enough water and ice cubes to cover the jelly. Pour the liquid over the jelly, and shake the pan to loosen the squares.

Divide the oranges equally among 8 bowls. Top with the jelly and liquid.

Serves 8.

Ruth J. Allen

Edward Hicks
(American, 1780-1849)
*The Residence of David Twining
in 1785*, 1845-48
Oil on canvas

26 × 29½ in. (66 × 75 cm.)
Howard N. Eavenson Memorial
Fund for the Howard N.
Eavenson Americana Collection,
1962

Edward Hicks, 1780–1849
The Residence of David Twining in 1785, 1845–1848

Edward Hicks, one of the foremost figures in American folk art, was, like John Kane, entirely self-taught. Unbound by aesthetic theories, his forthright vision emanated from the devout beliefs he held as an itinerant Quaker preacher.

Hicks earned his living by painting signs, coaches, and furniture. At one time in nineteenth-century Pennsylvania nearly every Bucks County tavern boasted one of his signs above its door.

In *The Residence of David Twining in 1785* the mature artist recollects the prosperous Quaker farm and adopted family of his boyhood. Figures from his memory inhabit an idealized countryside in which trees spread their branches in perfect symmetry and plow horses march in lock step. Nowhere in the real world do people live so utterly free of strife, nor do farm animals cluster in perfect contentment; but here, as in his other paintings, Hicks orders a gentle universe as he would have it.

I would not part with this child-like belief . . . for ten thousand times ten thousand worlds.
Edward Hicks

Bounty

Menu

Acorn Squash Soup

Mallard Duck Pie

Braised Lettuce and Carrots

Persimmon Pudding with Hard Sauce

Serves Four

Wine

Italian Chianti or

Barbaresco

In Edward Hicks's world, the evening meal was most often the satisfying result of a well-tended garden and a hunter's steady aim.

This American country menu celebrates the land's plentiful yields. Serving the golden soup in the squash's own green shell glorifies both the vegetable and the season, preparing the way for the unusual mallard pie.

The persimmon pudding is reminiscent of the rich and brilliant hues of autumn.

Acorn Squash Soup

4 small, about 3½ inches (9 cm) in diameter, acorn squashes with stems

1 1½-pound (680 g) acorn squash

1 medium onion, sliced

About 1½ cups (360 mL) chicken stock

½ cup (120 mL) heavy cream

¼ teaspoon (1.3 mL/ 0.6 g) nutmeg

Salt and pepper to taste

Preheat oven to 400° F (205° C).

Cut the tips from the bottoms of the small squashes so that they will sit firmly on a plate. Cut off the tops; reserve for lids. Scoop out the seeds and enough pulp so that each squash will hold ⅔ to ¾ cup (160 to 180 mL) liquid. Reserve the pulp for the soup.

Peel, seed, and cut the large squash into 1½ inch (3.8 cm) chunks. Combine with the reserved pulp, the onion, and 1½ cups (360 mL) of the stock. Cook over medium heat for 15 minutes.

In a food processor, blend the mixture for about 2 minutes, or until smooth; there should be about 3 cups of purée. Add the cream, nutmeg, salt, and pepper. For a thinner soup, add stock.

Fill the squash shells with water. Place on a greased pan or cookie sheet and bake for 15 minutes. Remove the shells from the oven. Drain the water. Fill the shells with the soup, sprinkle with nutmeg, and cover with the squash lids.

Note:
Acorn squash soup may also be served cold.

Serves 4.

Edith H. Fisher

Mallard Duck Pie

8 cloves garlic

1 teaspoon (5 mL) salt

Juice of 2 lemons

2 Mallard ducks

2 onions, sliced

3½ ounces (100 g) (5 slices) bacon

1 cup (240 mL) orange juice

Brandy **or** Madeira (optional)

6 to 8 juniper berries, crushed

Salt and pepper to taste

Unbaked pastry for top and bottom piecrusts (see Pâte Brisée, below)

Preheat oven to 500° F (260° C).

Make a paste of the garlic, 1 teaspoon (5 mL/6 g) salt, and lemon juice. Rub the insides and outsides of the ducks with the paste. Place them in a roasting pan. Bake for 15 minutes. Prick the ducks, and baste with the juices. Reduce the heat to 350° F (175° C), and continue roasting for 1 hour.

Sauté the onions with the bacon. Purée.

Remove the fat from the ducks; break the duck meat into very small pieces, and add to the onion purée. Add the orange juice and brandy or Madeira, if desired. Add the juniper berries. Season with salt and pepper.

Line an ungreased 2-inch (5 cm) deep clay or glass baking dish with half the pie pastry. Add the duck mixture. Cover with the remaining pastry. Make 4 or 5 slits in the top crust. Bake for 1 hour at 350° F (175° C).

Serves 4.

Teresa Heinz

Pâte Brisée:

12 tablespoons (180 mL/ 170 g) chilled unsalted butter

1½ cups (360 mL/200 g) all-purpose unbleached flour

½ cup (120 mL/48 g) plain bleached cake flour

2 tablespoons (30 mL/ 29 g) chilled vegetable shortening

2 pinches of sugar

¼ teaspoon (1.3 mL/ 1.5 g) salt

About ½ cup (120 mL) ice water

Cut the butter into 12 pieces.

In a food processor with a metal blade, place the flours, butter, shortening, sugar, and salt. Process, turning the switch on and off rapidly seven or eight times. With the machine running, pour in all but 1 tablespoon (15 mL) of the ice water. Process, turning the switch on and off, just until the dough begins to mass together but still has some unformed bits. Remove, and form rapidly into a ball. Wrap in wax paper, and refrigerate for at least 1 hour.

Makes one 10- or 11-inch (25 to 28 cm) pastry shell, **or** one 9- by 9-inch (23 by 23 cm) turnover, **or** two 8- or 9-inch (20 or 23 cm) pastry shells.

The Cookbook Committee

Braised Lettuce and Carrots

1 pound (455 g) carrots, peeled and cut into 2-inch (5 cm) lengths, **or** finger-size carrots

4 heads tight-formed Boston lettuce

7 tablespoons (105 mL/ 100 g) unsalted butter

1 stalk celery, minced

1 medium onion, minced

1 cup (240 mL) chicken stock

¼ teaspoon (1.3 mL/ 1.2 g) sugar

7 parsley sprigs

1 teaspoon (5 mL/1.5 g) thyme

1 bay leaf

Bring a large kettle of salted water to a boil. Add the carrots, and blanch for 4 minutes. Drain, and set aside. Return the kettle to a boil. Add the lettuce, and blanch for 2 minutes. Transfer to a bowl of ice water. Drain, and pat dry. Cut each head in half.

In a large heavy skillet, melt 3 tablespoons (45 mL/43 g) of the butter, and sauté the celery and onion until soft. In one layer, add the lettuce, cut sides down, and carrots. Add the stock, sugar, parsley, thyme, and bay leaf. Bring to a boil. Cover with a greased round of wax paper and the lid. Braise for 25 to 30 minutes, or until tender. Transfer the lettuce and carrots to a platter.

Strain the cooking liquid into a saucepan, and reduce until syrupy. Stir in the remaining butter until melted. Pour the hot sauce over the lettuce and carrots.

Serves 4.

Singer Euwer

Persimmon Pudding with Hard Sauce

2 or 3 (225 g) persimmons

½ cup (120 mL) milk

1 tablespoon (15 mL/14 g) unsalted butter, melted

1 cup (240 mL/225 g) granulated sugar

1 cup (240 mL/130 g) all-purpose flour

1 teaspoon (5 mL/4.4 g) baking soda

¼ teaspoon (1.3 mL/ 1.5 g) salt

Hard Sauce:
   1½ cups (360 mL/175 g) sifted confectioners' sugar

   ¼ pound (115 g) unsalted butter **or** margarine, softened

   2 teaspoons (10 mL) vanilla

Preheat oven to 350° F (175° C). Grease a 9-inch (23 cm) piepan.

Peel and mash the persimmons, or purée them in a blender or food processor; there should be 1 cup (240 mL). Combine the persimmons, milk, and 1 tablespoon (15 mL/ 14 g) butter.

In a large bowl, combine the granulated sugar, flour, baking soda, and salt. Stir into the persimmon mixture. Pour the combined mixture into the piepan. Place the piepan in a large shallow pan, and pour boiling water into the shallow pan to a depth of ½ inch (1.3 cm). Bake for 1 to 1¼ hours, adding water if needed. Remove to a wire rack.

To serve warm, cool slightly. To serve cold, cool completely, and refrigerate.

Hard Sauce:
In a small bowl, cream together the confectioners' sugar and ¼ pound (115 g) butter. Beat until fluffy. Beat in the vanilla.

To serve:
Cut the pudding into wedges, and top with the sauce.

Serves 4.

Mrs. John G. Zimmerman, Jr.

Georgia O'Keeffe
(American, b. 1887)
Gate of Adobe Church, 1929
Oil on canvas
20 × 16 in. (50.8 × 40.6 cm.)
Gift in memory of Elisabeth
Mellon Sellers from her
friends, 1974

Georgia O'Keeffe, 1887–
Gate of Adobe Church, 1929

It is impossible to imagine her anywhere other than the Southwest. Her red deserts, blue New Mexico skies, and sun-bleached skulls have become synonymous with this land of cactus and pueblos, but Georgia O'Keeffe was born in the Midwest and trained at the Art Students League in New York City and at the Art Institute of Chicago.

O'Keeffe introduced many to modern art with flowers painted so large that they seemed abstract despite the accuracy of their portrayal. While she was still in her twenties and teaching art in Texas, a friend sent some of her paintings to the famous photographer Alfred Stieglitz, whose gallery on Fifth Avenue in New York City was the center of the avant-garde art world in America. Stieglitz was the first in this country to exhibit Picasso, Matisse, and Cézanne. He became O'Keeffe's greatest champion and, in 1924, her husband.

Although they were devoted to each other, the marriage did not allow O'Keeffe the solitude which her painting required. In the summer of 1929 she set off alone for the Southwest and found there "the only place I have ever felt that I really belonged." *Gate of Adobe Church* dates from that solitary summer.

Anyone who doesn't feel the crosses simply doesn't get that country.
Georgia O'Keeffe

Abiquiu

Menu

Tortilla Salad with Guacamole

Abiquiu Chicken

Stuffed Chilies

Sopaipillas with Honey

Green Chili Sorbet

Serves Six

Beer

Mexican Varieties

This Mexican dinner rates *iolé!s* from its stylish setting to its surprising dessert. It is an evening done in bold strokes, seasoned liberally with the hot and the sweet.

Great glasses of frothy Mexican beer make an exceptionally refreshing accompaniment. Mild, slightly bitter Dos Equis and amber Tecate are favorites for quenching the fiery taste of chili peppers, which dominate Mexican cooking.

Dinner begins with a tortilla and guacamole salad. The chicken that follows is a hearty, piquant dish in which the bite of chili, garlic, and cumin is mellowed by orange juice, red wine, and brown sugar.

Before dessert, guests follow the Mexican tradition of filling their hot sopaipillas with honey. The popoverlike pastries are nestled in large peasant baskets lined with brightly colored tissue paper.

Dessert is a frosty reprise of earlier tastes and flavors. Unlike other vegetable ices, usually served early in the meal in place of cold soup, the chili sorbet is the evening's final adventure.

Tortilla Salad with Guacamole

Salad Dressing:

½ cup (120 mL) olive oil

2 tablespoons (30 mL) lemon juice

2 tablespoons (30 mL) red wine vinegar

½ teaspoon (2.5 mL/3 g) salt

½ teaspoon (2.5 mL/ 1.1 g) dry mustard

½ teaspoon (2.5 mL/ 1.3 g) paprika

1 clove garlic, minced

Guacamole:

1 avocado, peeled and mashed

Juice of ½ lime

3 scallions, minced (optional)

1 clove garlic, minced

¼ to ½ teaspoon (1.3 mL to 2.5 mL) Tabasco sauce

½ teaspoon (2.5 mL/ 1.2 g) chili powder

A pinch of sugar

A pinch of salt

1 head iceberg lettuce, shredded

6 corn tortillas

¼ cup (60 mL) vegetable oil

2 large tomatoes, peeled, seeded, and chopped

12 slices bacon, fried crisp and crumbled

1½ cups (360 mL/235 g) garbanzo beans

Salad Dressing:
Combine all ingredients. Mix well.

Guacamole:
Combine all ingredients. Mix well.

Assembly:
Toss the lettuce lightly with the salad dressing.

Fry the tortillas until they are crisp. Drain on paper towels. Place on plates.

Layer the ingredients on each tortilla in this order: lettuce, tomatoes, guacamole, bacon, and beans.

Serves 6.

Mrs. Brittan C. MacIsaac

Abiquiu Chicken

1½ cups (360 mL) red wine

¾ cup (180 mL) orange juice

3 tablespoons (45 mL/ 21 g) chili powder

⅓ cup (80 mL/45 g) chopped green chilies

3 tablespoons (45 mL) olive oil

1 large onion, chopped

3 cloves garlic, minced

1½ teaspoons (8 mL/1.1 g) oregano

2 teaspoons (10 mL/4.3 g) ground cumin

1½ tablespoons (23 mL/ 17 g) brown sugar

1 bay leaf

Grated rind of 1½ oranges

Salt to taste

2 3½-pound (1.59 kg) chickens, cut into serving pieces

Combine all the ingredients except the chicken. Pour the mixture over the chicken. Marinate in the refrigerator for 12 hours. Bake the chicken in a preheated 350° F (175° C) oven for 1 hour, basting frequently with the marinade.

Serves 6.

Singer Euwer

Stuffed Chilies

Green Chili Sauce:
3 tablespoons (45 mL) olive oil

¼ cup (180 mL/86 g) chopped scallions

3 cloves garlic, pressed

3 peeled, seeded, and chopped tomatoes **or** about ¾ cup canned tomatoes (180 mL/170 g)

1½ tablespoons (23 mL/ 5 g) chopped parsley

½ cup (120 mL/68 g) canned green chilies, chopped

1½ teaspoons (8 mL/ 4.2 g) ground coriander

2 whole cloves

Salt and pepper to taste

3 eggs separated

About ½ cup (120 mL/ 66 g) all-purpose flour

Salt and pepper to taste

6 peeled and seeded green chilies

1½ cups (360 mL/400 g) refried beans

About ¼ cup (60 mL) safflower oil

⅔ cup (160 mL) light cream

½ cup (120 mL/60 g) grated sharp Cheddar cheese

½ cup (120 mL/60 g) grated Monterey Jack cheese

Green Chili Sauce:
Heat the olive oil, and sauté the scallions and garlic until transparent. Add the remaining ingredients, and combine well. Simmer for 10 to 15 minutes.

Preheat oven to 350° F (175° C).

Beat the egg whites until stiff. With a fork, beat the egg yolks lightly, and fold them into the whites. Fold in ½ cup (120 mL) flour, salt, and pepper. Pour the batter into a shallow dish.

Stuff the chilies with the beans. Dredge them in flour, and roll them in the batter, turning them to coat them completely. With a slotted spoon, place each chili carefully on a saucer.

Heat the safflower oil in a skillet, and gently slide the chilies into the hot fat. Fry on both sides until golden, and transfer to a shallow baking dish. Pour first the cream, then the chili sauce over the top. Sprinkle with both cheeses. Bake for about 15 minutes, or until the cheese melts and the cream bubbles.

Serves 6.

Singer Euwer

105

Sopaipillas with Honey

1 tablespoon (15 mL/14 g) granulated sugar

3 cups (720 mL) lukewarm water

1 envelope (¼ ounce/7 g) dry yeast

6 cups (1.44 L/790 g) all-purpose flour

2 tablespoons (30 mL/29 g) unsalted butter **or** vegetable shortening

4 cups (960 mL) peanut oil

Confectioners' sugar, for garnish

2 cups (480 mL/455 g) honey

Dissolve the granulated sugar in the water. Add the yeast, and stir to dissolve. Let the mixture rest for about 3 minutes. Add 1 cup (240 mL/130 g) of the flour, and mix thoroughly.

Add the remaining flour, a cup at a time, mixing thoroughly with each addition (the dough will be slightly sticky). Shape the dough into a ball, brush with butter, and cover with buttered plastic wrap. Let it rise for 1½ hours in a draft-free place (the dough may be allowed to rise up to 4 hours before frying).

Lightly flour a work surface. Roll out the dough approximately ⅛ inch (0.3 cm) thick. If the dough is too sticky, knead in more flour. Cut the dough into 3-inch (8 cm) squares.

In a deep fryer, heat the oil to 400° F (205° C). To test the temperature, drop a small scrap of dough into the oil. When the oil is hot enough, the dough will dance and turn golden.

Drop the squares into the oil. They will puff up immediately. Fry until golden. Drain thoroughly on paper towels. Dust with confectioners' sugar, and serve hot with honey. The sopaipillas should be opened and the honey spooned inside.

Makes about 24.

The Cookbook Committee

Green Chili Sorbet

2 cups (480 mL/455 g) sugar

1 cup (240 mL) water

½ cup (120 mL) white vinegar

½ cup (120 mL/68 g) chopped green chilies (see Note)

1½ cups (360 mL/205 g) chopped green bell peppers

In a saucepan, dissolve the sugar in the water. Add the vinegar, chilies, and peppers. Simmer for about 5 minutes. Strain and cool.

Freeze in an ice cream freezer. First the mixture will become bubbly; then, suddenly, as it thickens, it will turn creamy white.

Note:
Prepared chilies may be found in the frozen or canned goods sections of supermarkets.

To prepare fresh chilies, cook them on a very hot griddle or under the broiler until the skins are dark on all sides. Layer the chilies between very damp paper towels, and freeze. When the chilies defrost, the skins will be easy to remove. Remove the ends and seeds.

Jalapeños may be substituted for green chilies, but the sorbet will have just the "bite," not the fruity flavor.

Serves 6 to 8.

Tom Brownell
Thunderbird Lodge
Taos Ski Valley, New Mexico

Augustus Saint-Gaudens
(American, 1848-1907)
Victory, 1902
Gilded bronze
41⅞ × 23 × 35 in.
(106.3 × 58 × 89 cm.)
Museum Purchase, 1919

Augustus Saint-Gaudens, 1848–1907
Victory, 1902

Despite his French name, Augustus Saint-Gaudens was actually born in Dublin and came to the United States when he was not yet six months old. Apprenticed at thirteen to a New York cameo cutter, Saint-Gaudens learned early the discipline of modeling and dimensional portraiture.

Saint-Gaudens was almost thirty when he met Stanford White, a principal, along with Charles McKim, in one of the most prestigious architecture firms of the day. The three became fast friends and business associates. McKim arranged the commissions, White designed the pedestals, and Saint-Gaudens executed the sculptures or reliefs. Their collaboration resulted in some of Saint-Gaudens's most celebrated works.

Victory, a golden angel, was part of a monument commissioned for the city of New York. The original stands today before an equestrian statue of General William Tecumseh Sherman in the small park in front of the Plaza Hotel at Fifth Avenue and Fifty-ninth Street. Cast in massive numbers, *Victory* was one of the most popular items sold at Tiffany's in 1902.

Ambrosia

Menu

Chilled Plum Soup

Squab with Apricots and Macadamia Nuts

Brown Rice

Purée of Broccoli

Torta da Alice

Serves Sixteen

Wine

French Beaujolais (main course)

California or Portuguese Vintage Port (dessert)

This formal supper retains the spirit but amends the quantities and numbers of courses of the typical *fin de siècle* dinner party of Saint-Gaudens's time. Fresh fruit, a green vegetable, and a unique choice of fowl are more in keeping with contemporary styles.

The first course is a tart soup, an unusual introduction to the squab. Rock Cornish game hens are a satisfactory substitute when pigeons are not available.

The golden-baked birds, seasoned with a fragrant combination of herbs and garnished with dried fruit, make a presentation worthy of applause. Besides juniper berries, the dish contains coriander leaves. Although most cooks are familiar with dried coriander, an herb which smells faintly of orange peel, this recipe calls for the fresh herb, frequently available in Asian markets, where it is known as Chinese parsley.

Chilled Plum Soup

12 cups (2.88 L) water

2¼ cups (540 mL/510 g) sugar

4½ pounds (2.04 g) small purple plums, halved and pitted

3 strips 2-inch (5 cm) -long lemon rind

3 cinnamon sticks

6 teaspoons (30 mL/20 g) arrowroot, dissolved in 3 tablespoons (45 mL) cold water

1½ cups (360 mL) port

4 cups (960 mL/1.04 kg) plain yogurt

Cinnamon (optional)

In a saucepan, combine the water and sugar. Bring to a boil over moderate heat, stirring until the sugar dissolves. Boil the syrup, undisturbed, for 5 minutes. Add the plums, lemon rind, and cinnamon sticks. Cook the mixture, covered, over moderate heat for about 30 minutes, or until the plums are very soft. Remove the lemon rind and cinnamon. In a food processor or food mill, purée the mixture. Return the purée to the pan.

Bring the purée to a boil, and stir in the dissolved arrowroot. Cook, stirring, for about 5 minutes, or until slightly thickened. Remove from the heat, and stir in the port. Refrigerate for at least 3 hours, or until well chilled.

Blend 1 cup (240 mL) of the plum purée into 3 cups (720 mL/780 g) of the yogurt, stirring until smooth. Combine with the rest of the soup. Serve in chilled glass bowls. Garnish with a dollop of the remaining yogurt and a dash of cinnamon, if desired.

Note:
This soup is an excellent late-summer or autumn appetizer.

Serves 16.

Abby McKinnon

Squab with Apricots and Macadamia Nuts

8 squabs

6 cups (1.44 L) white Burgundy **or** other full-bodied dry white wine

2 tablespoons (30 mL/ 21 g) juniper berries, crushed

2 teaspoons (10 mL/1.8 g) rosemary leaves

1 teaspoon (5 mL/1.1 g) coriander leaves

Flour

¾ cup (180 mL/170 g) vegetable shortening **or** bacon fat

5 cups (1.2 L) chicken stock

2 tablespoons (30 mL/3 g) dried tarragon

1 teaspoon (5 mL/2.4 g) nutmeg

3 tablespoons (45 mL/ 10 g) chervil

3 cups (720 mL/420 g) dried apricots

1 cup (240 mL/140 g) macadamia nuts, sliced and lightly toasted

One or two days before, cut the squabs in half. Place them in a deep container with a nonmetallic surface. Cover with the wine, juniper berries, rosemary, and coriander. Marinate in the refrigerator for 24 to 48 hours, turning frequently.

When ready to prepare, remove the squabs. Pat them dry, and set aside. Over medium heat, reduce the marinade to about 1 cup (240 mL). Strain, and reserve.

Preheat oven to 325° F (165° C).

Dredge the squabs heavily in flour. In a Dutch oven or casserole, brown them evenly in the shortening or bacon fat. Pour off the fat, leaving 2 tablespoons (30 mL) in the pan. Add the stock, reserved marinade, tarragon, nutmeg, chervil, and apricots. Bring to a boil, reduce to a slow simmer, and cover. Place the casserole in the oven, and bake for 1½ to 2 hours.

Transfer the squabs to a heated platter. Arrange the apricots in a border. Pour enough of the sauce over the top to glaze lightly.* If a thicker sauce is desired, reduce slightly over high heat. Garnish with the macadamia nuts.

Note:
The flavor improves when the squabs are made 1 or 2 days ahead.

Serves 16.

John Cheek

*Serve the remaining sauce on the side.

Purée of Broccoli

3 bunches (about 3¾ pounds) (1.70 kg) broccoli

3 medium onions, sliced

6 cups (1.44 L) chicken stock

9 tablespoons (135 mL/ 130 g) unsalted butter

Wash the broccoli. Peel the stems. Cut the florets and stems into fairly small pieces. Cook the broccoli and onions in the stock for about 10 minutes, or until tender but still green. Strain, reserving about ¾ cup (180 mL) of the stock.

In a food processor or blender, purée the broccoli and reserved stock to the desired consistency. Reheat, and add the butter. To retain green color, do not overcook.

Serves 16.

The Cookbook Committee

Torta da Alice (Chocolate Cake Roll)

Chocolate Filling:
   8 ounces (225 g) semisweet chocolate

   4 egg yolks

   2 cups (480 mL) milk

   1 tablespoon (15 mL/ 8 g) cornstarch

Cake:
   5 eggs, separated

   1 cup (240 mL/225 g) granulated sugar

   1 cup (240 mL/130 g) all-purpose flour

   1 teaspoon (5 mL/3.4 g) baking powder

   Confectioners' sugar

Chocolate Filling:
In the top of a double boiler, melt the chocolate. In a saucepan, beat the egg yolks. Add the milk, and mix. Add the cornstarch, and cook over medium heat until thickened. Stir to prevent separating. Add cornstarch mixture to the melted chocolate. Let the filling cool.

Cake:
Preheat oven to 350° F (175° C). Line a 15- by 12-inch (38 by 30 cm) jelly roll pan with wax paper. Grease and flour the paper.

Beat the egg yolks well. Add the granulated sugar, and beat until light. Add the flour and baking powder gradually.

In a separate bowl, beat the egg whites until stiff. Fold into the egg yolk mixture. Spread the batter evenly in the pan. Bake for about 15 minutes, but check at 12 minutes. Do not overbake.

Sprinkle a towel generously with confectioners' sugar. Turn the cake onto the towel. Pull off the paper quickly. With a sharp, long knife, trim all crisp edges so the cake will roll without breaking. Roll the cake in the towel, and let it stand for a few minutes. Unroll it, and spread it with the filling. Roll firmly, and wrap loosely in aluminum foil. Refrigerate until ready to serve.

Serves 8; make two to serve 16.

Teresa Heinz

113

Vincent van Gogh
(Dutch, 1853-1890)
The Plain of Auvers, 1890
Oil on canvas

28 ¾ × 36¼ in. (73 × 92 cm.)
Acquired through the generosity
of the Sarah Mellon Scaife
family, 1968

114

Vincent van Gogh, 1853–1890
The Plain of Auvers, 1890

For many people Vincent van Gogh is the prototypical tragic artist—impoverished, alone, and unrecognized in his lifetime. When he died at age thirty-seven, he left the record of a world twisted and full of torment.

Van Gogh was born in Holland, not far from the Belgian border. After several unsuccessful careers he took up painting with a singular zeal. He studied in Paris for two years and then moved south, driven by a northerner's hunger for the sun. He settled eventually in Auvers, a tiny French village near Paris bounded by the Oise Valley on one side and by an enormous wheat field on the other.

The light and color of Provence inspired his brilliant palette. Warmth and beauty were everywhere. His letters to his brother Theo spoke of hope and of new beginnings. But broken in health and in spirit, van Gogh was soon overtaken by the loneliness and melancholy which had plagued him throughout his short, troubled life.

The Plain of Auvers is a thickly impastoed landscape of wheat fields and twisted cypress, reflecting the artist's torment. It was painted only days before he sought his own death.

I am convinced that nature down here is just what one needs to give one color.
Vincent van Gogh

Paysage

Menu

Pasta with Fresh Tomatoes

Wheatberry Salad

Corn Bread with Cheese and Chilies

Summer Fruits with Crème Fraîche

Brownies

Serves Six

Wine

French Muscadet or

New York State Seyval Blanc

The golden wheat fields of van Gogh's landscape inspired the choice of wheatberries for this nutritious summer menu. Wheatberries are long nut-brown kernels of unprocessed wheat with the bran and germ intact. Once cooked, they are combined with a rainbow of marinated vegetables for a different kind of salad.

Use tightly lidded glass jars full of pastas, grains, and rice to stock your summer kitchen, and plant small clay pots with tarragon, burnet, rosemary, and chives for a ready supply of fresh seasonings.

Art is a little corner of creation seen through a temperament.
Emile Zola
Novelist

Pasta with Fresh Tomatoes

Sauce:

2 pounds (905 g) ripe tomatoes, peeled and seeded (reserve juice)

2 garlic cloves, minced

20 fresh basil leaves, minced

⅛ teaspoon (0.6 mL/ 0.1 g) minced oregano

1 tablespoon (15 mL/ 3 g) minced Italian parsley

1½ teaspoons (8 mL/ 9 g) salt

¼ teaspoon (1.3 mL/ 0.7 g) freshly ground pepper

5 tablespoons (75 mL) olive oil

½ pound (225 g) mozzarella cheese, diced

6 quarts (5.76 L) water

2 tablespoons (30 mL/ 36 g) salt

1 pound (455 g) small pasta shells

Sauce:
Chop the tomatoes into bite-size pieces. In a serving bowl, combine the tomatoes and the reserved juice. Add the remaining sauce ingredients. Mix well, and let stand at room temperature for at least 1 hour.

Bring the water and salt to a boil. Add the pasta, and cook until it is *al dente.* Drain it thoroughly, and toss it with the tomato mixture. Serve immediately on warm plates.

Serves 6.

Mrs. Brittan C. MacIsaac

The laws of color are unutterably beautiful, just because they are not accidental.
Vincent van Gogh

117

Wheatberry Salad

2 cups (480 mL/270 g)
wheatberries

2 cups (480 mL/350 g)
soybeans

Marinade:

¼ teaspoon (1.3 mL/
0.6 g) dry mustard

½ cup (120 mL) tarragon
vinegar

3 tablespoons (45 mL/
44 g) mayonnaise

½ cup (120 mL/130 g)
plain yogurt

Juice of 1 lime

A dash of basil

1 cup (240 mL/53 g)
chopped parsley

3 tablespoons (45 mL)
dry white wine

2 carrots, diced

1 green pepper, diced

4 scallions, diced

1 cup (240 mL) other
diced fresh vegetables

2 cups (480 mL/500 g)
cottage cheese

4 or 5 sprigs fresh
burnet,* for garnish
(optional)

2 or 3 sprigs fresh
tarragon, for garnish

Cook the wheatberries
and soybeans in water to
cover for a least 1 hour,
or until tender. Drain and
set aside.

Combine all the marinade
ingredients; mix well.
Combine with the cooked
wheatberries and
soybeans. Marinate at
room temperature for
several hours.

Add the carrots, green
pepper, scallions, any
other fresh vegetables, and
cottage cheese. Toss.

Garnish with fresh sprigs
of burnet, if desired, and
tarragon.

Serves 6.

Ellen C. Walton

*Burnet is an herb that
   can be found in gourmet
   food shops.

Corn Bread with Cheese and Chilies

1 cup (240 mL/230 g)
unsalted margarine **or**
butter

1 cup (240 mL/225 g)
sugar

4 eggs

4 ounces (115 g) canned
green chilies, chopped

16 ounces (455 g) canned
creamed corn

½ cup (120 mL/57 g)
shredded Monterey Jack
cheese

½ cup (120 mL/57 g)
shredded Cheddar cheese

1 cup (240 mL/132 g)
all-purpose flour

1 cup (240 mL/145 g)
yellow cornmeal

4 teaspoons (20 mL/13 g)
baking powder

¼ teaspoon (1.3 mL/
1.5 g) salt

Preheat oven to 350° F
(175° C). Grease an 8- by
12- by 2-inch (20 by 30 by
5 cm) pan.

Combine the margarine,
sugar, eggs, chilies, corn,
and cheeses. Sift the flour,
cornmeal, baking powder,
and salt; add to the egg
mixture. Pour into the
prepared pan.

Lower the heat to 300° F
(150° C). Bake for 1 hour.

Serve hot or cold.

Serves 4 to 6.

Teresa Heinz

Summer Fruits with Crème Fraîche

6 peaches

1 pint (480 mL/230 g) blueberries

1 pint (480 mL/230 g) raspberries

1 cup (240 mL) Crème Fraîche (see below)

Confectioners' sugar, for garnish

Slice the peaches. Mix them in a glass bowl with the blueberries and raspberries. Chill.

Serve with crème fraîche. Garnish with confectioners' sugar.

Serves 6.

The Cookbook Committee

Crème Fraîche:

1 cup (240 mL) heavy (not ultrapasteurized) cream

1 teaspoon (5 mL) buttermilk

Combine the cream and buttermilk. Heat until lukewarm, not over 85° F (29° C). Pour into a jar. Cover loosely. Let stand in a moderately warm place overnight, or until thickened. Cover, and refrigerate for at least 4 hours.

Makes about 1 cup (240 milliliters).

The Cookbook Committee

Brownies

4 ounces (115 g) unsweetened chocolate

½ pound (225 g) unsalted butter

2 cups (480 mL/455 g) granulated sugar

½ teaspoon (2.5 mL) vanilla

½ teaspoon (2.5 mL) almond extract

¼ teaspoon (1.3 mL/ 1.5 g) salt

1 teaspoon (5 mL/2.7 g) black pepper

4 large eggs

1 cup plus 2 tablespoons (270 mL/110 g) cake flour

1 cup (240 mL/105 g) chopped pecans

1 cup (240 mL/ 170 g) chocolate chips

Confectioners' sugar

Preheat oven to 350° F (175° C).

Line a 9- by 13-inch (23 by 33 cm) baking pan with foil. Grease the foil with a nonstick spray.

In a heavy-bottomed saucepan or the top of a double boiler, melt the chocolate and butter. Transfer to a mixing bowl. Stir in the granulated sugar, vanilla, almond extract, salt, and pepper. Beat in the eggs, one at a time. Fold in the cake flour. Add the pecans and chocolate chips, and mix to combine. Pour into the baking pan, and smooth the top. Bake in the lower third of the oven for 40 to 45 minutes. While the brownies are still warm, turn them onto a rack. Place a cutting board on top, and turn again.

Cut into squares with a long, thin knife. Sprinkle with confectioners' sugar.

Makes about 28.

Fred Anderson

John Frederick Kensett
(American, 1816-1872)
Long Neck Point from
Contentment Island, Darien,
Connecticut, c. 1872
Oil on canvas

15⅜ × 24⅜ in. (39 × 61.9 cm.)
Gift of the Women's Committee
of the Museum of Art, 1980

John Frederick Kensett, 1816–1872
Long Neck Point from Contentment Island, Darien, Connecticut,
circa 1872

Every summer John Kensett moved from his Manhattan studio to
Long Island Sound, where he pursued his vision of romantic realism.
Often accompanied by like-minded celebrants of the American spirit,
including Longfellow, Lowell, and Thackeray, he traveled throughout
New England and eastern Canada, recording what he saw. During
the winter months he converted his summer sketches into the
delicately colored paintings that earned him reputation and wealth.

Kensett was one of the leading figures in a loosely affiliated group,
now known as the Luminists, who worked between 1850 and 1880.
Their treatment of water, sky, and landscape is characterized by
strong horizontals and an overwhelming sense of peace and stillness.

Always serene and orderly, Kensett's paintings incorporated greater
and greater open space as the artist matured. *Long Neck Point from
Contentment Island, Darien, Connecticut,* painted during the last
summer of the artist's life, presents an almost uninterrupted
foreground and an endless sky.

Summer Twilight

Menu

Cold Tomato Soufflé

Grilled Swordfish Méditerranée

Risotto Gorgonzola

Marinated Vegetables

Mocha Rum Pots de Crème

Serves Four

Wine

French White Rhône Wine or

California Chardonnay

Dusk enhances the serenity of sand, sky, and ocean, a peaceful setting for a twilight picnic. The fire pit is dug, driftwood gathered, and the table set, all as the day ebbs into evening.

Fresh swordfish is one of the delights of summer. These paper-thin fish slices are grilled for only a few minutes over red, glowing coals. A zesty burst of fresh-cut lemon adds the final touch.

Everything else can be prepared at home. Tomato soufflé is delicate in flavor and texture but travels well. Risotto can be heated beside the fire until dinner is served.

Cold Tomato Soufflé

1 pound (455 g) ripe
tomatoes, peeled and
seeded

1 cup (240 mL/230 g)
thick mayonnaise

¼ cup (60 mL/29 g)
minced onion

Salt and pepper to taste

1½ tablespoons (⅜ ounce/
10.5 g) unflavored gelatin

¼ cup (60 mL) tomato
juice

½ cup (120 mL) heavy
cream, whipped

Chopped parsley, for
garnish

Dice half the tomatoes,
and refrigerate. Put the
remainder through a very
fine sieve. Combine the
mayonnaise with the
onion, salt, and pepper.

Combine the gelatin with
the tomato juice. Heat
to dissolve the gelatin,
and add to the sieved
tomatoes. Add the
mixture to the mayonnaise
mixture. Fold in the
whipped cream.

Using a double layer of
wax paper, make a collar
for a 1-quart (960 mL)
soufflé dish. The collar
should reach about
3 inches (8 cm) above the
dish. Attach it with string
or tape. Set a glass upright
in the center of the soufflé
dish. Fill the dish, around
the glass, with the soufflé
mixture. Refrigerate.

When ready to serve,
remove the glass. Season
the reserved diced
tomatoes with salt and
pepper. Spoon into the
center of the soufflé.
Sprinkle with parsley.

Note:
The soufflé may be
prepared the day before
serving.

Serves 4.

Mrs. Fred I. Sharp

Grilled Swordfish Méditerranée

2 pounds (905 g) boneless swordfish steaks, sliced ¼ inch (0.6 cm) thick

Olive oil

Lemon wedges

Brush each slice of swordfish liberally with the oil. Grill over very hot charcoal for 3 to 5 minutes on each side, or until light brown. Use tongs to turn the fish gently so it does not fall apart.

Garnish with lemon wedges.

Note:
This method of preparing swordfish is often used in Greece and Sicily. The fish is very moist and delicate.

Serves 4.

Edith H. Fisher

Risotto Gorgonzola

¼ teaspoon (1.3 mL/0.6 g) powdered saffron

About 3¼ cups (780 mL) unsalted chicken stock

2½ tablespoons (38 mL/ 36 g) unsalted butter

1½ tablespoons (23 mL/ 11 g) minced onion

1 cup (240 mL/200 g) rice

6 tablespoons (90 mL) dry white wine

½ cup (120 mL/60 g) crumbled Gorgonzola cheese

Freshly ground pepper

Preheat the oven to 400° F (205° C).

Combine the saffron with ¼ cup (60 mL) of the stock, and set aside.

In a heavy metal casserole, melt 1½ tablespoons 23 mL/21 g) of the butter. Add the onion. Cook, stirring, until it is soft but not browned. Add the rice, and stir without browning. Add the wine and the saffron mixture. Add 1½ cups (360 mL) of the stock. Cook over moderate to high heat, stirring frequently with a wooden spoon and adding stock as necessary until all liquid is absorbed (rice should not be soupy or mushy). Stir in ¼ cup (60 mL/30 g) Gorgonzola cheese.

In a shallow casserole, melt the remaining butter. Pour in the rice mixture. Sprinkle the pepper and the remaining Gorgonzola on top. Heat in the oven until the cheese is lightly browned and bubbly.

Note:
Excellent with grilled fish or meat.

Serves 4.

Edith H. Fisher

Marinated Vegetables

Asparagus

Cauliflower buds

Celery **or** fennel hearts

Broccoli florets

Sliced leeks

Sliced carrots

Mushrooms

Sliced cucumbers

½ cup (120 mL) Sauce Vinaigrette (see below)

Chopped parsley

Use any combination of the asparagus, cauliflower, celery or fennel, broccoli, leeks, and carrots, to yield 1 quart (960 mL/470 g). Simmer each vegetable separately in salted water for 3 to 5 minutes or until barely tender. Drain, and cool.

Mix the cooked vegetables with the mushrooms and cucumbers. Marinate them in the vinaigrette sauce in the refrigerator for at least 1 hour.

Spoon the marinated vegetables into a cold serving dish. Sprinkle with the parsley.

Serves 4.

The Cookbook Committee

Sauce Vinaigrette:

2 tablespoons (30 mL) wine vinegar **or** 1 tablespoon (15 mL) wine vinegar and 1 tablespoon (15 mL) lemon juice

6 tablespoons (90 mL) light olive oil **or** vegetable oil

¼ teaspoon (1.3 mL/1.5 g) salt

⅛ teaspoon (0.6 mL/0.3 g) freshly ground black pepper

1 tablespoon (15 mL/3 g) chopped parsley and/or other fresh herbs, such as chervil, chives, basil, tarragon, thyme, and marjoram, **or** 1 teaspoon of the above herbs, dried (5 mL/0.8 g)

1 tablespoon (15 mL/17 g) Dijon mustard

Place all the ingredients in a small mixing bowl. Beat vigorously with a wire whisk.

Makes about ½ cup (120 milliliters).

The Cookbook Committee

Mocha Rum Pots de Crème

2½ teaspoons (13 mL/ 3.6 g) instant decaffeinated coffee

1 tablespoon (15 mL) water

2½ tablespoons (38 mL) rum

2 ounces (57 g) German sweet chocolate

3 eggs, separated

The day before, in a double boiler, dissolve the coffee in the water and 1¼ tablespoons (19 mL) of the rum. Add the chocolate. When the chocolate has melted, set the mixture aside to cool.

Beat the egg whites for about 10 minutes, or until stiff and dry. Beat the egg yolks for at least 5 minutes, or until light yellow. Add the remaining rum to the egg yolks. Add the egg yolk–rum mixture to the cooled chocolate. Gently fold in the egg whites. Spoon into 4 pot de crème cups. Refrigerate for at least 24 hours.

Note:
May be prepared several days in advance.

Serves 4.

Mrs. David McCargo

Paul Cézanne
(French, 1839-1906)
Landscape near Aix, the Plain of the Arc River, 1892-95
Oil on canvas
31⅝ × 25⅛ in.
(80.3 × 63.8 cm.)
Acquired through the generosity of the Sarah Mellon Scaife family, 1966

Paul Cézanne, 1839–1906
Landscape near Aix, the Plain of the Arc River, 1892–1895

The name Paul Cézanne looms over modern art. Matisse called him "the great god of painting"; Picasso, "my one and only master."

Although he painted a select number of portraits and many still lifes, Cézanne was best known for his landscapes. His inspiration was Aix-en-Provence, in southern France, where he lived and worked for most of his life.

Cézanne attempted to reconcile the dynamics of light with the permanence and unity of the real world. He communicated space and volume not with line but with strokes of color, painstakingly applied.

Landscape near Aix, the Plain of the Arc River, a rich study of tonal values, executed with calm and confidence in pale greens, earth shades, and modulations of blue, is a classic example of Cézanne's post-Impressionist style.

*Long live the sun which
gives us such beautiful color.*
Paul Cézanne

La Vallée du Rhône

Menu

Scallops and Asparagus Terrine

Chicken du Roi René

Potatoes Dauphine

Green Beans Vinaigrette

Apple Snow

Serves Six

Wine

French Red Côtes du Rhône or

French Gigondas (main course)

Aromatic herbs, olive oil, and the firmest ripe tomatoes spark this imaginative menu. Entertaining late in the evening calls for a menu that can be prepared in advance. Here the terrine, chicken, and potatoes need only brief last-minute attention.

A profusion of mixed garden flowers is boldly scaled, but the food claims instant attention, arranged on crystal platters that show off its lusty colors and textures.

Named for a region in southeastern France, Potatoes Dauphine are an airy transformation of potatoes into light golden fritters. Green beans in a vinaigrette dressing are tossed with spicy pecans. And pale, frothy Apple Snow is a reminder of the artist's promise to surprise Paris with his apple.

With an apple I will astonish Paris.
Paul Cézanne

Scallops and Asparagus Terrine

Tomato Coulis:

¼ cup (60 mL/29 g) chopped shallots **or** scallions

5 tablespoons (75 mL/ 71 g) unsalted butter

2 cups (480 mL/450 g) (about 4) coarse-chopped tomatoes

½ teaspoon (2.5 mL/ 2.4 g) teaspoon sugar

Salt and pepper to taste

10 to 12 strips orange peel

1 teaspoon (5 mL/0.4 g) tarragon

Terrine:

10 ounces (285 g) sea (not bay) scallops

1 egg white

Salt and pepper

A pinch of nutmeg

1 cup (240 mL/120 g) ¼-inch (0.6 cm) -thick sliced asparagus

1 tablespoon (15 mL/ 14 g) unsalted butter

1 cup (240 mL) Crème Fraîche (see page 119) **or** sour cream

4 tablespoons (60 mL/ 57 g) unsalted butter, melted

⅓ cup (80 mL/36 g) freshly grated Parmesan cheese

Tomato Coulis:
Sauté the shallots or scallions in 3 tablespoons (45 mL/43 g) of the butter until softened but not browned. Add the tomatoes, sugar, salt, pepper, orange peel, tarragon, and the remaining butter. Cook over low heat, stirring occasionally, for about 20 minutes, or until reduced and thickened. Purée through a food mill, not a food processor.

Terrine:
Brush the scallops with the egg white. In a food processor, purée the scallops, 1 teaspoon (5 mL/6 g) salt, ¼ teaspoon (1.3 mL/0.7 g) pepper, and the nutmeg. Transfer the purée to a bowl. Cover and chill for at least 1 hour or overnight.

Preheat oven to 375° F (190° C). Grease a 1-quart (960 mL) rectangular terrine.

Blanch the asparagus. Drain, and toss with the 1 tablespoon (15 mL/14 g) butter. Add salt and pepper to taste.

Beat the crème fraîche or sour cream, ¼ cup (60 mL) at a time, into the scallops. Fold in the asparagus, and spoon into the terrine. Cover with greased wax paper and a lid. Set the terrine in a baking pan. Add enough hot water to reach halfway up the sides of the terrine. Bake for 35 to 40 minutes. Remove from the baking pan. Remove the lid and the paper. Cool for at least 30 minutes.

Preheat oven to 400° F (205° C). Grease a large pan.

Cut the terrine into 8 slices, and arrange 2 inches (5 cm) apart in the prepared pan. Brush with the melted butter. Sprinkle with Parmesan cheese. Bake for 20 to 25 minutes, or until puffed. Serve immediately with the tomato coulis.

Note:
The tomato coulis may be made a day ahead.

Serves 6 to 8 as a first course.

Mrs. George R. McCullough

Chicken du Roi René

1 3½-pound (1.59 kg) chicken, cut into serving pieces

2 small chicken breasts, split

Salt and freshly ground pepper

½ cup plus 2 tablespoons (150 mL/83 g) all-purpose flour

7 tablespoons (105 mL/ 100 g) unsalted butter

2 tablespoons (30 mL) olive oil

3 tablespoons (45 mL/ 22 g) minced shallots

½ cup (120 mL) Madeira **or** dry sherry

½ cup (120 mL/115 g) peeled and chopped tomatoes

1½ cups (360 mL) chicken stock

Bouquet Garni (see below)

¾ pound (340 g) mushrooms, quartered

1 tablespoon (15 mL) lemon juice

A pinch of cayenne

Season all the chicken with salt and pepper. Dust it with ½ cup (120 mL/ 66 g) of the flour, shaking off the excess.

In a large skillet, heat 4 tablespoons (60 mL/57 g) of the butter and the oil over moderately high heat. Sauté the chicken until golden brown, turning once. Remove it to a plate while preparing the sauce.

In the same skillet, heat the butter and oil, and sauté the shallots until tender but not brown. Add the remaining flour, blend well, and cook for 1 more minute. Add the Madeira or sherry, tomatoes, and stock. Bring to a boil, mixing well. Return the chicken to the skillet, and add the bouquet garni. Cover, and simmer gently for 20 to 25 minutes.

In a saucepan, melt the remaining butter. Add the mushrooms, and sauté for 3 minutes.

Arrange the chicken on a platter. Strain the sauce, removing the bouquet garni. Add the mushrooms with their liquid, the lemon juice, and cayenne. Combine well. Pour the sauce over the chicken.

Note:
May be prepared ahead. Just before serving, bring to a simmer on top of the stove; then place it, covered loosely with foil, in a preheated 350° F (175° C) oven. Heat for about 25 minutes.

May be frozen.

Serves 6 to 8.

Jane Citron Cooking Classes

Bouquet Garni:

2 sprigs parsley

⅓ bay leaf

1 sprig thyme **or** ⅛ teaspoon (0.6 mL/0.2 g) dried thyme

If all fresh herbs are used, tie them together with string.

If dried herbs are included, wrap them in cheesecloth, and tie securely.

The Cookbook Committee

Potatoes Dauphine

3 medium-size potatoes, peeled and quartered

Vegetable oil, for deep frying

Pâte à chou:

3 tablespoons (45 mL/ 43 g) unsalted butter

Salt

A dash of pepper

A pinch of nutmeg

½ cup (120 mL/66 g) all-purpose flour

2 large eggs

In a saucepan, boil the potatoes in ½ cup (120 mL) water for 25 minutes. Drain, and mash. Measure 1 cup (240 mL), season with salt and pepper to taste, and set aside.

In a deep fryer, preheat oil to 370° F (190° C).

To make a pâte à chou (dough):
In a heavy-bottomed saucepan, bring ½ cup (120 mL) of water, the butter, ½ teaspoon (2.5 mL/3 g) salt, pepper, and nutmeg to a boil.

Cook slowly until the butter has melted. Remove from the heat. Immediately add all the flour, beating vigorously with a wooden spoon for several seconds until thoroughly blended. Place over moderately high heat. Beat for 1 to 2 minutes, or until the mixture leaves the sides of the pan, forms a mass, and begins to film the bottom of the pan. Remove from the heat. Make a well in the center of the mixture. Immediately break the eggs into the well. Beat until smooth.

Assembly:
Beat together equal parts of the potatoes and pâte à chou. Drop by the teaspoonful into the preheated oil. Cook until nicely browned. Drain on paper towels. Sprinkle with salt (do not salt if the potatoes are to be frozen).

Note:
The cooked potatoes may be frozen. Reheat in 350° F (175° C) oven for 12 to 15 minutes. Drain on paper towels. Sprinkle with salt.

Serves 6 to 8.

Jane Citron Cooking Classes

Green Beans Vinaigrette

Vinaigrette Dressing:
2 teaspoons (10 mL/ 0.8 g) dried tarragon, crushed

2 teaspoons (10 mL/ 11 g) Dijon mustard

⅓ cup (80 mL) sherry vinegar **or** wine vinegar

¼ teaspoon (1.3 mL/ 1.5 g) salt

Pepper to taste

2 egg yolks

1¼ cups (300 mL) vegetable oil, or less (if desired)

Seasoned Pecans:
1½ cups (360 mL/155 g) pecans

½ teaspoon (2.5 mL/ 1.1 g) ground cumin

A dash of cayenne pepper to taste

A dash of marjoram **or** thyme to taste

⅓ cup (80 mL) vegetable oil, or less (if desired)

1 to 1½ pounds (455 to 680 g) green beans

Lettuce leaves

Vinaigrette Dressing:
Combine the tarragon, mustard, vinegar, salt, pepper, and egg yolks. Add the oil gradually, and blend thoroughly.

Seasoned Pecans:
Preheat oven to 350° F (175° C).

Toss the pecans and seasoning ingredients together. Place in a roasting pan, and bake until the mixture has been absorbed and the nuts are uniformly browned, about 20 minutes.

Beans:
Trim the beans, and cut them to a uniform size. Blanch them in boiling salted water, partially covered, for about 5 minutes (beans should be slightly crisp, not hard).

Drain in a colander, and cool under running cold water. Shake or pat dry. Toss the beans in the vinaigrette dressing.

To serve:
Drain the beans, toss them with the pecans, and place on lettuce leaves.

Note:
The beans may be marinated in the vinaigrette dressing for up to 24 hours.

Serves 4 to 8.

Mrs. Anthony J. A. Bryan

Apple Snow

5 or 6 medium McIntosh apples, peeled, cored, and cut in eighths

3½ tablespoons (53 mL) applejack **or** Calvados

A dash of salt

3 egg whites

3 tablespoons (45 mL/ 43 g) sugar

Ground nutmeg

6 thin apple slices with peel, for garnish

Cook the apples in very little water until they can be mashed to a slightly lumpy consistency (the applesauce should be fairly thick). Chill. Add the applejack or Calvados and salt.

Beat the egg whites until they stand in soft, stiff peaks. Gradually beat in the sugar. Fold in the applesauce mixture. Spoon into 6 bowls, preferably glass. Sprinkle with nutmeg. Garnish with the thin slices of apple.

Note:
May be prepared up to 2 hours ahead. Keep refrigerated until ready to serve.

Serves 6.

Edith H. Fisher

Maurice B. Prendergast
(American, 1859-1924)
Picnic, 1915
Oil on canvas
77 × 106½ in.
(195.6 × 270.5 cm.)

Gift from the people of
Pittsburgh through the efforts of
the Women's Committee,
Museum of Art, Carnegie
Institute, in honor of the Sarah
M. Scaife Gallery, 1972

Maurice B. Prendergast, 1859–1924
Picnic, 1915

A painter of daydreams, Maurice B. Prendergast was one of America's first Modernists. His style is built on undulating curves and sensuous movement. In flattened, artificial space he creates a textured, full-bodied fantasy reminiscent of tapestry or hand-screened fabrics.

Although the figures in *Picnic* appear to move freely, they are far from randomly placed. The setting may be dreamlike, but the dreamer was meticulously deliberate.

There is nothing like a good, old red wine for making the blood run.
Maurice B. Prendergast

Unhampered Picnic

Menu

Trout-stuffed Artichokes

Butterflied Pork with Mustard Sauce

Vegetable Rice Salad

Hazelnut Cheesecake

Serves Eight

Wine

Jug Wine (main course)

French Sauternes (dessert)

In Prendergast's time the Paris restaurant Ledoyen celebrated the opening of the Spring Salon by serving the first trout of the season. Here, teamed with artichokes, also at their best in springtime, the fish serves as a light introduction to an elaborate feast.

This picnic is designed to celebrate a special event. So take your prettiest quilt or rug, colorful glasses and napkins, and the most elaborate hamper or basket and have a happy time.

The love you liberate in your work is the only love you keep.
Maurice B. Prendergast

Trout-stuffed Artichokes

4 smoked trout, skinned and boned

¾ cup (180 mL) dry white wine **or** water, **or** half wine (90 mL) and half water (90 mL)

8 medium artichokes

2 tablespoons (30 mL) each white vinegar and lemon juice

8 tablespoons (120 mL/ 125 g) sour cream

2 teaspoons (10 mL/0.6 g) dillweed

4 teaspoons (20 mL/14 g) capers

8 lemon wedges

Poach the trout in the wine or water for 10 minutes. Cool in the poaching liquid. Flake a small amount of the fish, and reserve, if desired, for a garnish.

Trim the stems from the artichokes. Cut off the top third. Remove the tough outer leaves. Trim the tips of the remaining leaves with scissors. Place in a pot of water seasoned with vinegar and lemon juice.

Boil for 30 to 40 minutes, or until tender. Remove from the pot, and place upside down to drain.

In a blender or food processor, process the trout, sour cream, dill, and capers until smooth. When the artichokes are cool, remove the fuzzy choke, and spoon in the trout mixture. Garnish with reserved trout, if desired. Serve at room temperature or chilled, with a lemon wedge.

Note:
May be prepared several hours in advance. Fresh trout or other fresh fish may be substituted.

Serves 8.

Linda Youtzy

Butterflied Pork with Mustard Sauce

Mustard Sauce:
⅔ cup (160 mL/170 g) sour cream

⅔ cup (160 mL/155 g) mayonnaise

2 tablespoons (30 mL/ 14 g) dry mustard

1 tablespoon (15 mL/ 17 g) Dijon mustard

2 tablespoons (30 mL/ 15 g) fine-chopped scallions

1 tablespoon (15 mL) white vinegar

Salt to taste

½ cup (120 mL) soy sauce

½ cup (120 mL) bourbon

4 tablespoons (60 mL/ 44 g) brown sugar

5 to 6 pounds (2.27 to 2.72 kg) butterflied pork loins

Mustard Sauce:
Mix together the sour cream and mayonnaise until smooth. Combine with the remaining sauce ingredients.

Preheat oven to 350° F (175° C).

Mix the soy sauce, bourbon, and brown sugar. Marinate the meat in this mixture for several hours, turning occasionally.

Bake for about 1½ hours, or until the meat thermometer reads 185° F (85° C), basting frequently with the marinade. Carve the pork into thin, diagonal slices, and serve with the mustard sauce. May be served warm or at room temperature.

Serves 8.

The Cookbook Committee

Vegetable Rice Salad

Salad:

3 cups (720 mL/445 g) cooked rice, cooled

½ cup (or more to taste) (120 mL/24 g) scallions (stems only), chopped

10 ounces (285 g) frozen tiny green peas, defrosted

10 large radishes, cut into thin slices

10 ripe olives, sliced

1 to 2 teaspoons (5 mL/ 1.1 g to 10 mL/2.2 g) chopped parsley

14 cherry tomatoes, halved

½ cup (120 mL/61 g) chopped celery

½ teaspoon (2.5 mL/ 2.7 g) celery salt

Freshly ground black pepper

Dressing:

¾ cup (180 mL) vegetable oil

3 tablespoons (45 mL) lemon juice

4 tablespoons (60 mL) cider vinegar

2 teaspoons (10 mL/ 12 g) salt

1 teaspoon (5 mL/4.7 g) sugar

½ teaspoon (2.5 mL/ 1.3 g) paprika

Salad:
In a large bowl, combine the salad ingredients.

Dressing:
In a small bowl or jar, combine the dressing ingredients. Blend well.

Assembly:
Pour dressing over the salad, and toss gently. Cover and chill before serving.

Serves 6 to 8.

Mrs. Frederic L. Cook

Hazelnut Cheesecake

2 cups (480 mL/330 g) hazelnuts (filberts), with skins removed

2 packets (300 g) graham crackers

2 tablespoons (30 mL) Tía María **or** other coffee liqueur

2 tablespoons (30 mL/ 29 g) unsalted butter, melted

2 pounds (905 g) cream cheese

1⅓ cups (320 mL/305 g) sugar

4 eggs

Zest of 1 lemon

Preheat oven to 350° F (175° C). Grease a springform pan.

In a food processor, process 1 cup (240 mL/ 165 g) of the hazelnuts. Do not overgrind. Set aside.

Process and combine the graham crackers and ¼ cup (60 mL/40 g) of the remaining whole hazelnuts. Add the Tía María and butter. Spread in a thin layer on the bottom of the springform pan, reserving some of the crust for the sides.

In a food processor or electric mixer, combine the cream cheese and sugar; mix until soft. Add the eggs, one at a time. Stir in the lemon zest and the cup of ground hazelnuts set aside earlier. Pour the mixture into the springform pan. Set it into a larger pan filled with warm water to a depth of 2 inches (5 cm).

Bake for 1½ hours, or until the top is golden brown (bubbles and cracks may appear). Cool in the pan (cake will settle). Remove the ring, and press the reserved crust along the sides of the cake. Garnish with the remaining whole hazelnuts.

Serves 8 to 10.

Julia N. Williamson

Henri Matisse
(French, 1869-1954)
The Thousand and One Nights, 1950
Gouache on cut-and-pasted paper

54¾ × 147¼ in. (139 × 374 cm.)
Acquired through the generosity
of the Sarah Mellon Scaife
family, 1971

Henri Matisse, 1869–1954
The Thousand and One Nights, 1950

Even in his seventies, Matisse continued to grow as a master. No longer able to work at his easel, the artist instructed his nurse/assistants to color in gouache large pieces of paper with his favorite sapphire blues, fuchsias, blacks, and vibrant yellows. Matisse then cut the colors into shapes and, from his bed, directed their placement on paper or linen, arranging and rearranging until he achieved the composition he sought.

Although *The Thousand and One Nights* was created during the master's last years, it was inspired by his visits to Algeria almost a half century earlier. With fanciful shapes Matisse retells the story of Scheherazade, who quieted the bloodlust of a Moslem prince with her nightly tales of adventure. Five large rectangles depict the passage of night during which the clever princess wove her tale until "elle vit apparaître le matin, elle se tut discretèment [she saw the dawn approach, and she discreetly fell silent]."

Matisse, you were born
to simplify painting.
Gustave Moreau
Painter

Ghazal

Menu

Carrot Soup

Mussels Marinière

Coffee-Roasted Lamb

Eggplant Baskets with Pasta

Mixed Green Salad

Brie in Puff Pastry

Poached Pears

Serves Ten

Wine

French Pouilly Fuissé or

California Sauvignon Blanc (first course)

Italian Chianti (main course)

A dinner which has its beginnings in the fantasy tale of Scheherazade is bound to be extravagant. An imaginative buffet can be made as opulent as a seated dinner with considerably less effort.

Recalling Matisse's scale and colors, the table is covered with bright pink and magenta shawls and decorated with calla lilies in clear glass containers.

A large tureen of mussels is served with cocktails. Unlike a typical buffet, supper actually begins at the table with cold carrot soup at each place. After this colorful prelude, guests can help themselves to the entrée, vegetable, and salad.

Roasted to a delicate pink, lamb makes a handsome presentation served with eggplant, a traditional Middle Eastern combination.

Cutting into color reminds me of the direct carving of the sculptor.
Henri Matisse

Carrot Soup

6 tablespoons (90 mL/86 g) unsalted butter **or** margarine

¾ cup (180 mL/86 g) chopped onions

3 ribs celery, chopped

6 cups (1.44 L/740 g) sliced carrots

3 cups (720 mL) orange juice

3 cups (720 mL) chicken stock

3 cups (720 mL) light cream

1 tablespoon (15 mL/18 g) salt

¾ teaspoon (3.8 mL/1.8 g) nutmeg

¾ teaspoon (3.8 mL/2 g) pepper

1 tablespoon (15 mL/14 g) sugar

In a large saucepan, melt the butter or margarine. Add the onions and celery. Cook until tender. Add the carrots, and cook for 10 minutes. Add the orange juice and stock.

Cover, and simmer for 40 to 50 minutes, or until the carrots are tender.

Turn the mixture into a food processor, and process until smooth. Return to the saucepan, stir in the remaining ingredients. Heat thoroughly, but do not boil. Chill.

Note:
This soup may also be served hot.

Serves 10.

Mrs. Alvin M. Owsley

Mussels Marinière

9 dozen mussels

3 cups (720 mL) white wine

¾ cup (180 mL/86 g) chopped scallions, onions, **or** shallots

4 sprigs parsley

12 tablespoons (180 mL/170 g) unsalted butter

A dash of pepper (optional)

A dash of thyme (optional)

Clean the mussels, using a stiff wire brush or paring knife. Remove all the threads, barnacles, and residue. When they are clean, put them in fresh water in the refrigerator for an hour or two to remove any sand. Before they are cooked, rinse the mussels again.

Put the mussels, wine, scallions, parsley, butter, pepper, and thyme in a large pot. Cover, and steam for 5 to 10 minutes, or until the shells open. Discard unopened shells.

Note:
For other occasions, mussels marinière may be served in soup bowls with the broth, French bread, and a green salad.

Serves 10.

Cuppy Kraft

Coffee-Roasted Lamb

1 5-pound (2.27 kg) leg of lamb

1 clove garlic, slivered

Coarse salt

Freshly ground pepper

3 tablespoons (45 mL/ 51 g) Dijon mustard

4 tablespoons (60 mL/ 44 g) brown sugar

1 cup (240 mL) strong coffee

1 cup (240 mL) Burgundy

Preheat oven to 400° F (205° C).

Make small slits in the lamb, and insert slivers of garlic. Season generously with salt and pepper. Spread with the mustard. Sprinkle with the brown sugar.

Combine the coffee and wine.

Place the lamb, uncovered, in a roasting pan. Insert a meat thermometer, and bake for 1 hour, or until the thermometer reads 150° F (66° C). Baste every 15 minutes with the coffee and wine mixture.

Slice thin.

Note:
The lamb may be held up to 20 minutes before being sliced and served.

Serves 10.

Gay Arensberg

Mixed Green Salad

5 quarts (4.8 L) salad greens, any combination: lettuce (Bibb, Boston, leaf, iceberg, romaine, or escarole), chicory, Belgian endive, sorrel, watercress, young spinach, and dandelions, new nasturtium leaves and blossoms

Chives, shallots, parsley, tarragon, chervil, basil, and scallion bulbs to taste

1 clove garlic

½ cup (120 mL) Sauce Vinaigrette (see page 125)

Wash unblemished greens and dry thoroughly, using a salad shaker, wire basket, or towel to remove excess water.

Tear greens into bite-size pieces, place in a plastic bag and chill thoroughly in the refrigerator.

Rub salad bowl with a split clove of garlic. Toss greens lightly with the vinaigrette sauce. Serve immediately.

Serves 10.

The Cookbook Committee

Eggplant Baskets with Pasta

1 cup (240 mL/125 g) small pasta (ditalini 30 or elbow 24: yields 2 cups (480 mL), cooked)

10 small or 5 large eggplants

5 tablespoons (75 mL/71 g) unsalted butter

4 medium onions, minced

2 cloves garlic, minced

14 ounces (395 g) mozzarella cheese, cut into ½-inch (1.3 cm) cubes

1 cup (240 mL/110 g) freshly grated Parmesan cheese

⅓ cup (80 mL) milk

2 eggs, lightly beaten

3 to 4 tablespoons (45 mL/50 g to 60 mL/67 g) tomato paste

4 tablespoons (60 mL/13 g) minced parsley

Salt and pepper to taste

2 to 3 tomatoes, cut into thin slices

About 2 tablespoons (30 mL) olive oil

Preheat oven to 350° F (175° C). Lightly oil a shallow baking pan.

Cook the pasta according to the package directions. Set aside.

If using small eggplants, cut off the tops. Cut the large eggplants in half. Scoop out, and chop the pulp. Set aside the pulp and the shells.

In a skillet, melt the butter, and sauté the onions and garlic until they are golden. Add the eggplant pulp, and sauté for about 5 minutes. Transfer the mixture to a bowl, and let it cool. Stir in the cooked pasta and the cheeses. Combine the milk and eggs, and add to the mixture, along with the tomato paste, parsley, salt, and pepper.

Fill the reserved eggplant shells with the mixture. Top each with a thin slice of tomato. Season with salt and pepper, and brush lightly with the oil. Arrange them in the baking pan. Bake for about 40 minutes, or until the cheese is soft and the stuffing is hot.

Serves 10.

Edith H. Fisher

Brie in Puff Pastry

½ recipe (1 pound/455 g) Puff Pastry (see recipe below)

1 two-pound (905 g) wheel of ripe Brie cheese

1 egg

1 tablespoon (15 mL) milk **or** cream

Preheat oven to 425° F (220° C). Grease a baking sheet.

Divide the puff pastry into two equal portions. Roll each into a circle just larger than the wheel of cheese. Place the cheese on one circle, and cover it with the second circle.

In a bowl, combine the egg and milk or cream. Beat until well blended. Moisten the edges of the pastry with this egg wash, and seal the edges. Cut off the excess pastry. (The cheese may be refrigerated at this point and baked just before serving.)

Brush the top of the pastry with more egg wash. The wheel may be decorated with the pastry trimmings, cut into various shapes. Bake for about 25 to 30 minutes, or until puffed and browned.

Note:
Homemade puff pastry is preferable, but puff pastry may be purchased in bakeries or supermarkets.

Serve with crackers or slices of apple or pear. The cheese will be runny.

Serves 10 to 20.

Susan C. Johnson

Puff Pastry:

3 cups (720 mL/395 g) all-purpose unbleached flour

1 cup (240 mL/96 g) plain bleached cake flour

4 sticks (460 g) chilled unsalted butter

1½ teaspoons (8 mL/9 g) salt

1 cup (240 mL) ice water

Place the flours in a mixing bowl. Rapidly cut the sticks of chilled butter into lengthwise quarters; then dice. Add to the flour. If the butter has softened, refrigerate the bowl to chill the butter before proceeding. Add the salt. Blend by hand to make large flakes about 1 inch (2.5 cm) in size. Blend in the water, mixing just enough so that the dough masses roughly together but the butter pieces remain the same size.

Turn the dough out onto a lightly floured work surface. Rapidly push, pat, and roll it into a rectangle about 8 by 18 inches (20 by 46 cm). Lightly flour the top of the dough. Using a baking sheet, fold the bottom of the rectangle over the center, and fold the top down over it, as if folding a letter.

Lift the dough from the work surface with the baking sheet. Scrape the surface clean, flour it lightly, and return the dough to it so that the top flap is on the right. Lightly flour the top of the dough, and roll it out again into a rectangle. Fold again as before. Roll and fold two more times. The pastry should look like dough; however, large flakes of butter will still be scattered under the surface.

Wrap the dough in a plastic bag, and refrigerate for 40 minutes or longer. Roll out, and fold the dough two more times. Let the dough rest for 30 minutes. It is then ready for forming and baking.

Makes about 2 pounds (905 g).

The Cookbook Committee

Poached Pears

4½ cups (1.08 L) Beaujolais wine,

1 cup plus 2 tablespoons (270 mL/255 g) sugar

2¼ teaspoons (11 mL/6 g) cinnamon

2 cloves

3 slices orange

3 slices lemon

7 black peppercorns

10 large pears

Crème Anglaise:
   ¾ cup (180 mL/170 g) sugar

   6 egg yolks

   1½ teaspoons (8 mL/ 4.1 g) cornstarch

   2⅝ cups (630 mL) boiling milk

   1½ tablespoons (23 mL) vanilla extract **or** other flavoring

In a large saucepan, combine the Beaujolais wine, the 1 cup plus 2 tablespoons (270 mL/ 255 g) sugar, the cinnamon, cloves, orange, lemon, and peppercorns. Cook until the sugar and cinnamon are dissolved.

Peel the pears, leaving the stems on. Cook in the syrup for about 15 minutes, or until tender. Stir occasionally so the pears color evenly. Remove from the heat. Refrigerate in the syrup for several hours.

Crème Anglaise:
Gradually beat the ¾ cup (180 mL/170 g) sugar into the egg yolks, and continue beating for about 2 or 3 minutes, or until the mixture is pale yellow and forms a ribbon. Beat in the cornstarch. While still beating, slowly add the milk in a thin stream.

Pour the mixture into a saucepan. Set it over moderate heat, stirring continuously with a wooden spoon until the sauce thickens just enough to coat the spoon. Do not let the custard approach a simmer. Candy thermometer temperature should not exceed 170° F (77° C).

Cool, and strain the custard. Stir in the flavoring.

To Serve:
Place a chilled poached pear in a bowl. Surround with the crème anglaise. Top with pear syrup.

Serves 10.

Phyllis Beeson Susen

Recipes

Appetizers

Recipes in Menu Section

Stuffed Artichokes

Artichokes:

4 medium artichokes

Boiling water

1 teaspoon (5 mL/6 g) salt

2 tablespoons plus 1 teaspoon (35 mL) olive oil

1 clove garlic, peeled and halved

¼ teaspoon (1.3 mL/ 0.4 g) dried thyme

Stuffing:

⅓ cup (80 mL) olive oil

2 large ribs celery, cut into thin slices

2 cups (480 mL/105 g) minced parsley, lightly packed

1 large clove garlic, minced

1 large onion, minced

7 slices ⅜-inch (1 cm) -thick firm white bread, crust removed, crumbled into coarse pieces

½ cup (120 mL/54 g) grated Parmesan cheese

½ teaspoon (2.5 mL/3 g) salt

⅛ teaspoon (0.6 mL/0.3 g) pepper

½ teaspoon (2.5 mL/0.4 g) dried crushed oregano

Artichokes:

With a sharp knife, trim 1 inch (2.5 cm) from the top of each artichoke. Pull off the small bottom leaves. Cut off the stems, leaving a flat base. With kitchen shears, cut off the tips of the leaves.

Stand the artichokes upright in a saucepan. Add enough boiling water to reach halfway up the artichokes. Add the salt, 1 tablespoon (15 mL) of the oil, the garlic, and thyme. Cover, and boil gently for about 35 minutes, or until the artichoke bottoms are barely tender when pierced with a fork. Add water, if necessary, while the artichokes are cooking.

Remove the artichokes, and turn them upside down to drain. Turn them upright; remove and discard the small soft inner leaves attached to the choke or thistle portion. Scoop out and discard the choke.

Stuffing:
Preheat oven to 350° F (175° C).

Heat ⅓ cup (80 mL) of the oil in a 10-inch (25 cm) skillet over moderate heat. Add the celery, parsley, garlic, and onion, and cook for 5 to 10 minutes, or until the celery is tender. Remove from the heat, and stir in the bread crumbs, Parmesan cheese, salt, pepper, and oregano.

Spread the leaves of the artichokes, and spoon the stuffing into the centers. Pack any remaining stuffing among the outside leaves.

Drizzle 1 teaspoon (5 mL) of the olive oil over the outer leaves of each artichoke. Stand them in a shallow 8-inch (20 cm) -square baking dish. Cover tightly with foil. Bake for 45 minutes. Serve hot.

Serves 4

Mrs. George R. Gibbons, Jr.

Asparagus with Strawberry Vinaigrette

18 leaves Bibb lettuce

30 thick asparagus spears

1 cup (240 mL/115 g) sliced fresh strawberries

6 tablespoons (90 mL) olive oil

¼ cup (60 mL) heavy cream

2 tablespoons (30 mL) red wine vinegar

Salt and freshly ground pepper

6 sprigs parsley

Wash the lettuce, and dry thoroughly. Chill.

Wash, scrape, and trim the asparagus to 4½-inch (11 cm) lengths. Cook them in salted water for about 6 to 8 minutes, or until tender. Drain, and refrigerate.

Purée the strawberries. In a processor or blender, combine the oil, cream, vinegar, salt, and pepper. Add to the strawberry purée.

Arrange 3 leaves of lettuce on each of 6 plates. Arrange 5 asparagus spears on each, and spoon the sauce across the center. Garnish each serving with a sprig of parsley. Pass additional sauce.

Note:
This recipe should be prepared 2 hours before being served.

Serves 6.

The Cookbook Committee

Spicy Avocado Dip

1 avocado, chopped

1 cup (240 mL/255 g) sour cream

½ cup (120 mL) Mexican-type hot sauce

1 cup (240 mL/115 g) mozzarella cheese, shredded

In a shallow bowl, place a layer of avocado. Cover with the sour cream, and top with the hot sauce. Sprinkle with the cheese, and press lightly. Cover, and refrigerate overnight.

Note:
Serve the dip with corn chips.

Serves 12.

Mrs. Nathan W. Pearson

Baba Ghanouj

2 medium eggplants

1 cup (240 mL/75 g) minced mushrooms

2 tablespoons (30 mL) olive oil

Juice of 1 lemon

½ cup (120 mL/125 g) tahini*

3 medium garlic cloves, crushed

½ cup (120 mL/27 g) minced parsley

¼ cup (60 mL/29 g) minced scallions

Freshly ground pepper

Preheat oven to 400° F (205° C).

Cut the stems from the eggplants. Prick all over with a fork, and bake about 45 minutes, or until soft. Cool. Scoop out the flesh, keeping approximately half the seeds.

*Tahini is a thick paste made of ground sesame seeds. It can be found in health food stores.

Sauté the mushrooms in 1 tablespoon (15 mL) of the olive oil. Place in a food processor with the eggplant and all other ingredients except the remaining oil. Process until smooth. Chill. Before serving, dribble the remaining oil over the mixture.

Note:
Serve as a dip with sesame seed sticks, crackers, or raw vegetables.

Serves 12 to 16.

Mrs. Robert O. Read

Bovril Fingers

4 tablespoons (60 mL/57 g) unsalted butter

1½ tablespoons (23 mL/28 g) Bovril*

9 thin slices white bread

⅓ cup (80 mL/36 g) grated Parmesan cheese

Preheat oven to 200° F (93° C).

In a small skillet, melt the butter, and stir in the Bovril. Brush the bread slices with the mixture. Sprinkle them generously with the Parmesan. Cut off the crusts, and cut each slice into thirds. Place on an ungreased baking sheet. Bake for 1 hour.

Note:
A very addictive appetizer. Keeps well in a covered tin.

Makes 27.

Mrs. Richard S. Smith

*Bovril, a meat extract, is available in gourmet food shops.

Caponata

1 cup (240 mL) vegetable oil

1 medium unpeeled eggplant, cut into 1-inch (2.5 cm) cubes

1 cup (240 mL/115 g) coarse chopped onion

1 cup (240 mL/120 g) sliced celery

1 cup (240 mL/125 g) sliced carrots

1 cup (240 mL/165 g) seeded and cubed tomatoes

Salt and pepper to taste

2 tablespoons (30 mL/ 33 g) tomato paste

2 tablespoons (30 mL) red wine vinegar

24 small pitted green olives

½ cup (120 mL/82 g) capers, drained

2 tablespoons (30 mL/ 28 g) sugar

In a skillet, heat the oil, and sauté the eggplant for 10 minutes. With a slotted spoon, transfer the eggplant to a serving dish, leaving the oil in the skillet. Add the onion, celery, and carrots. Cook until the onion is soft. Do not overcook; the vegetables should be crisp. Add them to the eggplant.

In the skillet, add the tomatoes, salt, pepper. Cover, and cook over low heat for 5 minutes. Add the tomato paste, vinegar, olives, capers, and sugar. Cook for a few minutes. Combine with the eggplant mixture. Refrigerate.

Note:
May be made ahead and stored in the refrigerator for up to 1 week.

Use as an hors d'oeuvre, a vegetable, or a salad.

Serves 10 or more as an appetizer; 6 to 8 as a vegetable or a salad.

Jane K. Steinfirst

Caviar Mousse

¾ cup (180 mL/190 g) sour cream

¼ cup (60 mL/29 g) chopped onion

3 eggs, hard-cooked and halved

3 tablespoons (45 mL/ 44 g) mayonnaise

4 teaspoons (20 mL) fresh lemon juice

1½ teaspoons (8 mL/9 g) salt (optional)

½ teaspoon (2.5 mL) Worcestershire sauce

¼ teaspoon (1.3 mL/0.6 g) white pepper

2 or 3 drops of Tabasco sauce, or to taste

1½ teaspoons (⅛ ounce/ 3.5 g) unflavored gelatin

2 tablespoons (30 mL) cold water

2 ounces (57 g) black lumpfish caviar, rinsed

In a food processor or blender, purée, in batches, the sour cream, onion, eggs, mayonnaise, lemon juice, salt, if desired, Worcestershire, pepper, and Tabasco. Transfer to a large bowl.

In a small bowl, sprinkle the gelatin over the cold water. Soften for 5 minutes. Set the bowl of gelatin into a larger bowl of hot water. Stir until the gelatin has dissolved. Remove from the hot water. Let cool.

Stir the gelatin into the sour cream mixture. Gently but thoroughly fold in the caviar, reserving a small amount for a garnish. Transfer the mousse to a 2-cup (480 mL) decorative mold. Chill, covered, for at least 3 hours.

Note:
Serve with fresh thin-sliced pumpernickel bread. Garnish with the reserved black caviar.

May be made a day ahead.

Serves 25.

Anonymous

Pastry Cheese Triangles

8 ounces (225 g) frozen phyllo dough

2 cups (480 mL/230 g) shredded extra-sharp Cheddar cheese

8 ounces (225 g) cream cheese, softened

2 eggs

½ teaspoon (2.5 mL/1.2 g) minced onion

¼ pound (115 g) unsalted butter **or** margarine, melted

Defrost the phyllo dough according to package directions. Preheat oven to 400°F (205°C).

Beat together the Cheddar cheese, cream cheese, eggs, and onion.

Stack 2 sheets of phyllo dough. Brush the top sheet with some of the butter or margarine. Cut the dough lengthwise into 6 strips about 2½ inches (6 cm) wide. Cut the strips in half to make 12 2½-inch (6 cm) -wide strips.

On each strip, place 1 teaspoon (5 mL) cheese filling in a corner. Fold the opposite corner over the filling to make a triangle. Continue folding in triangles to the end of the strip (like folding a flag). When the strip is completely folded, brush it very lightly with the melted butter or margarine. Repeat with the remaining dough, filling, and butter. (Cover the unused dough and finished triangles with a slightly damp cloth to keep the dough from drying out.)

Cover. Chill or freeze until ready to bake. Bake on an ungreased baking sheet for 15 to 20 minutes.

Makes 60.

Ellen A. Roth, Ph.D.

Crab Mousse

1 10¾-ounce can (305 g) mushroom soup

8 ounces (225 g) cream cheese

1 envelope (¼ ounce/7 g) unflavored gelatin

3 tablespoons (45 mL) white wine **or** cold water

1 pound (455 g) fresh crabmeat

1 cup (240 mL/230 g) mayonnaise

1 cup (240 mL/120 g) minced celery

2 tablespoons (30 mL/ 17 g) chopped green pepper

1 scallion, chopped

A dash of Tabasco sauce

¼ teaspoon (1.3 mL/0.4 g) thyme

¼ teaspoon (1.3 mL/ 0.7 g) lemon-herb pepper

1 tablespoon (15 mL) lemon juice

1 teaspoon (5 mL/1.3 g) grated lemon rind

Green pepper, tiny pickle strips, pimiento, olive slices, fresh parsley, for garnish

Oil a 5-cup (1.2 L) fish mold or other container.

Heat the soup and cheese, and mix until smooth.

Dissolve the gelatin in the white wine or water. Add to the soup mixture, and mix well. Add the remaining ingredients. Pour the mixture into the mold, and chill for several hours.

Unmold on a platter, and garnish as desired.

Note:
A fish-shaped mold is appropriate. Use olive slices for the eye, parsley for the tail, and other garnishes as desired.

Serves 8 for salad; 30 for hors d'oeuvres.

Romaine Hon

Crab-Zucchini Tidbits

4 cups (960 mL/595 g) sliced zucchini

1 onion, chopped

1½ cups (360 mL/180 g) grated muenster, mozzarella, **or** brick cheese

7¾ ounces (220 g) crabmeat, drained

½ cup (120 mL) vegetable oil

3 eggs, lightly beaten

1 teaspoon (5 mL/0.8 g) oregano

1 teaspoon (5 mL/6 g) salt

½ teaspoon (2.5 mL/1.4 g) pepper

1½ cups (360 mL/215 g) Bisquick

Preheat oven to 400° F (205° C). Grease a 9- by 13-inch (23 by 33 cm) baking dish.

Place the zucchini and onion in water to cover, and bring to a boil. Boil for about 3 minutes, or until just transparent. Drain. Set aside to cool.

Combine the cheese, crabmeat, oil, eggs, seasonings, and Bisquick. Mix thoroughly. Fold in the zucchini and onion mixture. Turn into the baking dish, and bake for about 25 to 30 minutes, or until lightly browned. Cool slightly, and cut into 1½-inch (3.8 cm) squares.

Serve at room temperature.

Makes 4 dozen.

R. Jackson Seay

William J. Glackens
(American, 1870-1938)
In Town It's Different, 1898
Watercolor and gouache on paper
18 × 12 in. (45.7 × 30.5 cm.)
Andrew Carnegie Fund, 1906

Eggs with Caviar and Sauce Vinaigrette

6 eggs, extra-large, hard-cooked, at room temperature

3 ounces (85 g) sturgeon caviar

2 teaspoons (10 mL/6 g) all-purpose flour

1 teaspoon (5 mL) water

Frying Batter:
   About ½ cup (120 mL/ 66 g) all-purpose flour

   ½ teaspoon (2.5 mL/ 1.7 g) baking powder

   1 tablespoon (15 mL/ 14 g) unsalted butter, melted

   1 egg, beaten

   ½ cup (120 mL) beer

   2 cups (480 mL) vegetable oil

6 sprigs parsley

½ cup (120 mL) Sauce Vinaigrette (see page 125)

Cut the eggs, crosswise, one third of the way down from the top (pointed end). Carefully remove the yolks and discard. In each yolk cavity place 1 tablespoon (15 mL) of the caviar.

Make a paste of the flour and water, and liberally coat the edges of the egg whites. Replace the two sections so that they fit together and adhere tightly. Dust the eggs with flour and refrigerate for an hour or longer.

Frying Batter:
Sift together the ½ cup (120 mL/66 g) flour and baking powder into a bowl. Gradually stir in the butter, egg, and beer until the mixture is smooth. Let the batter stand for an hour or more.

In a deep fryer, heat the oil to 400° F (205° C). Dust each egg again lightly with flour. Stir the batter and coat each egg liberally with the batter. With a slotted spoon, gently place in oil and cook for 3 to 5 minutes, or until golden brown.

Garnish each egg with a sprig of parsley, and serve hot with the Sauce Vinaigrette.

Note:
If inexpensive caviar is used, rinse the caviar thoroughly in fresh water to remove extra saltiness.

Serves 6.

The Cookbook Committee

Lobster Spread

8 ounces (225 g) cream cheese

2 tablespoons (30 mL/ 29 g) mayonnaise

2 tablespoons (30 mL/ 33 g) chili sauce

1 tablespoon (15 mL/3 g) chopped parsley

1 tablespoon (15 mL/7 g) minced onion

½ teaspoon (2.5 mL/2.8 g) prepared mustard

A drop of Tabasco

1 pound (455 g) fresh or frozen lobster meat, cooked and cut into small pieces

Salt to taste

Combine all the ingredients well.

Note:
Serve with crackers or toast points.

Serves 12.

Susan C. Johnson

Mushroom Ragout

1 quart (960 mL) beef stock

1 cup (240 mL) dry red wine

1 pound (455 g) fresh mushrooms, cut into coarse slices

½ recipe (1 pound/455 g) Puff Pastry (see page 147)

Combine the stock, wine, and mushrooms. Simmer for 45 minutes to 1 hour, or until the liquid has reduced substantially and thickened slightly. (The broth should be glossy.)

While the broth simmers, roll puff pastry to a thickness of ⅛ inch (0.3 cm). Cut into 2- by 4½-inch (5 by 11 cm) sections. Place on a chilled baking sheet. Refrigerate until ready to bake.

Preheat oven to 425° F (220° C). Remove the pastry from the refrigerator. Bake until browned and flaky.

Remove from the oven, and transfer half to a warm serving plate. Spoon a generous amount of the mushroom ragout on top and around the sides. Top each with another piece of pastry. Serve immediately.

Note:
Domestic or wild mushrooms may be used, but wild chanterelles, morels, or porcini are preferable.

Serves 4 to 6.

The Cookbook Committee

Mushrooms and Shad Roe

25 medium mushroom caps

1 6-ounce (170 g) can shad roe

¼ cup (60 mL/58 g) mayonnaise

A drop of Worcestershire sauce

A drop of Tabasco sauce

Seasoned salt to taste

Lemon pepper to taste

About 1 tablespoon (15 mL) lemon juice

Paprika

Wipe the mushrooms. Peel, if desired. Set aside.

Gently mash the shad roe, and combine with the mayonnaise, Worcestershire, Tabasco, seasoned salt, and lemon pepper. Spoon the mixture into the mushroom caps. Sprinkle lemon juice and paprika on top.

Preheat the broiler to 550° F (290° C). Place the mushrooms on the middle rack. Broil for about 15 minutes. Watch carefully.

Makes 25.

Minnette D. Bickel

Sherried Mushrooms

4 ounces (115 g) unsalted butter **or** margarine **or** ¼ cup (60 mL) vegetable (not olive) oil

1 pound (455 g) mushrooms, chopped into coarse pieces

A pinch of cayenne pepper

½ to 1 teaspoon (2.5 mL/ 3 g to 5 mL/6 g) salt

½ teaspoon (2.5 mL/2.4 g) sugar

½ cup (120 mL) cooking sherry

In a skillet, heat the butter or margarine or oil. Combine all the ingredients except the sherry. Add them to the skillet, and stir-fry quickly until the mushrooms begin to dry and brown. Add the sherry, and stir until evaporated.

Note:
Serve hot or cold with crackers or toast points.

Leftover mushrooms may be frozen. Add them to casseroles, soups, or stews. They may also be reheated with cream and served on toast points or served cold from a small bowl, surrounded by crackers.

Serves 8.

Annette Malcolm Rathbun

Dilled Ricotta Torte

1½ cups (360 mL/170 g) stale whole wheat bread crumbs

1 cup (240 mL) ground almonds

8 tablespoons (120 mL/ 115 g) unsalted butter, softened

12 ounces (340 g) cream cheese, softened

1 cup (240 mL/255 g) whole milk ricotta cheese

2 eggs

2 tablespoons (30 mL) milk

1 tablespoon (15 mL/3 g) minced fresh dill

½ to ¾ teaspoon (2.5 mL/ 3 g to 3.8 mL/4.5 g) salt

1 teaspoon (5 mL/2.4 g) minced lemon zest

½ teaspoon (2.5 mL/1.2 g) freshly grated nutmeg

Freshly ground pepper

Dill sprigs **or** dill blossom for garnish

Preheat oven to 350° F (175° C). Lightly grease a 9-inch (23 cm) springform pan.

In a bowl, combine the bread crumbs, almonds, and butter. Press the mixture onto the bottom and 1 inch (2.5 cm) up the sides of the pan.

In a food processor with a metal blade, blend the cream cheese with all the remaining ingredients except the dill garnish. Process until smooth. Taste, and correct the seasoning if necessary.

Pour the mixture into the shell. Slide a pizza pan under the springform pan to catch any drippings, and bake for about 45 minutes, or until a knife inserted into the center comes out clean. The mixture will rise above the crumb/nut shell as it bakes and will fall as it cools.

Allow the torte to cool in the pan on a rack. Remove the sides of the pan, and transfer the torte to a serving plate. Garnish with sprigs of dill or a dill blossom. Serve warm or at room temperature.

Serves 12.

Mary C. Poppenberg

Salmon Mousse

1 7¾-ounce can (220 g) red sockeye salmon

½ pound (225 g) smoked salmon, sliced, **or** bits if available

1 envelope (¼ ounce/7 g) unflavored gelatin

1 tablespoon (15 mL) water

¼ cup (60 mL/13 g) fresh dill **or** 1 tablespoon (15 mL/ 1 g) dried dill

2 large shallots, peeled and halved

3 tablespoons (45 mL) lemon juice

½ cup (120 mL/115 g) mayonnaise

3 drops of Tabasco sauce, or to taste

1 cup (240 mL) heavy cream

Thin-sliced cucumbers **or** watercress, for garnish (optional)

Oil a 4-cup (960 mL) mold.

Drain the canned salmon, reserving the liquid. Mix together the drained and smoked salmon, and set aside.

Pour the reserved salmon juice into a measuring cup. Add enough water to bring the liquid to ½ cup (120 mL). Soften the gelatin in 1 tablespoon (15 mL) water.

In a food processor, process the dill and shallots together for 20 seconds.

In a saucepan, combine the salmon juice and lemon juice. Bring to a boil. Add to the processor along with the gelatin, and blend for 20 seconds. Add the salmon, mayonnaise, and Tabasco. Blend for 60 seconds. With the machine running, pour the cream through the feed tube. Process until smooth. Add more Tabasco if desired.

Pour into the mold. Refrigerate for at least 4 hours. Garnish with cucumbers or watercress, if desired.

Serves 16 to 20.

Betty W. Eslick

Sautéed Scotch Salmon

6 thin, about ⅛-inch (0.3 cm) -thick, slices smoked Scotch or Nova Scotia salmon

About 2 teaspoons (10 mL) lemon juice

2 teaspoons (10 mL/6 g) all-purpose flour

Unsalted butter, for sautéing

3 slices toasted black bread

3 tablespoons (45 mL/ 47 g) sour cream

1 tablespoon (15 mL/10 g) capers

3 tablespoons (45 mL/ 21 g) chopped onion

6 lemon slices

Sprinkle each slice of salmon with lemon juice, and dip in flour. In a buttered skillet, sauté the salmon quickly over medium heat.

Remove crust from bread and cut bread into 6 strips to fit salmon slices. Place 1 slice of salmon on each strip. Garnish with sour cream, capers, onion and lemon.

Makes 6 hors d'oeuvres.

Adrienne F. Porter

Seviche

1 pound (455 g) bay scallops

3 hot green Italian peppers

3 hot red Mexican peppers **or** 1 tablespoon (15 mL/ 5 g) red pepper flakes

1 medium onion, cut into thin slices

1 cup (240 mL) fresh lime juice

1 teaspoon (5 mL/6 g) salt, or to taste

¼ cup (60 mL/13 g) minced cilantro* **or** parsley

4 to 8 limes, sliced

Drain the bay scallops.

Split the peppers, and remove the seeds. Slice them into thin strips.

*Cilantro can be found in Oriental and Mexican markets. It is often used interchangeably with parsley.

Combine the scallops, peppers or pepper flakes, onion, lime juice, salt, and 2 tablespoons (30 mL/7 g) of the cilantro or parsley. Chill for at least 4 hours.

Garnish with the remaining cilantro or parsley and lime slices.

Note:
Serve as an hors d'oeuvre or a salad.

Recipe may be doubled. It does not freeze well.

Serves 6 to 8.

Mrs. A. James Starr

Shrimp Rémoulade

¾ cup (180 mL/175 g) mayonnaise

1 teaspoon (5 mL/6 g) salt

2 teaspoons (10 mL/4.5 g) dry mustard

6 scallions, minced

2 stalks celery, cut into thin slices

1 teaspoon (5 mL/2.5 g) paprika

2 drops of Tabasco sauce

3 sprigs parsley, minced

1 pound (455 g) (about 24) medium-size cooked fresh shrimp

Combine the mayonnaise, salt, mustard, scallions, celery, paprika, Tabasco, and parsley, and pour over the shrimp. Refrigerate for at least 4 hours before serving.

Serves 4 to 6.

Mrs. William B. Renner

Soups

Almond Soup

½ pound (225 g) almonds, blanched and toasted

3 cups (720 mL) chicken stock

1 large potato, chopped into coarse pieces

1 medium onion, chopped into coarse pieces

Bouquet Garni:
   3 tablespoons (45 mL/ 23 g) chopped carrot

   3 tablespoons (45 mL/ 23 g) chopped celery

   1 bay leaf

   2 peppercorns, crushed

   2 sprigs parsley

1 cup (240 mL) heavy cream **or** half-and-half (optional)

½ cup (120 mL) heavy cream, whipped, for garnish (optional)

Sliced toasted almonds, for garnish (optional)

Pulverize the almonds. Set aside.

In a large pot, bring the stock to a boil. Add the potato, onion, and bouquet garni, which should be wrapped in cheesecloth and tied securely. Reduce the heat, and simmer for 20 to 30 minutes, or until the vegetables are tender. Add the almonds. Simmer for 5 minutes. Drain, and reserve the liquid. Discard the bouquet garni. Purée the vegetables, and return them to the liquid.

For a creamier texture, if desired, add the heavy cream or half-and-half.

Garnish with whipped cream or sliced toasted almonds, if desired.

Note:
May be served hot or cold.

Serves 4 to 6.

John Cheek

Chilled Apricot Soup

3 cups (720 mL/380 g) very ripe apricots, peeled, pitted, and chopped into coarse pieces

1 cup (240 mL) dry white wine

Juice and grated zest of 1 lemon

¼ to ½ teaspoon (1.3 mL/ 0.6 g to 2.5 mL/1.2 g) ground ginger

¼ to ½ teaspoon (1.3 mL/ 0.7 g to 2.5 mL/1.4 g) cinnamon

A pinch of ground cloves

1 cup (240 mL) light cream

In a saucepan, bring to a boil the fruit, wine, and lemon juice. Reduce the heat, and simmer until the fruit is soft. Cool. Pour into a blender. Add the lemon zest, ginger, cinnamon, and cloves. Purée on low speed until smooth. Add the cream.

Strain well, pressing the mixture against the sides of a strainer. Cover, and chill before serving.

Note:
Fresh peaches, plums, or cherries, or canned apricots, rinsed and drained, may be substituted for the fresh apricots.

Serves 4 to 6.

The Cookbook Committee

Chilled Avocado Soup

3 medium-size or 6 small avocados

2 tablespoons (30 mL) lemon juice

2 medium cucumbers, peeled and seeded

1 medium onion, sliced

1 clove garlic

3 cups (720 mL) chicken stock, fat removed

2 tablespoons (30 mL/ 7 g) fresh mint

1 tablespoon (15 mL/3 g) chopped chervil **or** parsley

A pinch of tarragon

1 cup (240 mL) heavy cream

Cayenne pepper and salt to taste

Mint leaves, whipped cream, and lemon and lime slices, for garnish.

Cut medium-size avocados in half, being careful not to damage the skin so the shells may be used for serving. (With small avocados, cut off the top, leaving the bottom two-thirds for serving.)

Carefully remove and discard the pits. Scrape away the pulp from inside the shells without puncturing the skin.

Chop the avocado meat into coarse pieces. Sprinkle it with the lemon juice to prevent discoloration. Chop the cucumbers into coarse pieces or dice them, and add to the avocados. Set aside.

Simmer the onion and garlic in the stock to cover until tender. Cool, and drain.

In stages, purée the avocados, cucumbers, onion, and garlic in the stock. Add the fresh mint, chervil or parsley, tarragon, and cream. Mix well. Season with cayenne and salt. Chill for at least 12 hours.

Serve the soup in the avocado shells or in soup bowls. Garnish with mint leaves, whipped cream, and slices of lemon or lime.

Note:
Serve the avocado shells on a bed of ice.

Serves 10.

Mrs. Anthony J. A. Bryan

Bisque of Bay Scallops

2 cups (480 mL/505 g) bay scallops with liquid

6 tablespoons (90 mL/86 g) unsalted butter

5 tablespoons (75 mL/41 g) all-purpose flour

2 tablespoons (30 mL/15 g) minced shallots

1 clove garlic, minced

A pinch of allspice **or** ground cloves

¼ teaspoon (1.3 mL/0.2 g) thyme

⅛ teaspoon (0.6 mL/0.1 g) marjoram

⅛ teaspoon (0.6 mL/0.1 g) rosemary

½ cup (120 mL) dry white wine

½ cup (120 mL) clam juice

2 cups (480 mL) milk **or** half-and-half

Salt to taste

Tabasco sauce to taste

Drain the scallops, reserving the liquid.

In a heavy saucepan, melt the butter. Add the flour, and cook until it begins to brown. Reduce the heat. Add the shallots and garlic; cook until they are transparent. Add the herbs. Deglaze with the white wine. Add the clam juice and scallop liquid. Set aside.

Scald the milk or half-and-half. Bring the scallop liquid mixture to a boil. Add the milk or cream gradually, stirring constantly to blend. Reduce the heat, and simmer slowly for 10 minutes. Do not allow to boil again. Add the scallops, and continue to simmer for about 5 minutes. Do not overcook the scallops, or they will become tough. Add the salt and Tabasco.

If a smooth texture is desired, purée and strain the bisque mixture. Serve very hot.

Serves 4 to 6.

The Cookbook Committee

Chilled Borscht

2 cups (480 mL/200 g) shredded cabbage

3 tablespoons (45 mL/ 43 g) unsalted butter

1½ cups (360 mL/220 g) cooked julienne beets

¼ cup (60 mL/23 g) minced leeks

¼ cup (60 mL/29 g) minced onion

¼ cup (60 mL/30 g) minced celery

2 cups (480 mL) bottled beet juice

3 tablespoons (45 mL) red wine vinegar

1 teaspoon (5 mL/4.7 g) sugar

Salt and pepper to taste

Sour cream

In a saucepan, blanch the cabbage for 2 minutes; drain. Melt the butter. Add the cabbage, beets, leeks, onion, and celery. Cook until soft. Add the beet juice, vinegar, sugar, salt, and pepper. Simmer for 1 hour.

Let the soup cool. Chill, covered, for at least 4 hours. Serve in chilled bowls; top each serving with a dollop of sour cream.

Serves 4 to 6.

Mrs. Robert O. Read

Meissen Factory
(German, 1710-   )
Monteith, c. 1730-40
Porcelain
7½ × 12 in. (19.1 × 30.5 cm.)
Ailsa Mellon Bruce Collection, 1970

Cream of Carrot Soup

4 tablespoons (60 mL/ 57 g) unsalted butter

1 pound (455 g) carrots, sliced

1 large onion, sliced

2 quarts (1.92 L) chicken stock

1 cup (240 mL/200 g) rice

½ teaspoon (2.5 mL/1.1 g) curry powder

½ teaspoon (2.5 mL/0.2 g) marjoram

1 cup (240 mL) heavy cream

1 teaspoon (5 mL/6 g) salt

½ teaspoon (2.5 mL/1.2 g) white pepper

In a large saucepan, melt the butter. Add the carrots and onion. Cook for 10 minutes over low heat, stirring frequently. Add the stock and rice. Bring to a boil. Add the curry and marjoram. Cover, and simmer for 1 hour.

Purée in a blender or food processor. Stir in the cream, and season with the salt and pepper. Soup should be quite thick. If it is too thick, it may be thinned with additional chicken stock.

Note:
Cream of carrot soup may be made ahead and reheated. It may also be served cold.

Serves 8 to 10.

Mrs. Fred I. Sharp

Creamy Corn Chowder

1 pound (455 g) unsalted butter

5 cups (1.2 L/575 g) chopped onions

Scant 1¾ cups (420 mL/230 g) all-purpose flour

4½ quarts (4.32 L) chicken stock, heated

3 cups (720 mL/365 g) chopped celery

3 cups (720 mL/410 g) chopped green peppers

16 to 18 17-ounce (480 g) cans creamed corn

7½ pounds (3.40 kg) frozen or fresh corn kernels

Salt and pepper to taste

2½ cups (600 mL) light cream

Chopped parsley

Crumbled bacon, crisp-fried

In a skillet, melt ¾ pound (340 g) of the butter. Add 4 cups (960 mL/460 g) of the onions, and sauté until golden. Whisk in the flour, and cook, stirring, for about 15 minutes, or until smooth. Transfer the mixture to a large kettle, and stir in the stock. Set aside.

In the skillet, melt the remaining butter. Add the remaining onions, the celery, and peppers, and sauté until soft but not browned. Add to the chicken broth mixture. Add the creamed corn and corn kernels. Season with salt and pepper. Return the chowder to the heat, and heat thoroughly. Stir in the cream just before serving.

Serve from a large tureen with bowls of parsley and bacon bits for garnish.

Serves 70.

Ellen C. Walton

Crabmeat and Tomato Soup

¼ pound (115 g) unsalted butter

½ cup (120 mL/58 g) chopped shallots **or** onion

1 cup (240 mL/140 g) any combination of julienne carrots, parsnip, celery, or leeks

4 cups (960 mL/905 g) peeled and chopped tomatoes with juice

Juice of 1 orange (about 3 tablespoons)

2 cloves

2 bay leaves

½ teaspoon (2.5 mL/0.2 g) marjoram

⅛ teaspoon (0.6 mL/0.3 g) each of allspice, cayenne pepper, and nutmeg

⅛ teaspoon (0.6 mL/0.3 g) saffron (optional)

1 teaspoon (5 mL/4.7 g) sugar (optional)

1 to 1½ cups (240 mL to 360 mL) beef **or** chicken stock

1 to 1½ cups (240 mL to 360 mL) heavy cream

½ pound (225 g) lump crabmeat, preferably jumbo

Salt and pepper to taste

In a saucepan, melt 2 tablespoons (30 mL/29 g) of the butter. Add the shallots or onion and the julienne vegetables, and sauté until soft but not browned. Add the tomatoes, orange juice, spices, and sugar, if desired. Simmer slowly. Reduce to 2½ cups (600 mL).

Remove the cloves and bay leaves. Purée and strain the mixture, forcing as much residue as possible through the strainer. Blend in the stock. Heat to boiling, and reduce the heat. Heat the soup slowly; do not boil. Add the cream, and set aside.

Melt the remaining butter. Sauté the crabmeat until thoroughly heated. Remove from the heat, and divide it among the soup bowls. Pour melted butter over the crabmeat. Reheat the soup. Add salt and pepper. Pour into the soup bowls.

Note:
Before the cream is added, the soup mixture may be refrigerated and kept for as long as 2 days before recipe is completed.

Serves 4 to 6.

Mrs. Anthony J. A. Bryan

Cream of Eggplant Soup

2 pounds (905 g) eggplant

2 or 3 medium onions

4 very ripe medium tomatoes

2 sweet red peppers

3 cloves garlic

Vegetable **or** olive oil

5 cups (1.2 L) vegetable **or** chicken stock

1 teaspoon (5 mL/0.8 g) basil

¼ teaspoon (1.3 mL/0.1 g) marjoram **or**
1½ tablespoons (23 mL/5 g) fresh mint (substitute for basil and marjoram)

2 tablespoons (30 mL/33 g) tomato purée

⅓ cup (80 mL) fresh orange juice

Salt and pepper to taste

Parmesan cheese or plain yogurt, for garnish

Preheat oven to 350° F (175° C).

Do not peel the vegetables or puncture skins. Oil the vegetables heavily. In a pan, roast them whole and uncovered as follows:

eggplant	1 to 1½ hours
onions	15 to 35 minutes
tomatoes	10 to 20 minutes
peppers	15 to 20 minutes
garlic	5 to 15 minutes

Test each vegetable for doneness by pressing firmly on the skin; it should give freely. When each is done, remove it from the oven, and cool.*

Cut the eggplant in half lengthwise, and remove the pulp; discard the skin. Peel the onions and garlic. Peel and seed the tomatoes and peppers. Chop all the vegetables into coarse pieces.

*Vegetables may also be roasted on an outdoor grill.

In a large pot, heat the stock. Add the vegetables, basil and marjoram, or mint. Bring to a boil quickly. Reduce to a simmer. Cook for 3 minutes. Add the tomato purée and orange juice. Remove from the heat. Cool, purée, and strain.

To serve hot:
Reheat the soup to the boiling point. Correct the seasoning, and serve topped with Parmesan cheese or yogurt.

To serve cold:
Chill. Correct the seasoning, and serve topped with yogurt.

Serves 6 to 8.

The Cookbook Committee

Country Herb Soup

¾ pound (340 g) pinto beans, soaked overnight

1 pound (455 g) ham, cut into ½-inch (1.3 cm) cubes

1 quart (960 mL) water

2¾ cups (660 mL) tomato juice

1 quart (960 mL) chicken stock

3 medium onions, chopped

3 cloves garlic, minced

1 teaspoon (5 mL/0.8 g) dried oregano

½ teaspoon (2.5 mL/1.1 g) ground cumin

½ teaspoon (2.5 mL/0.4 g) dried rosemary

½ teaspoon (2.5 mL/1.1 g) celery seeds

3 tablespoons (45 mL/ 10 g) chopped parsley

¼ cup (60 mL/34 g) chopped green pepper

¼ cup (60 mL/44 g) dark brown sugar

1 tablespoon (15 mL/7 g) chili powder

1 teaspoon (5 mL/6 g) salt

1 bay leaf, crumbled

½ teaspoon (2.5 mL/0.7 g) dried thyme

½ teaspoon (2.5 mL/ 0.4 g) dried basil

½ teaspoon (2.5 mL/0.2 g) dried marjoram

¼ teaspoon (1.3 mL/0.6 g) curry powder

4 whole cloves

1 cup (240 mL) dry sherry

1 scallion, chopped

Combine all the ingredients except the sherry and scallion. Simmer, partially covered, for 3 hours. Add the sherry just before serving. Sprinkle each serving with chopped scallion.

Note:
May be frozen.

Serves 12.

Mrs. W. H. Krome George

Hunt Chowder

1 pound (455 g) sausage

2 cups (480 mL) water

2 15½-ounce (440 g) cans red kidney beans

1 28-ounce (795 g) can tomatoes

1 onion, chopped

1 bay leaf

½ clove garlic, minced

Salt to taste

½ teaspoon (2.5 mL/0.7 g) thyme

⅛ teaspoon (0.6 mL/0.3 g) pepper

⅛ teaspoon (0.6 mL/0.3 g) caraway seeds

A pinch of crushed red pepper

1 cup (240 mL/140 g) diced potatoes

½ green pepper, chopped

In a skillet, brown the sausage. Drain and crumble.

In a large pan, combine the sausage, water, and all the remaining ingredients except the potatoes and green pepper. Simmer for 1 hour. Add the potatoes and green pepper, and simmer for 20 minutes.

Note:
This is a robust winter soup. The flavor improves when it is prepared a day ahead.

Serves 6.

Mrs. G. Jack Tankersley

Zupa Krupnik (Polish Barley and Vegetable Soup)

⅔ cup (160 mL/100 g) fine pearl barley, washed

11 cups (2.64 L) beef stock

5 tablespoons (75 mL/ 71 g) unsalted butter **or** margarine

1 medium onion, minced

2 carrots, cut into thin slices

2 celery stalks with leaves, sliced

2 potatoes, peeled and sliced

½ pound (225 g) mushrooms, sliced

Salt and pepper to taste

4 tablespoons (60 mL/ 63 g) sour cream

Fresh dill **or** parsley, for garnish

In a stockpot, combine the barley and 3 cups (720 mL)of the stock. Bring to a boil, cover, and simmer for 1 hour, or until the barley is tender. Remove from the heat.

In a skillet, heat 3 tablespoons (45 mL) of the butter or margarine, and sauté the onion until softened. Add the carrots, celery, and potatoes. Cover, and cook for 15 minutes. Transfer the vegetables to the stockpot.

Add the remaining butter to the skillet, add the mushrooms, and sauté until browned. Transfer to the stockpot, and add the remaining 8 cups (1.92 L) of stock. Add the salt and pepper. Bring to a boil, and simmer for 15 minutes, stirring frequently.

In a small bowl, blend the sour cream with ½ cup (120 mL) of the hot soup, and stir into the soup. Serve hot, garnished with dill or parsley.

Serves 8.

Clare Hoffman

Mushroom Bisque

7 tablespoons (105 mL/ 100 g) unsalted butter

1 cup (240 mL/89 g) chopped scallions, bulbs and stems

1 pound (455 g) mushrooms, chopped

4 tablespoons (60 mL/ 33 g) all-purpose flour

2 cups (480 mL) chicken stock

2 cups (480 mL) half-and-half

½ teaspoon (2.5 mL/ 3 g) salt

¼ teaspoon (1.3 mL/0.7 g) white pepper

4 tablespoons (60 mL) sherry

In a large saucepan, melt the butter. Add the scallions; cook for 5 minutes. Add the mushrooms; cook for 4 minutes. Add the flour, and stir. Cook for 2 to 3 minutes.

In a saucepan, heat the stock and half-and-half. Add to the mushroom mixture in a steady stream, stirring. Simmer for 5 minutes, stirring constantly. Add the salt, pepper, and sherry. Serve hot.

Serves 6 to 8.

Evie Bippart

Mushroom Soup

6 ounces (170 g) dried mushrooms*

Cognac, brandy, dry white wine, **or** water

6 cups (1.44 L) chicken **or** beef stock

Soak the mushrooms overnight in cognac, brandy, wine, or water to cover. Drain, reserving liquid. Pour the liquid through cheesecloth to remove any residue. In a large saucepan, heat the stock and mushroom liquid to boiling. Add the mushrooms. Simmer until tender. Serve very hot.

Serves 6 to 8.

The Cookbook Committee

*Use any combination of porcini, morel, chanterelle, girolle, or other varieties of dried Asian mushrooms. Because of drying techniques and variations, mushrooms may vary greatly in cooking time. Follow package directions when available.

Oysters and Artichoke Soup

¼ pound (115 g) unsalted butter

1½ cups (360 mL/135 g) chopped scallions, including 2 bulbs

2 cloves garlic, minced

3 tablespoons (45 mL/ 25 g) all-purpose flour

3 14-ounce (395 g) cans artichoke hearts, rinsed, drained, and quartered

6 cups (1.44 L) chicken stock

1 teaspoon (5 mL/1.5 g) crushed red pepper

½ teaspoon (2.5 mL/1 g) anise seed

1 teaspoon (5 mL/6 g) salt

1 quart (960 mL/1.01 kg) oysters, halved, with liquor

Lemon slices

In a large heavy pot, melt the butter, and sauté the scallions and garlic for 3 to 5 minutes, stirring constantly. Add the flour; stir until blended. Stir in the artichokes, stock, and seasonings. Cook for 20 minutes. Add the oysters and oyster liquor. Simmer for 10 minutes; do not boil.

The soup may be puréed and served in mugs, topped with a lemon slice.

Note:
If possible, prepare a day ahead.

Serves 12 to 14.

Mrs. Frederic L. Cook

Sausage and Lentil Soup

2 tablespoons (30 mL) olive oil

1 pound (455 g) chorizo (spicy Spanish sausage) **or** pepperoni

7 ounces (200 g) smoked ham, minced

2 large onions, minced

1 large green pepper, minced

1 medium carrot, minced

2 garlic cloves, minced

1 bay leaf

¾ teaspoon (3.8 mL/0.8 g) fresh thyme **or** ¼ teaspoon (1.3 mL/0.4 g) dried thyme

1 teaspoon (5 mL/2.1 g) whole cumin seed, ground

8 to 9 cups (1.92 to 2.16 L) chicken stock

1 1-pound can (455 g) tomatoes

1¼ cups (300 mL/225 g) dried lentils

Salt and freshly ground pepper to taste

12 large spinach leaves, shredded

In a 6- to 8-quart (5.76 to 7.68 L) saucepan, heat the oil over medium heat. Add the sausage, and cook until almost all the fat has been rendered. Transfer the sausage to a platter. Drain off all but 2 tablespoons (30 mL) of the fat from the saucepan. Add the ham, onions, green pepper, and carrot to the saucepan.

Cover, and cook for 15 minutes, stirring occasionally. Stir in the garlic, bay leaf, thyme, and cumin. Cover, and cook for another 5 minutes.

Cut the sausage into thin slices. Add it to the saucepan along with the stock, tomatoes, and lentils. Cover partially, and simmer gently for about 2 hours, or until the lentils begin to dissolve. Add salt and freshly ground pepper.

Remove any fat from the surface. Add the spinach leaves. Serve immediately.

Chinese Spinach Soup

Note:
Soup may be made up to the point at which the spinach is added and then refrigerated for up to 3 days before being finished.

Serves 8 to 10.

The Cookbook Committee

1 tablespoon (15 mL/8 g) cornstarch

1 tablespoon (15 mL/9 g) Sichuan peppercorns*

¾ pound (340 g) ground pork

4 cloves garlic, minced

3 scallions, minced

1-inch (2.5 cm) slice ginger root, peeled and minced

2 eggs

3 tablespoons (45 mL) soy sauce

1 tablespoon (15 mL) sesame oil

1 teaspoon (5 mL) vinegar

1 pound (455 g) packaged won ton skins*

6 cups (1.44 L) beef stock

1 cup (240 mL) cold water

2 cups (480 mL/95 g) fresh spinach, cut into ¼-inch (0.6 cm) strips

Dust a baking sheet with the cornstarch.

*Can be purchased in Asian food stores.

In a dry pan, cook the peppercorns over medium heat until they smoke. With a mortar and pestle, crush them lightly. Set aside.

In a bowl, mix the pork, garlic, scallions, ginger, 1 of the eggs, the soy sauce, sesame oil, vinegar, and peppercorns.

Spoon 1 teaspoon (5 mL) of the filling onto the center of each won ton square. Beat the remaining egg lightly, and rub a little of it around the perimeter of each square. Fold the dough over the filling to enclose it, pressing the edges together to seal. Place the finished won tons on the baking sheet. Cover with plastic wrap until ready to use.

Bring the stock to a boil. Add all the won tons. Bring to a boil again, and immediately add the cold water. Cover, bring to a boil a third time (the won tons are now cooked), and remove from the heat.

Place strips of fresh spinach in each soup bowl. Add 4 won tons and the broth. Serve immediately.

Serves 8.

Pamela Johnson

Split Pea Soup for Seventy

12 quarts (11.52 L) water

6 quarts (5.76 L) chicken stock

6 pounds (2.72 kg) dried split peas

4 onions, stuck with 3 cloves each

4 cups (960 mL/490 g) chopped celery

12 leeks, sliced

6 cups (1.44 L/740 g) chopped or sliced carrots

2 teaspoons (10 mL/2.9 g) thyme

4 bay leaves

A dash of cayenne pepper

Salt and pepper to taste

12 medium potatoes, peeled and chopped or sliced

35 hot dogs, cooked and sliced (optional)

In a large pot, combine the water and stock. Add the peas, bring to a boil, and simmer, uncovered, for approximately 1 hour, stirring occasionally. Add the onions, celery, leeks, 3 cups (720 mL/370 g) of the carrots and the seasonings. Simmer, covered, for 2 hours.

In a separate pot, cook the potatoes and remaining carrots in water to cover until just tender. Set aside.

In a blender, purée the soup. Just before serving, add the reserved potatoes and carrots and, if desired, the sliced hot dogs.

Note:
For smaller groups, this recipe can be easily reduced.

Serves 70.

Ellen C. Walton

Tomato Curry Soup

6 large ripe tomatoes, peeled

1 medium onion

1 tablespoon (15 mL) Worcestershire sauce

1 teaspoon (5 mL/4.7 g) sugar

1 teaspoon (5 mL/6 g) salt

6 tablespoons (90 mL/87 g) mayonnaise

About 1 tablespoon (15 mL/7 g) curry powder

3 tablespoons (45 mL/10 g) chopped parsley

The day before, put the tomatoes and the onion through a food mill, using the coarse blade. (Do not use a blender; the mixture will be too thin.)

In a bowl, blend the tomato-onion mixture with the Worcestershire, sugar, and salt. Cover, and chill overnight.

Combine the mayonnaise and the curry powder to taste. Add the parsley. Fill a soup cup with the tomato mixture, and top with 1 tablespoon (15 mL/15 g) of the curry mayonnaise.

Serves 4 to 6.

Suzanne O. Wolfe

Garden Fresh Tomato Soup

5 pounds (2.27 kg) tomatoes, cored and quartered

2 medium onions, sliced

½ cup (120 mL) vegetable oil

1 clove garlic

¼ cup (60 mL/13 g) parsley

3 to 4 cups (720 mL/375 g to 960 mL/500 g) shredded and drained zucchini (optional)

5 cups (1.2 L/585 g) cherry tomatoes

5 beef bouillon cubes

Bouquet Garni:
  4 bay leaves

  8 cloves

  ¼ teaspoon (1.3 mL/ 0.1 g) marjoram

  ¼ teaspoon (1.3 mL/0.4 g) thyme

  Salt and sugar to taste

In an 8-quart (7.68 L) pot, place the tomatoes, onions, oil, garlic, and parsley. Cook, covered, over medium-low heat until the tomatoes begin to soften. Bring to a boil, and add the zucchini, if desired. Cook until all ingredients are soft.

Put the vegetables through a food mill to remove the skins and seeds. Return the mixture to medium heat. Add the cherry tomatoes, bouillon cubes, and bouquet garni, which should be wrapped in cheesecloth and tied securely. Cook for about 30 minutes, or until the cherry tomatoes soften. Add salt and sugar. Remove the bouquet garni before serving.

Note:
May be frozen.

Serves 12.

Paul G. Wiegman

Summer Tomato Soup with Diced Ham

2 pounds (928 g) ripe tomatoes

1 tablespoon (15 mL/ 12 g) sugar

2 teaspoons (10 mL/ 12 g) salt

½ teaspoon (2.5 mL) onion juice

Juice and grated rind of ½ lemon

½ to ¾ cup (125 to 185 mL) heavy cream

2 slices cooked ham, diced

¼ to ½ cucumber, peeled, seeded, and diced

Fine-chopped parsley

In a blender or food processor, purée the tomatoes. Strain them through a fine sieve; there should be about 2½ cups (600 mL). Chill thoroughly.

Just before serving, add the sugar, salt, onion juice, lemon juice, and rind. Beat until smooth. Stir in enough cream to reach the desired consistency. Add the ham and cucumber.

Serve chilled. Garnish with parsley.

Serves 4.

Mrs. T. D. Mullins

Bavarian Trout Soup

1 tablespoon (15 mL/14 g)
unsalted butter

1 small shallot

1 cup (240 mL) water

1 cup (240 mL) dry
white wine

1 teaspoon (5 mL/2.8 g)
peppercorns

½ teaspoon (2.5 mL/
3 g) salt

1 clove

1 small bay leaf

1 12-inch (30 cm) -long
trout

1 teaspoon (5 mL/1.1 g)
coarse-chopped dill

½ small bunch watercress,
chopped

1 egg yolk

½ cup (120 mL) heavy
cream

In a skillet large enough
to accommodate the trout,
melt the butter, and sauté
the shallot. Add the water,
wine, peppercorns, salt,
clove, bay leaf, and trout.
Simmer for about 5
minutes, or until the trout
is done.

Remove the trout. Skin
and debone it, and divide
it among 4 soup cups.

Add the dill and
watercress to the broth.
Combine the egg yolk and
heavy cream, and add to
the broth. Heat, but do
not bring to a boil.

Strain, reserving the
watercress and dill for
garnish. Pour over the
trout, and serve
immediately.

Serves 4.

Willi Daffinger
Rolling Rock Club

Rembrandt Harmensz Van Rijn
(Dutch, 1606-1669)
Christ with the Sick around Him,
c. 1649
Etching
10⅞ × 15⅝₁₆ in.
(27.6 × 38.9 cm.)
Bequest of Charles J.
Rosenbloom, 1974

Pasta and Grains

Capellini and Scallops Pesto

2 cups (480 mL/105 g) stemless parsley

4 fresh spinach leaves

¼ cup (60 mL/13 g) fresh basil leaves

1 teaspoon (5 mL/6 g) salt

½ teaspoon (2.5 mL/1.4 g) freshly ground pepper

3 cloves garlic

6 tablespoons (90 mL/ 51 g) pine nuts (pignoli)

½ cup (120 mL) olive oil

Freshly grated Parmesan cheese

6 tablespoons (90 mL/ 86 g) unsalted butter

1 pound (455 g) bay scallops

6 shallots, chopped

½ teaspoon (2.5 mL/ 0.5 g) bouquet garni

About 1 cup (240 mL) dry white wine

1 pound (455 g) capellini **or** thinnest pasta available

Place the parsley in a food processor. Process, turning on and off several times.

Add the spinach, basil, salt, pepper, garlic, and pine nuts. Turn the processor on and off several times until the mixture is ground fine.

With the processor running, pour the oil through the tube. Scrape the sides, and continue processing until the mixture becomes a smooth, thick purée. Add 2 tablespoons (30 mL/ 14 g) of the Parmesan cheese, and process the pesto just long enough to mix.

In a saucepan, melt 2 tablespoons (30 mL/29 g) of the butter. Add the scallops, shallots, and bouquet garni. Barely cover with the wine. Simmer, stirring, for 5 to 6 minutes.

Cook the capellini until it is *al dente* according to package directions. Rinse with hot water, and drain thoroughly. Add the remaining butter. Stir in the pesto sauce and scallops. Pass a bowl of freshly grated Parmesan cheese.

Serves 6.

William P. Hackney

175

Cold Fettucine with Tuna

1 pound (455 g) fettucine

6 tablespoons (90 mL) olive oil

2 cloves garlic, minced

2 ounces (57 g) pine nuts (pignoli)

1 cup (240 mL/225 g) peeled, seeded, and chopped tomatoes

1 cup (240 mL/155 g) canned tuna, in chunks and drained

½ red pimiento, cut into thin strips

6 black olives, chopped

1 tablespoon (15 mL/3 g) chopped parsley

2 tablespoons (30 mL) red wine vinegar

Salt and freshly ground pepper to taste

Parsley, for garnish

Cook the fettucine until it is *al dente* according to package directions. Drain.

In a skillet, heat the oil, and sauté the garlic and pine nuts over low heat for about 5 minutes, or until the garlic is translucent and the nuts are golden. Add the tomatoes, and cook for a few seconds. Transfer to a large bowl. Cool.

Add the pasta to the pine nut mixture, and toss gently to coat. Add the tuna chunks, pimiento, olives, parsley, and vinegar. Blend. Season with salt and plenty of fresh pepper. Garnish with additional parsley. Serve at room temperature.

Serves 4.

Singer Euwer

Fettucine à la Française

8 ounces (225 g) fettucine

6 tablespoons (90 mL/ 86 g) unsalted butter

3 ounces (85 g) Roquefort or Danish bleu cheese, crumbled

1 cup (240 mL/53 g) chopped parsley

Freshly ground black pepper

Freshly grated Parmesan cheese (optional)

Cook the fettucine until it is *al dente* according to package directions. While it is cooking, place the butter on a serving platter. Set the platter on top of the fettucine pot to warm the platter and melt the butter.

When the pasta is cooked, drain it immediately, and place it on the warmed platter. Toss with the melted butter. Add the crumbled cheese, and toss again to melt the cheese.

Add the parsley, and toss lightly, allowing most of the parsley to remain on top as a garnish. Serve at once. Pass freshly ground pepper and the Parmesan cheese, if desired.

Serves 4.

Beth Smith

Fettucine Verde with Scallops

6 tablespoons (90 mL/86 g) unsalted butter

1 cup (240 mL/53 g) minced parsley

3 shallots, minced

1 cup (240 mL) dry white wine

1½ pounds (680 g) sea scallops, cut horizontally in ¼-inch (6 mm) medallions, **or** tiny bay scallops, dried on paper towels

1 cup (240 mL) half-and-half

1 cup (240 mL) heavy cream

2½ cups (600 mL/270 g) freshly grated Parmesan cheese

Freshly grated nutmeg

Salt and pepper to taste

1½ pounds (680 g) spinach fettucine **or** part tomato fettucine, cooked until it is *al dente* according to package directions

Sliced and sautéed mushrooms (optional)

Parsley, for garnish

In a skillet, heat 4 tablespoons (60 mL/57 g) of the butter, and sauté ½ cup (120 mL/27 g) of the minced parsley and shallots for about 5 minutes, or until the shallots are soft. Over high heat, add the wine, and reduce, stirring, to about 1½ cups (360 mL). Add the scallops. Cook over moderate heat, stirring, for about 1 minute. Add the half-and-half and cream. Simmer for 2 minutes. Remove from the heat. Stir in 2 cups (480 mL/215 g) of the Parmesan cheese, the remaining minced parsley, nutmeg, salt, and pepper.

Toss the fettucine with the remaining butter and the mushrooms, if desired. Transfer to a hot platter.

Pour the sauce over the fettucine; mix thoroughly.

Garnish with parsley. Serve Parmesan cheese on the side.

Note:
Cold marinated vegetables in a pesto-based dressing are a good accompaniment.

Serves 4 to 6.

Susan C. Santa-Cruz

Winslow Homer
(American, 1836-1910)
Fisher Girls, 1882
Pencil on paper
8¼ × 11¾ in.
(20.9 × 29.8 cm.)
Carnegie Special Fund, 1904

Frank Lloyd Wright
(American, 1867-1959), designer
Side Chair, c. 1904
Oak and leather
40½ × 15 × 18¾ in.
(102.9 × 38.1 × 47.6 cm.)
AODA Purchase Fund, 1982

Green Noodles and Shrimp

1 pound (455 g) green noodles

6 tablespoons (90 mL/ 86 g) unsalted butter

1 medium onion, chopped

1 clove garlic, minced

1 pound (455 g) shrimp, cooked, shelled, and deveined

3 tablespoons (45 mL) sherry

A dash of nutmeg

4 tablespoons (60 mL/ 33 g) all-purpose flour

2 cups (480 mL) milk

1 cup (240 mL/120 g) grated medium-sharp Cheddar cheese

1 teaspoon (5 mL/6 g) Dijon mustard

1 cup (240 mL/120 g) chopped celery

1 cup (240 mL/105 g) chopped pecans

½ pound (225 g) mushrooms, sliced

Preheat oven to 400° F (205° C). Grease a 9- by 13-inch (23 by 33 cm) baking dish.

Cook the noodles according to package directions. In a saucepan, melt 2 tablespoons (30 mL/29 g) of the butter. Add the onion and garlic; cook until soft. Add the shrimp, sherry, and nutmeg; cook for 5 minutes.

In another saucepan, melt the remaining butter. Stir in the flour. Add the milk, stirring constantly until the white sauce has thickened.

Add ¾ cup (180 mL/90 g) of the Cheddar cheese and the mustard; stir until blended. Remove from the heat. Stir in the celery, pecans, and mushrooms.

Alternate layers of sauce, shrimp, and noodles in the baking dish, ending with sauce. Sprinkle the remaining cheese on top. Bake for 35 minutes.

Note:
May be refrigerated before baking.

Serves 6 to 8.

Judith M. Davenport

178

Noodle Mushroom Ring

½ pound (225 g) medium noodles

Salt

2½ tablespoons (38 mL/ 36 g) unsalted butter

2 tablespoons (30 mL/ 17 g) all-purpose flour

½ cup (120 mL) milk

⅓ cup (80 mL) heavy cream

Freshly ground pepper to taste

A pinch of cayenne pepper

A dash of freshly grated nutmeg

1 egg, slightly beaten

⅓ cup (80 mL/36 g) grated Parmesan cheese

Filling:
  2 tablespoons (30 mL/ 29 g) unsalted butter

  8 cups (1.92 L/610 g) thin-sliced mushrooms

  1 tablespoon (15 mL) lemon juice

  2 tablespoons (30 mL/ 15 g) minced shallots

⅓ cup (80 mL) dry sherry

Salt and freshly ground pepper to taste

1 cup (240 mL) heavy cream

1 teaspoon (5 mL/3.3 g) arrowroot

Chopped parsley, for garnish

Preheat oven to 375° F (190° C).

Cook the noodles in boiling salted water for 5 minutes. Drain. Rinse under cold water. Drain again.

Grease a 4-cup (960 mL) mold with 1 tablespoon (15 mL/14 g) of the butter.

In a saucepan, melt the remaining butter. Add the flour, stirring. Continue stirring rapidly, adding the milk and heavy cream. Add salt to taste, pepper, cayenne, and nutmeg.

Stir the egg into the Parmesan cheese. Combine with the white sauce and the noodles. Pour the mixture into the mold. Smooth the top. Bake for 30 to 35 minutes, or until set.

Filling:
In a skillet, melt the butter. Add the mushrooms and lemon juice. Cook until the liquid has almost evaporated. Add the shallots; stir. Add all but 1 tablespoon (15 mL) of the sherry. Bring to a boil. Add the salt, pepper, and cream. Bring to a boil again.

Combine the reserved sherry and the arrowroot. Stir into the sauce. Cook briskly until slightly thickened.

Assembly:
Unmold the noodle ring onto a platter. Spoon the mushroom filling into the center. Sprinkle with the parsley.

Serves 4 to 6.

Mrs. Arthur M. Scully, Jr.

Pasta with Mussels

2 pounds (905 g) mussels

3 tablespoons (45 mL/ 25 g) all-purpose flour

2 tablespoons (30 mL) olive oil

2 tablespoons (30 mL/ 29 g) unsalted butter

¾ cup (180 mL/86 g) chopped onion

4 chopped shallots

2 to 3 cloves garlic, chopped

1½ (360 mL) cups dry white wine

½ cup (120 mL) fish stock

Bouquet Garni (see page 131)

2 large tomatoes, peeled, seeded, and chopped

A dash of saffron or curry

3 to 4 tablespoons (45 mL/50 g to 60 mL/67 g) tomato sauce

1 cup (240 mL) heavy cream

1 pound (455 g) flat noodles (rolled Mafaldina)

½ cup (120 ml/27 g) minced Italian parsley

Discard any mussels that are open and do not close when put in cold water. Scrub the usable mussels with a brush under cold running water.

With a knife, scrape off any seaweed or barnacles. Pull off the wispy beards. Soak for 1 to 2 hours in cold water to which the flour has been added to eliminate any sand remaining in the shells. Rinse again in cold water.

In a large pot, heat the oil and butter. Stir in the onion, shallots, and garlic. Cook slowly, for 4 to 5 minutes, or until wilted. Add the wine, stock, and bouquet garni. Bring to a boil. Lower the heat, and simmer for 5 minutes. Add the mussels, and cover. Boil for 3 to 4 minutes, or until the mussels open. Discard any mussels that do not open. Remove the mussels to a plate. When they are cool enough to handle, remove the top shell from each, and discard.

Add the tomatoes, saffron or curry, and tomato sauce to the pot. Cook, uncovered, over high heat for 3 to 5 minutes, or until reduced or slightly thickened. Discard bouquet garni. Add the cream, and continue cooking over high heat until the sauce coats the spoon.

While the sauce cooks, cook the pasta until it is *al dente* according to package directions. Drain.

Return the mussels in the half shell to the sauce to warm for 1 or 2 minutes. Add the parsley, and mix.

Arrange the pasta and mussels on a heated plate. Cover with the sauce, and serve immediately.

Serves 4.

Jane Citron Cooking Classes

Pasta with Salmon and Peas

¼ pound (115 g) unsalted butter

1 clove garlic

1 pound (455 g) salmon steak, skinned, boned, and cut into 1-inch (2.5 cm) cubes

Salt to taste

1 pound (455 g) fresh peas, shelled and cooked

⅓ cup (80 mL/18 g) chopped parsley

1 pound (455 g) pasta shells, ziti, **or** penne

Freshly ground pepper

2 tablespoons (30 mL) lemon juice

In a large skillet, melt the butter. Add the garlic and the salmon. Stir gently. Cook for 1 to 2 minutes, or until just done. Add the salt, peas, and parsley. Cook, stirring, for 1 minute.

Cook the pasta until it is *al dente* according to package directions. Drain. Add to the salmon mixture. Add the pepper and lemon juice. Serve hot.

Serves 6.

The Cookbook Committee

Seafood Primavera with Pasta Shells

¾ pound (340 g) small pasta shells

3 tablespoons (45 mL) safflower oil

2 tablespoons (30 mL) vegetable oil

8 scallions, chopped

1 large clove garlic, minced

2 cups (480 mL) clam juice

12 ounces (340 g) preferably bay scallops, sliced

1½ pounds (680 g) large raw shrimp, peeled and deveined

2 large carrots, cut into 3-inch (8 cm) julienne lengths

2 large unpeeled zucchini, cut into 3-inch (8 cm) julienne lengths

Herb Dressing:
  1 large clove garlic, minced

  ½ cup (120 mL/27 g) chopped parsley

  1½ tablespoons (23 mL/ 5 g) dillweed

  2 ounces (57 g) grated Parmesan cheese

½ cup (120 mL) clam juice

⅓ cup (80 mL) safflower oil

2 teaspoons (10 mL) lemon juice

1 teaspoon (5 mL/ 6 g) salt

Freshly ground pepper

1 cup (240 mL/53 g) minced parsley

1½ tablespoons (23 mL/ 5 g) dillweed

1½ teaspoons (8 mL/ 9 g) salt

Freshly ground pepper

Cook the pasta until it is *al dente* according to package directions. Toss with the safflower oil.

In a skillet, heat the vegetable oil. Add the scallions and garlic, and sauté until soft. Add the clam juice, and heat. Add the scallops, and simmer until they are firm and opaque. Remove, and cool. Add the shrimp, and simmer until opaque.

Remove, and cool. Add the carrots, and cook for about 5 minutes; carrots should be firm. Remove. Add the zucchini, and cook for 20 seconds. Drain.

Herb Dressing:
Combine all the ingredients. Blend well.

Assembly:
Combine the seafood and vegetables. Add the parsley, dill, salt, pepper, and pasta. Toss with the herb dressing, and refrigerate.

Note:
Herb dressing may be made the day ahead. Vegetables may be prepared ahead, and the seafood cooked in the morning.

Serves 10.

The Cookbook Committee

Summer Pasta

Dressing:
2 cups (480 mL/465 g) mayonnaise

1 cup (240 mL) vegetable oil

½ cup (120 mL) white wine

1 teaspoon (5 mL/4.7 g) sugar

1 pound (455 g) spaghetti, cooked until it is *al dente* according to package directions and chilled

2 cups (480 mL/225 g) sliced black olives

1 cup (240 mL/94 g) thin-sliced celery

1 cup (240 mL/115 g) thin-sliced red onions

1½ cups (360 mL/179 g) thin-sliced radishes

1 to 2 tablespoons (15 mL/3 g to 30 mL/6 g) chopped fresh dill

1 teaspoon (5 mL/2.7 g) freshly ground black pepper

1 tablespoon (15 mL/13 g) garlic salt

1 cup (240 mL/140 g) dry roasted sunflower nuts **or** chopped walnuts

½ cup plus 2 tablespoons (150 mL/33 g) chopped parsley

1 to 2 cups (240 mL/120 g to 480 mL/240 g) sliced or diced blanched vegetables (optional)

1 to 2 cups (240 mL/105 g to 480 mL/210 g) shredded cooked chicken (optional)

1 egg, hard-cooked and diced, for garnish

Dressing:
Mix all the ingredients until well blended.

In a large bowl, toss the chilled spaghetti with the olives, celery, red onions, radishes, dill, pepper, garlic salt, nuts, and ½ cup (120 mL/27 g) parsley. Fold in the vegetables and chicken, if desired, with half the dressing. Chill for several hours to allow the flavors to mingle.

Garnish with the egg and the remaining parsley. Serve with the remaining dressing on the side.

Serves 6 to 8.

Ricka Feely

Rice Ring

1 cup (240 mL/200 g) long-grain rice

2 cups (480 mL) water

Salt

2 tablespoons (30 mL/29 g) unsalted butter

¼ pound (115 g) mushrooms, chopped

3 to 6 fresh or canned artichoke hearts, diced

1 tomato, peeled and diced

1 cup (240 mL/115 g) fresh or frozen peas

¼ cup (60 mL) hot bouillon

Pepper to taste

¼ cup (60 mL/31 g) grated Parmesan cheese

Chopped parsley, for garnish

In a saucepan, combine the rice, water, and 1 teaspoon (5 mL/6 g) of the salt. Bring to a full boil. Reduce the heat, cover, and simmer for about 20 minutes, or until the water is absorbed and the rice is dry and flaky.

Preheat oven to 350° F (175° C). Grease a 6-cup (1.44 L) mold.

Melt the butter, and sauté the mushrooms for 3 minutes. Add the artichoke hearts, tomato, peas, and bouillon. Simmer for 2 minutes. Combine the rice with the mushroom mixture. Season with salt and pepper to taste, and Parmesan cheese.

Spoon the mixture into the prepared mold, and smooth firmly with a spoon. Set in a large baking dish with 1 inch (2.5 cm) hot water. Bake for 30 minutes. Unmold on a serving platter. Garnish with parsley.

Note:
May be prepared a day or two ahead and served hot or cold. A nice accompaniment for seafood.

Serves 6 to 8.

Susan C. Johnson

Scallion Rice

2 tablespoons (30 mL) vegetable oil

1 cup (240 mL/200 g) rice

¾ cup (180 mL/87 g) chopped scallions

½ cup (120 mL/68 g) chopped green pepper

¼ cup (60 mL/13 g) chopped parsley

2 cups (480 mL) chicken stock

1 teaspoon (5 mL/6 g) salt

¼ teaspoon (1.3 mL/ 0.7 g) pepper

Preheat oven to 375° F (190° C).

In a large skillet, heat the oil, and sauté the rice, stirring, until lightly browned. Stir in the scallions, and cook until soft. Mix in the green pepper, parsley, stock, salt, and pepper. Pour into a 6-cup (1.5 L) casserole. Cover, and bake for 30 to 40 minutes. Toss lightly with a fork before serving.

Serves 4 to 6.

Kathleen E. Lee

Valencian Rice

6 tablespoons (90 mL/ 86 g) unsalted butter

2 tablespoons (30 mL/ 14 g) fine-chopped onion

1 cup (240 mL/225 g) tomatoes, peeled and cubed

1 cup (240 mL/200 g) rice

2 small zucchini, cubed

2½ cups (600 mL) chicken stock

1 teaspoon (5 mL/1.5 g) dried thyme

2 tablespoons (30 mL/7 g) minced parsley

2 chopped pimientos

1 10-ounce (285 g) package frozen peas

Salt and pepper

Preheat oven to 400° F (205° C).

In a flameproof casserole, melt the butter, and cook the onion, stirring, until it is wilted. Add the tomatoes, and cook, stirring, until most of the liquid has evaporated.

Add the rice, and stir until each grain is well coated with butter. Add the remaining ingredients, and bring to a boil. Cover the casserole, place it in the oven, and bake for about 20 minutes, or until the moisture is absorbed and the rice is tender. Stir well.

Note:
For variety, browned pork chops may be added before baking, or shrimp may be added halfway through.

Serves 4.

Mrs. Danforth P. Fales

Spaghetti Carbonara

1 pound (455 g) thin
spaghetti

6 tablespoons (90 mL/
86 g) unsalted butter

2 tablespoons (30 mL)
white wine

2 egg yolks

½ cup (120 mL)
heavy cream

¼ pound (115 g) sliced
bacon, fried and crumbled

¾ cup (180 mL/94 g)
grated Parmesan cheese

Salt and freshly ground
pepper to taste

Cook the spaghetti for
4 minutes in at least
6 quarts (5.76 L) boiling
salted water. Drain.

In a large heavy skillet,
combine the butter and
wine. Reduce quickly over
high heat. Turn the heat
to medium, and add the
spaghetti. Cook for 2
minutes, coating well.

Combine the egg yolks
and cream. Add to the
spaghetti mixture quickly
so the eggs do not scramble.
Add the bacon and
cheese. Season with
pepper. Serve immediately
on warm plates.

Serves 6 to 8.

Elizabeth Cramer

Spinach and Wild Rice Casserole

1 package white and
wild rice mix

2⅓ cups (560 mL)
beef stock

2 10-ounce (285 g) packages
frozen chopped spinach

8 ounces (225 g) cream
cheese, softened

Salt to taste

2 to 3 tablespoons
(30 mL/29 g to 45 mL/
43 g) unsalted butter

1 pound (455 g)
mushrooms, cut into
thin slices

Preheat oven to 350° F
(175° C). Grease a 2-quart
(1.92 L) casserole.

Cook the rice according
to package directions,
substituting the stock for
water. Cook the spinach
until tender. Drain well,
combine with the cream
cheese, and add the salt.

Melt the butter, and sauté
the mushrooms until
golden. In the casserole,
layer half the rice, half the
spinach, and half the
mushrooms. Repeat the
layers. Cover, and bake
for 40 minutes.

Serves 6 to 8.

Mrs. George R. McCullough

Eggs and Cheese

Breakfast Party Casserole

Scrambled Eggs:
8 dozen eggs

½ cup (120 mL) evaporated milk

¾ pound (340 g) unsalted butter

White Sauce:
1½ pounds (680 g) unsalted butter

3 to 4 cups (720 mL/ 395 g to 960 mL/530 g) all-purpose flour

3 quarts (2.88 L) milk

Salt and pepper to taste

Mushroom Sauce:
1 pound (455 g) unsalted butter

5 to 6 pounds (2.27 to 2.72 kg) mushrooms, sliced

1½ cups (360 mL/175 g) chopped onions

1½ to 2 cups (360 to 480 mL) sherry

5 to 6 cups (1.2 L/600 g to 1.44 L/720 g) grated Cheddar cheese

The day before, grease 4 9- by 13- by 2-inch (23 by 33 by 5 cm) casseroles.

Scrambled Eggs:
Combine the eggs and milk. In a large skillet, heat the butter. Add the eggs, and scramble lightly. Set aside. This will have to be done in batches.

White Sauce:
Melt the butter over low heat. With a wire whisk, stir in the flour. Add the milk, a little at a time, stirring constantly to keep the mixture smooth. Add the salt and pepper. Continue cooking, stirring, until the sauce thickens.

Mushroom Sauce:
In a large skillet, melt the butter, and sauté the mushrooms and onions. Stir in the sherry and the white sauce.

Assembly:
Assemble the casseroles in layers, beginning with the eggs, then the mushroom sauce, and last the grated cheese. Repeat, ending with the cheese. Cover, and refrigerate overnight.

To bake, place the casseroles in a cold oven. Turn the heat to 300° F (150° C), and bake for approximately 1 hour.

Serves 50.

Ellen C. Walton

Cheddar Cheese Soufflé

1 tablespoon (15 mL/14 g) unsalted butter

½ cup (120 mL/62 g) grated Parmesan cheese

6 eggs

½ cup (120 mL) heavy cream

½ cup (120 mL/135 g) Dijon mustard

½ teaspoon (2.5 mL/3 g) salt

A dash of pepper

½ pound (225 g) sharp Cheddar cheese

11 ounces (310 g) cream cheese

Preheat oven to 375° F (190° C). Grease a 6-cup (1.44 L) soufflé dish with the butter. Coat the dish with ¼ cup (60 mL/31 g) of the Parmesan cheese.

In a food processor with a metal blade, mix the eggs, cream, remaining Parmesan, mustard, salt, and pepper. Process until smooth. With the processor running, add chunks of the Cheddar cheese and cream cheese until mixed. Pour the mixture into the soufflé dish. Bake for 40 to 45 minutes. Serve at once.

Note:
Serve with broiled tomato, a salad, and French bread.

Serves 4 to 6.

R. Jackson Seay

Corned Beef Quiche

1 unbaked 9-inch (23 cm) pie shell (see Pâte Brisée, page 98)

¼ to ½ pound (115 to 225 g) corned beef, minced

1 cup (240 mL/115 g) shredded Cheddar **or** Swiss cheese

2 tablespoons (30 mL/ 17 g) all-purpose flour

¼ teaspoon (1.3 mL/1.5 g) salt

A dash of nutmeg

2 eggs, beaten

1¼ cups (300 mL) milk

Preheat oven to 450° F (230° C).

Bake the pie shell for 7 minutes. Remove from the oven. Reduce the oven temperature to 325° F (165° C).

Place the corned beef in the shell. Top with the cheese.

Combine the flour, salt, nutmeg, eggs, and milk. Pour over the corned beef mixture. Return the quiche to the oven, and bake for about 40 minutes, or until the filling is set. Serve warm or cold.

Serves 6 to 8.

Ann and David Wilkins

Corn, Cheese, and Chili Pie

3 large eggs

1 8-ounce (225 g) can creamed corn

1 10-ounce (285 g) package frozen corn, defrosted and drained, **or** 1 7-ounce (200 g) can corn, drained

¼ pound (115 g) unsalted butter **or** margarine, melted

½ cup (120 mL/73 g) yellow cornmeal

1 cup (240 mL/255 g) sour cream

4 ounces (115 g) Monterey Jack cheese, cut into ½-inch (1.3 cm) cubes

4 ounces (115 g) canned green chilies, diced

½ teaspoon (2.5 mL/3 g) salt

¼ teaspoon (1.3 mL) Worcestershire sauce

Preheat oven to 350° F (175° C). Grease a 10-inch (25 cm) quiche or pie pan.

In a large mixing bowl, beat the eggs. Add all the remaining ingredients, and stir until thoroughly blended. Pour the mixture into the baking dish. Place on the center rack of the oven. Bake for about 1 hour, or until firm. Let stand for 10 minutes before serving.

Note:
May be kept up to 3 days in the refrigerator or up to 3 months in the freezer. If it is frozen, defrost, then heat it at 350° F (175° C) for about 20 minutes.

Serves 6 to 8.

Mrs. John P. Davis, Jr.

Grits Soufflé

1 cup (240 mL) milk

1 cup (240 mL) water

½ cup (120 mL/85 g) regular or instant grits

3 egg yolks, well beaten

2 tablespoons (30 mL/29 g) unsalted butter

3 tablespoons (45 mL/23 g) grated sharp yellow cheese

1½ teaspoons (8 mL/9 g) salt

¼ teaspoon (1.3 mL/0.6 g) paprika

3 egg whites

Preheat oven to 350° F (175° C). Grease a 1½-quart (1.44 L) soufflé dish.

In the top of a double boiler, heat the milk and water. Add the grits. Cook for 1 hour, stirring (if using instant grits, cook for 5 to 10 minutes). Remove from the heat.

Add the egg yolks, butter, cheese, salt, and paprika. Beat the egg whites until stiff, and fold them into the grits. Pour into the baking dish. Bake for 45 minutes.

Serves 3 to 4.

Scona Lodge

Huevos Rancheros

2½ tablespoons (38 mL) olive oil

2 tablespoons (30 mL/ 15 g) minced onion

1 fresh hot chili, seeded and minced

2 cloves garlic, minced

1 cup (240 mL/265 g) tomato **or** chili sauce

1 tablespoon (15 mL/2 g) dried oregano

¼ teaspoon (1.3 mL/1.5 g) salt

4 eggs

2 cups (480 mL) peanut oil

4 tortillas

8 slices avocado

Sour cream

In a skillet, heat the olive oil, and sauté the onion until transparent. Add the chili and garlic. Cook for about 1 minute. Add the tomato or chili sauce, oregano, and salt. Cook for about 4 minutes, or until thickened.

Break the eggs over the sauce. Cook, covered, for about 3½ minutes. Remove from the heat.

In a wok or deep fryer, heat the peanut oil until almost smoking. Carefully float 1 tortilla at a time in the oil until crisp and golden. Turn, and fry the second side for about 30 seconds. Drain thoroughly on paper towels.

Divide the tortillas among 4 plates. Place an egg on each tortilla. Cover with the sauce. Garnish with avocado slices and a dollop of sour cream.

Serves 4.

The Cookbook Committee

Sausage Frittata

1 pound (455 g) link or bulk, mild or hot Italian sausage

½ pound (225 g) pepperoni (optional)

24 ounces (680 g) ricotta cheese

8 ounces (225 g) grated mozzarella cheese

12 eggs

Preheat oven to 350° F (175° C). Grease a 9- by 13-inch (23 by 33 cm) baking pan.

Remove any casings from the sausage. Brown the sausage in its own fat. Drain, and set aside to cool.

Peel the pepperoni stick, if desired. Slice, brown, and drain. Cool.

Mix together the sausage, pepperoni, and cheeses. Pat into the baking dish.

Beat the eggs. Pour them over the sausage and cheese mixture. Lift along the edges with a spatula to let the eggs run under the mixture. Bake for about 50 minutes, or until the eggs are set. The frittata should not get too brown. Cool slightly; then cut into squares.

Serve hot or cold.

Note:
Serve for luncheon with a tossed salad and hot rolls.

Serves 12 (1½-inch [3.8 cm] squares) for hors d'oeuvres; 8 to 10 (3- to 4-inch [8 to 10 cm] squares) for luncheon.

Carolyn A. Tumolo

Meats

Beef Braciola

3 to 4 pounds (1.36 to 1.81 kg) sirloin, round steak, **or** any lean beef, sliced ½ inch (1.3 cm) thick

Salt and pepper to taste

⅓ cup (80 mL) olive oil

½ cup (120 mL/58 g) minced onion

3 to 6 cloves garlic, minced

2 10-ounce (285 g) packages frozen chopped spinach, defrosted and squeezed dry

1 cup (240 mL/110 g) freshly grated Parmesan **or** Romano cheese

1 teaspoon (5 mL/0.8 g) basil

1 teaspoon (5 mL/2.1 g) crushed fennel seeds

½ pound (225 g) mushrooms, stems removed

½ cup (120 mL) dry red wine

2 cups (480 mL) beef stock

2 tablespoons (30 mL) brandy (optional)

¼ cup (60 mL/33 g) all-purpose flour

Preheat oven to 375° F (190° C).

Place 1 slice of beef at a time on a flat surface, and pound it until ¼ inch (0.6 cm) thick. Season with salt and pepper. In a saucepan, heat 4 tablespoons (60 mL) of the oil. Add the onion and garlic, and sauté until the onion is transparent. Remove from the heat. Set aside.

Combine the spinach and cheese. Add the onion mixture, basil, and fennel. Mix well.

Spread the spinach mixture on the steaks. Roll them, and secure with toothpicks or string. In a large ovenproof skillet, heat the remaining oil, and brown the beef rolls on all sides. Remove the rolls, and keep them warm.

Add the mushroom caps to the skillet. Sauté them for a few minutes over high heat. Remove. Deglaze the skillet with the wine. Reduce it to almost a syrup, and add 1½ cups (360 mL) of the stock and the brandy, if desired. Continue cooking, uncovered, to reduce further.

Mix the flour with the remaining stock, stirring briskly to avoid lumps. Add to the stock mixture. Return the beef rolls and mushrooms to the skillet. Bring the liquid to a boil, cover, and place in the oven.

Bake for about 1 hour. Check occasionally, and add stock or water if the gravy becomes too thick.

Note:
Serve with pasta and freshly grated Parmesan cheese, a green salad, and hot Italian bread.

Serves 6 to 8.

Katy Hinds

Marinated Beef Tenderloin

4½ to 5 pounds (2.04 to 2.27 kg) beef tenderloin

Pepper

¼ cup (60 mL) Kitchen Bouquet

¾ cup (180 mL) soy sauce

2 tablespoons (30 mL) Worcestershire sauce

The day before, sprinkle the meat with pepper. Combine the remaining ingredients, and pour over the meat. Cover, and marinate in the refrigerator for 24 hours.

Remove the meat from the refrigerator 2 to 3 hours before cooking to bring to room temperature.

Preheat oven to 450° F (230° C).

Drain the meat. Roast, uncovered, for 20 minutes. Turn the oven off. Do not open the oven door. Leave the roast in the oven 15 minutes longer. Serve immediately.

Serves 8.

Mrs. Thomas P. Preston

Red Hot Chili

2 pounds (905 g) ground beef

1 pound (455 g) ground pork

1 tablespoon (15 mL/18 g) salt

2½ ounces (71 g) chili con carne seasoning

1 teaspoon (5 mL/2.8 g) ground cardamom

2 teaspoons (10 mL/4.5 g) turmeric powder

1 large onion, chopped

2 to 3 cloves garlic, minced

½ green pepper, seeded and minced (optional)

2 to 3 hot red jalapeño peppers, minced, **and/or** hot pepper sauce to taste

1 28-ounce (795 g) can plum tomatoes, undrained and chopped into coarse pieces

1 cup (240 mL) dry red wine

2 to 3 15-ounce (425 g) cans kidney beans, drained, **or** 12 ounces (340 g) dried kidney beans

In a large Dutch oven brown the meat. Add the salt, chili con carne seasoning, cardamom, turmeric, onion, garlic, and green pepper. Season with jalapeño peppers or hot pepper sauce to taste. Cook for 10 minutes. Stir in the tomatoes; cook an additional 10 minutes. Add the wine and beans and cook for 10 more minutes (if dried beans are used, cook at least 1 hour longer, or until the beans are tender).

Note:
If dried kidney beans are used, soak them overnight in cold water before cooking.

Serve with rice.

Very hot. French bread and cold beer will soothe the palate.

Makes 2½ to 3 quarts (2.4 to 2.88 liters). Freezes well.

Beth Adams

Lamb with Garlic and Rosemary

1 or 2 cloves garlic

1 5- to 6-pound (2.27 to 2.72 kg) leg of lamb, boned and butterflied

Fresh or dried rosemary

Freshly ground black pepper

Salt (optional)

Lemon slices and watercress, for garnish

Preheat oven to 500° F (260° C). Line a roasting pan with foil.

Split the garlic in half, and rub it over the lamb. Slice the garlic into slivers, and tuck them into tiny slits under the fat or in the pockets formed by the boning. Sprinkle both sides with rosemary, pepper, and salt, if desired.

Place the lamb in the roasting pan. Roast for 35 to 45 minutes, depending on desired doneness (lamb will be medium at 45 minutes). Remove to a serving platter. Decorate with lemon and watercress.

Strain the juices into a saucepan. Skim off the fat. Serve separately.

Serves 10 to 12.

Mrs. O. Harry Gruner III

Lamb Chops Supreme

8 lamb chops

½ teapoon (2.5 mL/3 g) salt

¼ teaspoon (1.3 mL/0.7 g) pepper

¼ pound (115 g) bleu cheese

A drop of Tabasco sauce

1 teaspoon (5 mL) Worcestershire sauce

½ cup (120 mL) beef stock (canned, **or** made from a bouillon cube)

Preheat oven to 350° F (175° C).

Season the chops with the salt and pepper. Combine the cheese, Tabasco, and Worcestershire, and spread the mixture on the chops.

Place them in a shallow baking dish, and pour the stock over them. Bake for 1 hour and 15 minutes.

Serves 4.

Mrs. William N. Steitz

Steamed Leg of Lamb with Pesto Stuffing

⅓ cup (80 mL) dry white wine

½ cup (120 mL) Italian olive oil

1½ cups (360 mL/80 g) (about 1 bunch) fresh basil **or** parsley, packed firm

2 teaspoons (10 mL/6 g) minced garlic

2 teaspoons (10 mL/1.8 g) dried rosemary

1 teaspoon (5 mL/6 g) salt

Freshly ground pepper

1½ cups (360 mL/68 g) fresh bread crumbs

⅓ cup (80 mL/45 g) pine nuts (pignoli)

1 5- to 6-pound (2.27 to 2.72 kg) leg of lamb, boned and butterflied

3 cups (720 mL) water

2 tablespoons (30 mL/ 29 g) unsalted butter

In a food processor, combine the wine, oil, basil or parsley, garlic, rosemary, salt, and pepper, and process until well blended. Remove 2 tablespoons (30 mL) of the mixture, and set aside.

Add first the bread crumbs, then the pine nuts to the food processor. Process for about 5 seconds, or until the stuffing is just blended.

Spread the stuffing evenly over the lamb. Roll the lamb, and tie it securely with string. Rub the surface with the reserved herb mixture. Insert a meat thermometer into the center.

In the bottom of a steamer, bring the water to a boil. Place the lamb on the steamer rack. Cover. Reduce the heat to medium. Cook for about 1 hour, or until the meat thermometer reads 145°F (63° C). Check periodically to see that the water has not boiled away; if the heat is adjusted properly, the liquid should not evaporate. When the lamb is done, remove to a warm serving platter. Allow it to rest for about 20 minutes before carving.

Pour the liquid from the bottom of the steamer into a glass measuring cup. Skim off the fat. Pour into a small saucepan, and heat to boiling. Whisk in the butter until smooth. Transfer to a warm sauceboat.

Note:
Serve with steamed vegetables such as new potatoes, sweet carrots, yellow squash, snow peas, or asparagus tips.

Serves 10.

Bettie Studer

Meat Pie

Filling:

1 tablespoon (15 mL/ 14 g) unsalted butter

1 medium onion, minced

2 pounds (905 g) ground round **or** ground sirloin steak

1 egg

¼ pound (115 g) grated Swiss cheese

1 teaspoon (5 mL/1.5 g) thyme

½ teaspoon (2.5 mL/ 0.8 g) sage

½ teapoon (2.5 mL/3 g) salt

½ teaspoon (2.5 mL/ 1.4 g) pepper

Pastry:

1½ cups (360 mL/200 g) all-purpose flour

¼ teaspoon (1.3 mL/ 1.5 g) salt

¼ pound (115 g) unsalted butter, frozen

¼ cup (60 g) ice water

1 egg, beaten

Filling:
Preheat oven to 375° F (190° C).

Melt the butter, and sauté the onion until transparent. Add the meat, and cook until it is no longer pink. Drain off the excess fat. Place the mixture in a large bowl to cool. Add the remaining ingredients. Mix well, and set aside.

Pastry:
Place the flour and salt in a processor with a steel blade. Cut the butter into teaspoon-size pieces, and place on top of the flour. Process, turning the motor on and off quickly 6 times. Add the water, and process until the pastry forms a ball. Use at once, refrigerate, or freeze.

Assembly:
Roll out the dough into a 24-inch square, ⅛ inch thick (61 cm by 0.3 cm). Spoon the meat mixture into the center of the dough. Bring up the corners to cover the meat,

pinching the seams to seal. Brush with the beaten egg. Prick steam holes in the top, and bake 20 to 25 minutes, or until golden brown.

Note:
Variation: For an elegant bombe, roll out half the pastry to form a circle. Place it on an ungreased baking sheet. Mound the meat filling in the center. Roll out the remaining pastry, and place it on top of the meat mixture, creating a bombe. Shape the pastry, and crimp the top and bottom edges together. Decorate with flowers, butterflies, or other shapes cut out of the pastry. Continue as directed above for completing and baking.

Both the pie and the bombe may be frozen before being baked.

Serves 6.

R. Jackson Seay

W. Eugene Smith
(American, 1918-1978)
Smoky City, 1955-57
Photograph
23¾ × 19⅞ in.
(60.3 × 50.5 cm.)
Museum Purchase: Gift of Vira I. Heinz Fund of the Pittsburgh Foundation, 1982

Sechuan Pork with Peanuts

Sauce:

1 teaspoon (5 mL/2.7 g) cornstarch

1 tablespoon (15 mL) dry sherry

1½ tablespoons (23 mL) soy sauce

2 teaspoons (10 mL) red wine vinegar

2 teaspoons (10 mL/ 9 g) sugar

¼ teaspoon (1.3 mL/ 1.5 g) salt

1 teaspoon (5 mL) sesame oil

1 tablespoon (15 mL) soy sauce

1 tablespoon (15 mL/8 g) cornstarch

2 tablespoons (30 mL) vegetable oil

1 pound (455 g) boneless pork loin, cut into ¼-inch (0.6 cm) cubes

4 cups (960 mL) water

4 to 6 dried chili peppers **or** sesame-chili oil to taste

3 slices ginger root, minced

½ cup (120 mL/72 g) coarse-chopped peanuts

Sauce:
Combine all the ingredients, and mix well.

In a bowl, combine the soy sauce, cornstarch, and 1 tablespoon (15 mL) of the oil. Mix well. Add the pork, and marinate for 30 minutes or longer in the refrigerator.

In a saucepan, bring the water to a boil. Add the meat, and stir to separate. Return to a boil, and cook for 1 minute. Drain, and set aside.

Heat a skillet over high heat. Add the remaining oil, and turn the heat to low. Add the peppers, and press them into the oil with a large spoon; or add the sesame-chili oil. Add the ginger, and stir briskly. Turn the heat to high, add the meat, and cook for 45 seconds. Stir in the sauce. Spoon the mixture into a serving dish, and sprinkle it with the peanuts.

Note:
Chili peppers are hot; use them to taste. For a milder flavor, use the sesame-chili oil.

Serves 4.

Rebecca Henry

John Wakelin and William Tayler (English, London, working 1776-1792)
Dessert Basket and Stand, 1788
Silver and glass
7⅛ × 15⅛ × 10⅞ in.
(18.1 × 38.4 × 27.6 cm.)
Gift of Mrs. Paul Block, 1976

Barbecued Ribs

½ cup (120 mL) soy sauce

⅓ cup (80 mL) wine vinegar

2 cloves garlic, minced

¼ cup (60 mL/61 g) grated onion

4 to 5 pounds (1.81 to 2.27 kg) spareribs

Sauce:
½ cup (120 mL) white vinegar

¼ cup (60 mL/44 g) brown sugar

½ cup (120 mL/135 g) ketchup

2 tablespoons (30 mL/ 34 g) prepared mustard

Black pepper to taste

2 tablespoons (30 mL) reserved soy sauce marinade

½ cup (120 mL) pan drippings

Preheat oven to 400° F (205° C).

Combine the soy sauce, vinegar, garlic, and onion. Brush the ribs with the marinade, and let stand for 30 minutes.

Place the ribs and marinade in a roasting pan. Reserve 2 tablespoons (30 mL) of the marinade for the sauce. Bake for 1 to 1½ hours, depending on the crispness preferred.

Sauce:
In a saucepan, combine the vinegar, sugar, ketchup, mustard, pepper, and reserved marinade. Cook until thick. Add the pan drippings. Cook for 10 minutes.

Serves 4.

Saul Drucker

Sausage and Wild Rice Casserole

1½ pounds (680 g) bulk sausage

1 cup (240 mL/200 g) wild rice, well rinsed

1 1-pound (455 g) can tomatoes

1 cup (240 mL/115 g) chopped onion

3 teaspoons (15 mL/17 g) mild mustard

2 to 3 teaspoons (10 mL/ 4.5 g to 15 mL/7 g) curry powder

1 teaspoon (5 mL/1.5 g) thyme

1 teaspoon (5 mL/5 g) celery salt

8 ounces (225 g) tomato sauce

¼ cup (60 mL/27 g) grated Parmesan cheese

Preheat oven to 350° F (175° C).

In a 2-quart (1.92 L) casserole, combine all the ingredients except the tomato sauce and Parmesan cheese. Bake, covered, for 50 minutes.

Stir the mixture, and bake, uncovered, for an additional 15 minutes. Add tomato sauce as needed to keep rice moist. Stir in the cheese. Bake for 15 minutes longer.

Serves 5 or 6.

Jane Reeves Thompson

Green Pepper Steak

⅓ cup (80 mL) soy sauce

1 clove garlic, mashed

1 cup (240 mL) water

1½ pounds (680 g) flank steak, cut diagonally into paper-thin slices

¼ cup (60 mL) peanut oil

2 medium green peppers, cut into thin slices

1 medium onion, cut into thin slices

5 stalks celery, cut diagonally into thin slices

1 tablespoon (15 mL/8 g) cornstarch

2 cups (480 mL/295 g) hot steamed rice

Tomato wedges, for garnish

In a shallow casserole, mix the soy sauce, garlic, and ½ cup (120 mL) of the water. Add the steak. Marinate for 15 minutes. Drain, reserving the liquid.

In a large skillet, heat the oil on the highest heat. Brown the meat quickly for 2 minutes. Push the meat to one side of the pan. Add the peppers, onion, and celery. Cook for 2 minutes, or until the vegetables are crisp-tender.

Mix the cornstarch and the remaining water. Add to the reserved marinade, and stir the mixture into the meat and vegetables. Cook until the liquid is thickened.

Arrange on hot rice, and garnish with tomato wedges.

Serves 4.

Mrs. Daisuke Nakada

Minced Veal

1½ pounds (680 g) veal tenderloin or cutlets

6 tablespoons (90 mL/ 86 g) unsalted butter

¼ cup (60 mL/29 g) minced onions

¼ cup (60 mL) brandy

¼ cup (60 mL/33 g) all-purpose flour

½ teaspoon (2.5 mL/3 g) salt

¼ teaspoon (1.3 mL/0.6 g) white pepper

1½ cups (360 mL) dry white wine

1 cup (240 mL) heavy cream

1 tablespoon (15 mL/3 g) minced parsley

Trim the veal, and cut it into strips about ¼ inch wide by 1½ inches long (0.6 by 3.8 cm).

In a large skillet, heat the butter. Add the veal and onions. Cook, stirring constantly, for 3 to 4 minutes, or until the meat looks white. Add the brandy to the meat mixture; heat and ignite it. Then sprinkle it with the flour, salt, and pepper. Add the wine and cream. Cook over low heat, stirring constantly, until the mixture thickens; do not boil. Sprinkle with the parsley, and serve *immediately*. The meat will toughen if allowed to stand after cooking.

Serves 4 to 6.

Mrs. Rolf K. Bungeroth

Veal Stew

¼ cup (60 mL/31 g) all-purpose flour, sifted

¼ teaspoon (1.3 mL/0.6 g) nutmeg

1 teaspoon (5 mL/6 g) salt

1½ pounds (680 g) boneless veal, cut into cubes

4 tablespoons (60 mL/57 g) unsalted butter **or** margarine

1 cup (240 mL) chicken stock

½ cup (120 mL) sherry

¼ pound (115 g) mushrooms, sliced

1 tablespoon (15 mL/7 g) minced onion

1 tablespoon (15 mL/3 g) minced parsley

Combine the flour, nutmeg, and salt. Dredge the veal in the flour mixture.

In a Dutch oven, heat the butter or margarine, and brown the veal. Add the stock, sherry, mushrooms, onion, and parsley. Cover, and simmer for 1½ to 2 hours.

Serves 4.

Helen M. Erzen

Veal à la Waller

2 tablespoons (30 mL/10 g) regular or infant's oatmeal

Salt and pepper

3 bananas, cut in half crosswise

1 egg, beaten

¼ cup (60 mL) vegetable oil

1½ pounds (680 g) veal fillet, cut into 6 pieces

1 tablespoon (15 mL/8 g) all-purpose flour

3 slices bacon

1 tablespoon (15 mL/7 g) chopped onion

1 tablespoon (15 mL/9 g) chopped green pepper

⅓ cup (80 mL) sherry

1 cup (240 mL) canned **or** homemade brown gravy

Preheat oven to 350° F (175° C).

If regular oatmeal is used, pulverize it in a blender. Season to taste with salt and pepper. Dip the banana sections into the egg, then into the oatmeal. Heat ⅛ cup (30 mL) of the oil, and brown the bananas, turning frequently.

Roll 1 piece of veal around each banana section; secure with thread. Coat the veal with seasoned flour. Heat the remaining oil, and brown the veal. Arrange the veal in an 8- by 12-inch (20 by 30 cm) casserole. Cover with the bacon.

Combine the onion, green pepper, sherry, and gravy. Pour over the veal. Cover with foil. Bake for 1 to 1½ hours, or until tender.

Note:
Serve with wild rice.

Serves 6.

Mrs. Richard S. Smith

Poultry and Game

Chicken Breast Saltimbocca

1 cup (240 mL/130 g) all-purpose flour

6 whole chicken breasts, skinned, boned, and halved

5⅓ tablespoons (80 mL/ 76 g) unsalted butter

Salt and pepper to taste

¼ cup (60 mL/29 g) chopped shallots

3 large cloves garlic, minced

½ pound (225 g) mushrooms, sliced

½ cup (120 mL) dry white wine

1 cup (240 mL) chicken stock

1 teaspoon (5 mL/1.1 g) fresh thyme **or** ½ teaspoon (2.5 mL/0.7 g) dried thyme

1 teaspoon (5 mL/1.1 g) fresh oregano **or** ½ teaspoon (2.5 mL/0.4 g) dried oregano

2 tablespoons (30 mL/ 16 g) cornstarch

¼ cup (60 mL) water

½ cup (120 mL) dry sherry

½ cup (120 mL) light cream

12 thin slices (5 ounces/140 g) prosciutto ham

6 slices (170 g) Monterey Jack cheese, cut in half

Preheat oven to 375° F (190° C). Grease a 9- by 13- by 2-inch (23 by 33 by 5 cm) baking dish.

Flour the chicken. In a skillet, melt the butter, and brown the chicken lightly. Transfer the chicken to the baking dish, leaving the butter in the skillet. Season the chicken with salt and pepper. Set aside.

In the skillet, sauté the shallots and garlic until soft. Add the mushrooms, wine, stock, and herbs. Bring to a boil, and cook for 10 minutes.

Dissolve the cornstarch in the water. Add it to the sauce. Cook, stirring, until slightly thickened. Stir in the sherry and cream. Season with salt and pepper.

Place 1 slice of ham and 1 slice of cheese on each piece of chicken. Pour the sauce over the chicken. Cover with foil. Bake for 20 minutes. Remove the foil. Bake for about 10 minutes longer, or until browned.

Note:
After sauce has been made, chicken and sauce may be refrigerated until 30 minutes before serving, at which point oven should be preheated.

Serves 6.

Woodene Merriman

Coronation Chicken

2 3 to 3½-pound (1.36 to 1.59 kg) chickens

1 cup (240 mL) white wine

Bouquet Garni (see page 131)

3 chicken bouillon cubes

2 tablespoons (30 mL) vegetable oil

¼ cup (60 mL/29 g) minced onion

1 tablespoon (15 mL/7 g) curry powder

2 teaspoons (10 mL/11 g) tomato purée

½ cup (120 mL) water

¾ cup (180 mL) red wine

1 bay leaf

A pinch each of salt, pepper, and sugar

½ lemon, for juice

2 slices lemon

2 to 3 tablespoons (30 mL/41 g to 45 mL/ 61 g) apricot jam

2 cups (480 mL/465 g) mayonnaise

¼ cup (60 mL) heavy cream, lightly whipped, **or** sour cream

Place the chickens in a large pot, and cover them with cold water. Add the white wine and bouquet garni. Heat to a very slow boil. Add the bouillon cubes, and poach the chickens for 1 hour. Cool in the broth. Set aside.

In a saucepan, heat the oil. Add the onion, and cook gently for 3 to 4 minutes. Add the curry, and cook for 1 to 2 minutes longer. Add the tomato purée, water, red wine, and bay leaf. Bring to a boil. Add the salt, pepper, sugar, 2 squeezes of lemon juice, and 2 slices of lemon. Simmer, uncovered, for 5 to 10 minutes to reduce. Add the apricot jam. Strain, and cool.

In a bowl, add the sauce slowly to the mayonnaise. Adjust the seasonings, and add the whipped or sour cream.

Carve the chicken. Arrange on a large platter, dark slices on the bottom, white on top. Cover with the curry sauce. Pass the remaining sauce.

Note:
To make a delicious broth, add the discarded bones to the chicken stock.

This is the Cordon Bleu recipe for chicken salad served at Queen Elizabeth's coronation. Serve with a salad made with rice, peas, cucumbers, parsley, mixed herbs, and a well-seasoned French dressing.

Serves 6.

Mrs. T. D. Mullins

Curried Chicken

¼ pound (115 g) unsalted butter **or** margarine

1 3½-pound (1.59 kg) chicken, cut into pieces

1 carrot, chopped

1 onion, chopped

1 stalk celery, chopped into coarse pieces

1 unpeeled apple, chopped into coarse pieces

1 to 2 tablespoons (15 mL/7 g to 30 mL/ 14 g) curry powder

1 cup (240 mL) orange juice

Peel of 1 orange, cut into thin strips

⅓ cup (80 mL/100 g) chopped chutney

1 tablespoon (15 mL/8 g) cornstarch (optional)

In a large skillet, heat the butter or margarine. Brown the chicken. Remove the chicken from the pan. Add the chopped vegetables and apple to the skillet, and sauté for 5 minutes. Add the curry to taste. Stir in the orange juice, orange peel, and chutney. For a thicker sauce, mix the cornstarch and ¼ cup (60 mL) of the orange juice; stir into the sauce.

Return the chicken to the sauce. Simmer, covered, for 30 minutes.

Serves 4 to 6.

Mrs. George R. McCullough

Chicken Danica

1 broiler chicken, cut into 6 pieces **or** 3 chicken breasts, halved, with or without skin

½ cup (120 mL/66 g) all-purpose flour

¼ cup (60 mL) vegetable oil

½ pint (240 mL/255 g) sour cream

¼ pound (115 g) bleu cheese, crumbled

1 teaspoon (5 mL/4.4 g) garlic salt

Preheat oven to 350° F (175° C). Grease a 2-quart (1.92 l) casserole.

Coat the chicken with the flour. In a skillet, heat the oil, and brown the chicken on all sides over high heat. Transfer to the casserole. Combine the sour cream, bleu cheese, and garlic salt. Pour over the chicken. Cover, and bake for about 1 hour, or until tender. The sauce will separate slightly.

Note:
Serve over rice.

Serves 6.

Eva Lu Damianos

Ginger Chicken with Broccoli

⅓ cup (80 mL/34 g) pecan halves

2 tablespoons (30 mL/29 g) unsalted butter

2 tablespoons (30 mL) olive oil

4 large cloves garlic, minced

5 whole chicken breasts, split

1 to 1½ pounds (455 to 680 g) broccoli, pared, and stems and florets cut into 1½-inch (3.8 cm) pieces

1 medium onion, minced

1 tablespoon (15 mL/8 g) pared and minced ginger root **or** 1½ teaspoons (8 mL/3.6 g) powdered ginger

1 cup (240 mL) chicken stock

Salt and pepper to taste

In a small, ungreased skillet, toast the pecans over medium heat for about 5 minutes, or until they are golden brown. Shake the pan frequently.

In a large heavy skillet, heat the butter and oil over medium-low heat. Add the garlic, and cook until it begins to color. Remove the garlic with a slotted spoon; and set aside. Turn the heat to medium-high. Add the chicken pieces, and brown. Remove to a warm platter. Leave 3 tablespoons (45 mL) drippings in the skillet; pour out and reserve the remainder.

Return the skillet to the heat. Add the broccoli. Stir-fry for about 4 minutes, or until the florets brighten. Remove with a slotted spoon. Add 2 tablespoons (30 mL) of the reserved drippings to the skillet. Add the onion, and sauté for about 5 minutes, or until golden. Add the ginger and sauté for about 1 minute. Add the stock, garlic, and chicken. Cover, and simmer for about 10 minutes, or until the meat is firm, not springy. Add the broccoli, and cook for 5 to 10 minutes, or until the broccoli is crisp-tender.

Arrange the chicken and vegetables on a warm platter. Sprinkle the pecans over the top. Keep warm.

Skim and discard the fat from the pan juices. Add salt and pepper. Boil until juices are reduced by half. Pour over the chicken.

Serves 5 or 6.

Mrs. O. Harry Gruner III

Minted Chicken

Coarse salt

1 3-pound (1.36 kg) chicken

½ cup (120 mL/27 g) fresh mint, including stems

1 tablespoon (15 mL/14 g) unsalted butter, cut into small pieces

Preheat oven to 400° F (205° C).

Salt the chicken generously inside and out. Place the mint and butter in the cavity. Place the chicken in a casserole. Cover, and bake for 1 hour.

Serves 4.

Gay Arensberg

Rollatini of Chicken Breast

3 whole chicken breasts, skinned, boned, and split

¾ cup (180 mL/99 g) all-purpose flour

10 tablespoons (150 mL/145 g) unsalted butter

1 tablespoon (15 mL) vegetable oil

Freshly ground pepper

1 teaspoon (5 mL) lemon juice

½ pound (225 g) mushrooms, cut into thin slices

⅓ cup (80 mL) dry Marsala **or** dry white wine

3 slices ham, each slice cut into 6 strips

7 ounces (200 g) fontina **or** Parmesan cheese: 6 ounces (170 g) slivered with a vegetable peeler, 1 ounce (28 g) grated

4 to 6 scallions, minced

¼ cup (60 mL/12 g) minced chives

¼ cup (60 mL/13 g) chopped parsley

½ teaspoon (2.5 mL/0.5 g) basil (optional)

Preheat oven to 400° F (205° C).

Slice each half chicken breast into thirds, about ¼ inch (0.6 cm) thick. Coat with the flour.

In a skillet, heat 4 tablespoons (60 mL/57 g) of the butter and the oil over high heat. As the foam subsides, add the chicken slices in batches, and sauté quickly on both sides. Transfer to a warm platter. Sprinkle with freshly ground pepper.

In the same skillet, add the lemon juice and 2 tablespoons (30 mL/29 g) of the butter. Sauté the mushrooms. Add the wine, and deglaze the pan, stirring quickly. Set aside.

Cover each chicken slice with a strip of ham and some slivered cheese. Top with scallions, chives, parsley, and basil, if desired. Roll, and fasten with skewers.

Place the rolled chicken in a shallow baking dish. Brush each roll lightly with the mushroom-wine sauce. Sprinkle the tops with the grated cheese, and dot with the remaining butter. Pour the remaining wine sauce around the rolls. Bake for 6 to 8 minutes. Serve immediately.

Makes 18 rolls.

Mrs. Robert O. Read

Stuffed Chicken Suprêmes

3 carrots, cut into julienne strips

3 stalks celery, cut into julienne strips

3 chicken breasts, boned, skinned, and split

Salt and pepper to taste

6 tablespoons (90 mL/86 g) unsalted butter

½ pound (225 g) fresh snow peas, trimmed on the diagonal

Vegetable oil

2 cups (480 mL) chicken stock

2 cups (480 mL) Crème Fraîche (see page 119)

Bring a small amount of water to a boil. Add the carrots and celery, and blanch for 1 minute. Drain, and set aside.

Pull the fillet partially away from each chicken suprême, making a pocket. Sprinkle all over with salt and pepper. Fill the pockets with 1 tablespoon (15 mL) of the carrot and celery mixture. Close and press the edges together.

Place 1 tablespoon (15 mL/14 g) of the butter on each suprême. Wrap each tightly in a 10-inch (25 cm) sheet of durable plastic wrap. Twist and tie each end.

In a heavy saucepan, bring to a boil just enough water to cover the suprêmes. Add the wrapped suprêmes, reduce the heat to simmer, and poach for 8 to 10 minutes, turning once. Remove from the wrappers, and slice each suprême on the diagonal into quarters.

Lightly sauté the snow peas in a small amount of oil. Set aside.

Simmer the stock until reduced to 1½ cups (360 mL). Add the crème fraîche, and cook the sauce for a few minutes longer, stirring.

Pour the sauce onto a large platter. Arrange the sliced suprêmes on top of the sauce. Surround with the snow peas.

Note:
Serve with wild rice.

Serves 6.

Dana Kline

Suprêmes of Chicken with Fresh Figs in Gin

18 fresh figs

1 cup (240 mL) gin

6 chicken breasts, boned, skinned, and split

1 teaspoon (5 mL) lemon juice

6 tablespoons (90 mL/ 86 g) unsalted butter

½ cup (120 mL) chicken stock

½ cup (120 mL) dry vermouth

1½ cups (360 mL) heavy cream

Salt and pepper to taste

Wash the figs. Pierce several times, and soak in the gin for 2 to 3 hours.

Preheat oven to 400° F (205° C).

Rub the chicken suprêmes with the lemon juice. In an ovenproof dish with a lid, heat the butter. Add the suprêmes, and cook for 2 minutes, turning often. Cover, and bake for 8 minutes. Remove the suprêmes from the baking dish, and keep them warm.

Add the stock and vermouth to the baking dish. Boil rapidly, stirring, and reduce to ½ cup (120 mL). Add the cream, salt, and pepper. Pour the sauce over the suprêmes. Surround with drained figs. Serve hot.

Note:
Serve with wild rice and almonds.

Fresh peaches, fresh apricots, or canned plums may be substituted for the figs.

Serves 6.

Edith H. Fisher

Chicken Tortilla Casserole

5 whole chicken breasts, skinned

Chicken stock to cover

1 10¾-ounce (305 g) can of cream of chicken soup

1 10¾ ounce (305 g) can of cream of mushroom soup

1 cup (240 mL/255 g) sour cream

1 15-ounce (425 g) can pitted ripe olives

1 4-ounce (115 g) can whole or chopped green chilies

1 onion, chopped

6 corn tortillas, cut into ½-inch (1.3 cm) strips

10 ounces (285 g) sharp Cheddar cheese, grated

Poach the chicken in the stock for about 20 minutes, or until tender. When it is cool enough to handle, cut into bite-size pieces. Reserve the stock for another use.

Preheat oven to 350° F (175° C).

Combine the cream soups and sour cream. Mix in the olives, chilies, and onion. Spread a small amount of sauce on the bottom of an ungreased casserole. Top with layers of tortillas, chicken, sauce, and cheese. Repeat the layers. Top with the grated cheese. Cover the casserole, and bake for 45 minutes.

Note:
May be prepared up to 2 days in advance and refrigerated.

Serve with grapefruit and avocado salad.

Serves 8.

Mrs. Aiken W. Fisher

Chicken Livers on Sautéed Toast

4 slices bread, cut into triangles

Unsalted butter, for sautéing bread

4 tablespoons (60 mL/ 57 g) unsalted butter

1 pound (455 g) chicken livers, cut into bite-size pieces

2 thin slices ham, slivered

1 teaspoon (5 mL/1.1 g) chopped fresh sage **or** ½ teaspoon (2.5 mL/0.8 g) dried sage

Salt and pepper to taste

1 tablespoon (15 mL) sweet sherry

Heat butter (amount will depend on the dryness and texture of the bread), and sauté the bread on both sides until browned. Set aside.

In a skillet, heat the 4 tablespoons (60 mL/ 57 g) of butter. Cook the chicken livers, ham, and sage over medium heat for approximately 5 minutes. Season with salt and pepper.

Arrange the bread on a warm platter. Top with the chicken livers. Add the sherry to the pan juices. Heat, stirring. Pour over the livers. Serve immediately.

Serves 4.

Mrs. Robert O. Read

Duck à l'Orange

2 5-pound (2.27 kg) ducklings

1 teaspoon (5 mL/6 g) salt

1 tablespoon (15 mL) lemon juice

1 teaspoon (5 mL) soy sauce

1½ cups (360 mL) water

Juice and grated rind of 1 orange

¼ cup (60 mL) orange juice

2 tablespoons (30 mL/ 29 g) unsalted butter

2 tablespoons (30 mL/ 17 g) all-purpose flour

1 cup (240 mL) dry white wine

Orange slices for garnish

The day before, preheat oven to 350° F (175° C).

Remove the giblets and neck of the ducklings. With a sharp knife, score the duckling skin lengthwise. Rub with ½ teaspoon (2.5 mL/3 g) of the salt, the lemon juice, and soy sauce. Place on a wire rack in a shallow pan, breast side up. Add 1 cup (240 mL) of the water to the pan. Roast for about 2½ hours, or until tender (allow 25 to 30 minutes per pound).

While the duck is roasting, combine the orange juice, rind, and additional orange juice. Set aside. In a saucepan, melt the butter, add the flour, and stir until smooth. Remove from the heat. Add the juices, the remaining salt, and the wine. Stir until smooth. Set aside.

When the duck is tender, remove it from the oven. Pour off all the fat and liquid into a container, and refrigerate until the fat rises to the top. Add the remaining water to the roasting pan, and deglaze. Add to the wine sauce.

Carve the duck, and arrange in a casserole. Remove the congealed fat from the refrigerated pan drippings; discard the fat and add the remaining liquid to the wine sauce.

Heat to boiling. Simmer for 5 minutes. Pour over the duck. Cover and refrigerate overnight. Reheat the duck for 20 to 30 minutes before serving. Garnish with orange slices.

Serves 4 to 6.

Mrs. Rolf K. Bungeroth

Larry Jordan
(American, b. 1934)
Duo Concertantes, 1962-64
16 millimeters, 10 minutes, black & white, sound
Director's Discretionary Fund and National Endowment for the Arts, 1977

Roast Duckling with Raspberry or Maple Bourbon Sauce

Stock:
Duck necks and giblets

4 quarts (3.84 L) water

1 onion

2 carrots

3 stalks celery, including leaves

2 or 3 4-pound (1.81 kg) ducklings, excess fat removed

Salt and pepper to taste

2 cups (480 mL) water

6 tablespoons (90 mL) soy sauce

Raspberry Sauce:
1 quart (960 mL/460 g) fresh **or** frozen raspberries with juice

2 cups (480 mL) duck stock

1 cup (240 mL) port, Burgundy, **or** Madeira

or

Maple Bourbon Sauce:
2 cups (480 mL) duck stock

1 cup (240 mL) pure maple syrup

1 cup (240 mL) bourbon

2 to 3 cups (480 mL/295 g to 720 mL/445 g) cooked rice

Stock:
Combine all the ingredients. Simmer for 2 hours. Strain.

Preheat oven to 400° F (205° C).

Season the ducklings with salt and pepper. Place them, breast side down, on a rack in a roasting pan. Add the water. Roast, uncovered, for 40 minutes. Remove the ducks from the oven. Pour off the fat. Turn the ducks, breast side up, on the rack. Prick them with a fork, and brush with the soy sauce. Return them to the oven, and roast for 2 hours longer. Pour off fat after 1 hour. Remove from the oven, and cool.

While the ducks are roasting, prepare one of the following sauces:

Raspberry Sauce:
Combine all the ingredients. Simmer for 30 to 40 minutes, or until reduced by one-third.

Maple Bourbon Sauce:
Combine all the ingredients. Simmer for 30 minutes.

When the ducks are cool, cut them in half, and remove the spine and rib bones (they will pull out easily).

To serve:
Reheat the ducks for 30 minutes at 350° F (175° C). Arrange them on a platter over rice. Spoon some of the sauce on top. Pass the remaining sauce.

Serves 4 to 6.

Linda Youtzy

Moravian Rabbit Stew

½ cup (120 mL/58 g) coarse-chopped onion

½ cup (120 mL) brandy

2 tablespoons (30 mL) vegetable oil

½ teaspoon (2.5 mL/3 g) salt

¼ teaspoon (1.3 mL/0.7 g) pepper

1 or 2 2-pound (905 g) rabbits, cut into serving pieces

1 cup (240 mL/170 g) diced uncooked bacon

Flour, for dredging

4 tablespoons (60 mL/ 57 g) unsalted butter

1 clove garlic, minced

2 tablespoons (30 mL/ 12 g) slivered celery

2 tablespoons (30 mL/ 18 g) slivered carrot

2 tablespoons (30 mL/ 11 g) slivered parsnip

3 tablespoons (45 mL/ 17 g) slivered leek

⅔ cup (160 mL/72 g) coarse-diced tart apple

24 whole fresh mushrooms

1½ cups (360 mL) cider

½ tablespoon (8 mL/2 g) minced parsley

1 teaspoon (5 mL/1 g) thyme

2 bay leaves

The day before, in a large bowl, combine the onion, brandy, oil, salt, and pepper. Add the rabbit, and marinate for 24 hours in the refrigerator, stirring occasionally.

Remove the rabbit from the marinade, and pat dry. Strain the marinade, reserving both the marinade and the onion.

In a Dutch oven, fry the bacon until crisp. Remove the bacon, drain, and reserve. Dredge the rabbit in flour, and brown it evenly in the bacon drippings until crisp. Remove, and set aside. Add the butter, reserved onion, and the garlic to the Dutch oven, and sauté until transparent. Add the celery, carrot, parsnip, and leek; sauté until limp. Add the apple and mushrooms,

and cook until hot. Add the cider, parsley, thyme, bay leaves, marinade, bacon, and rabbit.

Bring the mixture to a boil, reduce to a simmer, and cook over low heat for 1 to 2 hours, or until the meat is tender.

Serves 4 to 6.

John Cheek

Rock Cornish Game Hen with Apricot Sauce

---

4 Rock Cornish game hens

1 package white and wild rice mix

¼ pound (115 g) unsalted butter

1 cup (240 mL) white wine

2 cups (480 mL) apricot nectar

3 drops Angostura bitters

Preheat oven to 375° F (190° C).

Prepare the rice mix according to package directions, and stuff the hens. Melt the butter with the white wine, apricot nectar, and bitters. Baste the hens four times during cooking. Bake for 1 hour.

Serves 4.

Robin Gemmett

Turkey and Vegetables Poached in Wine

Turkey:
1 6- to 8-pound (2.72 to 3.63 kg) turkey breast **or** 1 4-pound (1.81 kg) whole boned turkey

3 cups (720 mL) chicken stock

2 cups (480 mL) dry white wine

3 stalks celery

3 carrots

1 onion

2 cloves garlic, minced

4 sprigs parsley

1 bay leaf

10 black peppercorns

1 tablespoon (15 mL/ 18 g) salt

Vegetables:
1 medium cauliflower, broken into florets

6 slender carrots, cut into 1-inch (2.5 cm) sections

½ pound (225 g) green beans, ends trimmed

2 small zucchini, sliced

2 stalks celery, cut into ½-inch (1.3 cm) sections

1 red or green pepper, seeded and sliced

Tarragon Mayonnaise:
2 cups (480 mL/465 g) mayonnaise

1 tablespoon (15 mL/ 17 g) Dijon mustard

3 tablespoons (45 mL/ 10 g) fresh tarragon **or** 1½ teaspoons (8 mL/ 0.6 g) dried tarragon, softened in 1 teaspoon (5 mL) lemon juice

Turkey:
The day before, in a stockpot, place the turkey and all remaining ingredients. Bring to a boil. Lower the heat, and simmer for 1 hour, or until the turkey is completely done, or when thermometer reads 165° F (74° C). Remove from the heat. Cool slightly in the liquid, and marinate for at least 24 hours in the refrigerator.

Remove the turkey from the liquid. Remove the bones. Wrap the turkey tightly in foil. Place in the refrigerator until ready to serve.

Strain the liquid, pressing down on the solids to extract all the juices, and reserve the liquid. Discard the solids.

Vegetables:
Bring the poaching liquid to a boil. Poach each vegetable, except the pepper, separately until just tender. Remove the vegetables from the liquid, and place them in a large bowl. Add the pepper to the vegetables. Cool the poaching liquid slightly, and pour over the vegetables. Cover, and refrigerate.

Tarragon Mayonnaise:
Combine all ingredients, and chill.

To serve:
Cut the turkey into ½-inch (1.3 cm) slices. Drain the vegetables. Arrange the turkey on a platter, and surround it with vegetables. Serve with the tarragon mayonnaise.

Serves 8.

Woodene Merriman

Fish and Shellfish

Baked Fish Fillets

Bread crumbs

1½ pounds (680 g) fillets of sole **or** flounder

1 tablespoon (15 mL) white wine vinegar

1 tablespoon (15 mL) Worcestershire sauce

1 tablespoon (15 mL) lemon juice

1 teaspoon (5 mL/6 g) salt

½ cup (120 mL/115 g) melted unsalted butter

1 teaspoon (5 mL/6 g) prepared mustard

A dash of pepper

Paprika

Preheat oven to 450° F (230° C).

Cover the bottom of a shallow baking dish with bread crumbs. Place the fish fillets on top, and sprinkle with more crumbs.

Combine the remaining ingredients, except for the paprika. Mix until smooth. Pour over the fish. Sprinkle with paprika. Bake for 20 minutes, basting several times.

Serves 4.

Virginia H. Grosscup

Franz Kline
(American, 1910-1962)
Siegfried, 1958
Oil on canvas
102⅞ × 81¼ in.
(261.3 × 206.4 cm.)
Gift of Friends, 1959

209

Grilled Bluefish

1½ to 2 pounds (680 g to 905 g) (2 fillets) bluefish

Salt and pepper to taste

Garlic powder to taste

1 cup (240 mL/230 g) mayonnaise

¼ cup (60 mL/68 g) Dijon mustard

Juice of 1 lemon

1 tablespoon (15 mL/3 g) fresh dill

½ cup (120 mL/115 g) melted unsalted butter

Lemon wedges

Parsley

Preheat a charcoal grill.

Season the bluefish with salt, pepper, and garlic powder.

Combine the mayonnaise, mustard, lemon juice, and dill. Generously brush both sides of the fillets with the mixture. Place the fillets, flesh side down, directly on the grill, Cook for approximately 5 minutes, depending on the thickness. Turn, and cook the other side.

Remove to a serving platter, and drizzle with the melted butter. Garnish with lemon wedges and parsley, and serve at once.

Serves 4.

Judith M. Davenport

Broiled Fish with Dill Sauce

2 tablespoons (30 mL/7 g) chopped fresh dill

1 teaspoon (5 mL/1.9 g) dillseed

2 tablespoons (30 mL/7 g) chopped parsley

2 tablespoons (30 mL) lemon juice

1 teaspoon (5 mL/2.5 g) paprika

Salt and freshly ground pepper to taste

¼ pound (115 g) unsalted butter **or** margarine, melted

1 3-pound (1.36 kg) halibut, mackerel, **or** salmon

Preheat broiler to 400° F (205° C). Cover broiler pan with foil.

Combine the herbs, lemon juice, seasonings, and butter.

Place the fish on the broiler pan. Spread half the sauce on one side of the fish. Broil for 15 minutes. Turn, and spread with the remaining sauce. Broil for about 15 minutes, or until the fish flakes easily.

Serves 6.

Mrs. John T. Galey

Peixe "Avo Maria" (Grilled Stuffed Fish)

2¼ cups (540 mL) olive oil

1 cup (240 mL/110 g) chopped green olives

¾ cup (180 mL) lemon juice

7 cloves garlic, chopped

½ cup (120 mL/27 g) chopped parsley

2 loaves Italian bread, torn into small pieces

1 5-pound (2.27 kg) whole red snapper, grouper, striped bass, **or** rockfish

Salt and freshly ground pepper to taste

Preheat a charcoal grill.

Combine 2 cups (480 mL) of the oil, the olives, ½ cup (120 mL) of the lemon juice, the garlic, parsley, and bread. Spoon into the fish cavity.

Combine the remaining oil, remaining lemon juice, salt, and pepper. Grill the fish for about 10 minutes on each side, or until fish flakes easily, basting frequently.

Serves 6 to 8.

Teresa Heinz

Steamed Monkfish with Ginger Sauce

¼ pound (115 g) unsalted butter

3 to 4 tablespoons (45 mL/21 g to 60 mL/28 g) fresh ginger root, peeled and grated

4 cloves garlic, crushed

½ teaspoon (2.5 mL/0.8 g) dried chili flakes **or** ½ teaspoon (2.5 mL/1.4 g) jalapeño peppers, minced

½ cup (120 mL) soy sauce

½ cup (120 mL) white wine (optional)

⅓ cup (80 mL/45 g) diced sweet red **or** green peppers

2 tablespoons (30 mL/15 g) diced scallions

1 to 1½ pounds (455 to 680 g) monkfish tails **or** other firm-fleshed whitefish fillets, cut into 8 pieces

In a saucepan, melt the butter, and add the ginger, garlic, and chili flakes or jalapeño peppers.

Simmer for about 10 minutes. Do not allow the butter to brown. Add the soy sauce and wine. Do not boil. Just before serving, add the sweet peppers and scallions.

Steam the fish over boiling water for 2 to 3 minutes. Place the fish fillets on individual plates. Spoon the sauce over the fillets, and serve as a first course.

Serves 8.

Ardsheal House
Kentallen of Appin, Scotland

Scalloped Oysters

2 pints (960 mL/1.01 kg) oysters with liquor

1 cup (240 mL) half-and-half

4 tablespoons (60 mL/57 g) unsalted butter

5 ounces (140 g) crushed oyster crackers

¼ cup (60 mL/13 g) chopped parsley

½ teaspoon (2.5 mL/3 g) salt

1 teaspoon (5 mL) Worcestershire sauce

A drop of Tabasco sauce

Paprika

Preheat oven to 350° F (175° C). Grease a 6-cup (1.44 L) shallow baking dish.

Drain the liquor from the oysters, and reserve ½ cup (120 mL). Combine the reserved oyster liquor with the half-and-half, and set aside. In a medium-size saucepan, melt the butter. Stir in the crackers, parsley, and salt. Mix well.

Spread half of the cracker mixture in the baking dish. Spoon the oysters on top. Cover with the remaining cracker mixture. Stir the Worcestershire and Tabasco into the cream mixture. Pour over the oysters. Sprinkle with paprika. Bake for about 30 minutes, or until the top is golden.

Serves 6 to 8.

Susan C. Johnson

Broiled Scallops

½ cup (120 mL) dry vermouth

½ cup (120 mL) olive oil

½ teaspoon (2.5 mL/1.4 g) minced garlic

½ teaspoon (2.5 mL/3 g) salt

2 tablespoons (30 mL/7 g) minced parsley

1½ pounds (680 g) sea scallops

Prepare a marinade of the vermouth, oil, garlic, salt, and parsley. Add the scallops, and refrigerate for several hours.

Preheat broiler.

Place the scallops and marinade in a shallow pan, and set under the broiler, 2 inches (5 cm) from the heat. Broil for 5 to 6 minutes, turning once.

Note:
Bay scallops may also be used.

Serves 4.

Mrs. Fred I. Sharp

Vineyard Scallops

1 scant tablespoon (15 mL/14 g) unsalted butter

¼ teaspoon (1.3 mL/0.7 g) all-purpose flour

⅓ cup (80 mL) fine white wine

½ pound (225 g) bay scallops

Parsley, for garnish

In a skillet, melt the butter over low heat. Stir in the flour to make a very thin roux. Add the wine, and simmer, stirring. Add the scallops, and warm through, stirring gently a couple of times. Garnish with parsley. Serve in individual ramekins, accompanied by the rest of the bottle of wine.

Serves 2.

Richard Dilworth Edwards

Party Seafood Gumbo

4 slices Country Smoked Virginia ham, ⅛ inch (0.3 cm) thick, about 1 pound (455 g)

Bacon fat (optional)

3 large onions, chopped

4 10-ounce (285 g) packages frozen whole okra **or** 50 to 60 fresh okra pods

3 28-ounce (795 g) cans Italian-style tomatoes

3 bay leaves

4 or 5 peppercorns

2 or 3 cloves

1 tablespoon (15 mL/14 g) sugar

1 tablespoon (15 mL) Worcestershire sauce

7 to 10 drops Tabasco sauce or to taste

1 teaspoon (5 mL/1.5 g) thyme

1 pound (455 g) claw crabmeat or other less expensive variety, picked over to remove shells

4 pounds (1.81 kg) medium raw shrimp, cleaned and deveined

1 quart (960 mL/1.01 kg) oysters with liquor

Salt to taste

About 8 cups (1.92 L/1.18 kg) cooked rice

Trim the fat from the ham. Cut the ham into 1-inch (2.5 cm) pieces. Place 4 tablespoons (60 mL/57 g) fat in a large kettle; add bacon fat, if necessary. Heat the fat. Add the onions, and cook until translucent.

Add the ham, okra, tomatoes, and enough water to make 4 quarts (3.84 L) of mixture. Add the bay leaves, peppercorns, cloves, sugar, Worcestershire, Tabasco, and thyme. Simmer for 1 hour, uncovered. Add the crabmeat and shrimp. Cook for 20 minutes. Add the oysters with liquor. Cook for 10 minutes. Correct the seasonings; add salt to taste.

Serve topped with rice, or pass the rice separately.

Note:
This is a North Carolina version of the traditional New Orleans gumbo. It may be made 3 to 4 days in advance and will keep frozen for 6 months with no change in flavor.

Serves 25.

Minnette D. Bickel

213

Shrimp and Asparagus

1½ pounds (680 g) asparagus

1 tablespoon (15 mL/9 g) sesame seeds

⅓ cup (80 mL) vegetable oil

2 small onions, sliced

1½ pounds (680 g) large raw shrimp, shelled and deveined

4 tablespoons (60 mL) soy sauce

1¼ teaspoons (6 mL/8 g) salt

Peel the asparagus, and discard the tough ends. Cut into 2-inch (5 cm) pieces.

In a 12-inch (30 cm) ungreased skillet, heat the sesame seeds, and toast until golden, shaking the skillet occasionally. Remove the seeds, and set aside.

In the same skillet, heat the oil over medium-high heat. Add the asparagus, onions, and shrimp. Stir for 5 to 10 minutes, or until the shrimp are pink and the vegetables crisp-tender. Stir in the sesame seeds, soy sauce, and salt until barely mixed. Serve immediately.

Note:
Serve with herb or garlic toast and a tossed green salad.

Serves 6.

Mrs. Paul B. Steele, Jr.

Shrimp in Garlic and Wine

1 pound (455 g) (10 to 15) raw shrimp

3 tablespoons (45 mL/ 43 g) unsalted butter

1 teaspoon (5 mL/2.8 g) minced garlic

¼ cup (60 mL) white wine

1 teaspoon (5 mL/1.1 g) chopped parsley

¼ cup (60 mL) water

2 tablespoons (30 mL/ 14 g) bread crumbs

Salt to taste

Shell and devein the shrimp.

Heat a skillet, and add the butter. When the butter is hot, sauté the shrimp for 3 to 4 minutes on each side. With a slotted spoon, remove the shrimp to a warm platter.

Add the garlic to the skillet. Cook for several minutes. Add the wine, and deglaze the pan. Add the parsley, water, bread crumbs, and salt. Simmer for 1 or 2 minutes, correct the seasonings, and pour over the shrimp.

Serves 2.

Mrs. Fred I. Sharp

Greek Shrimp

6 tablespoons (90 mL) olive oil

1 medium onion, chopped

1 clove garlic, minced

1 28-ounce (795 g) can tomatoes

¼ teaspoon (1.3 mL/1.2 g) sugar

1 teaspoon (5 mL/6 g) salt

½ teaspoon (2.5 mL/1.4 g) pepper

2 tablespoons (30 mL/29 g) unsalted butter

2 pounds (905 g) shrimp, shelled and deveined

3 tablespoons (45 mL) ouzo

1 tablespoon (15 mL) brandy

¼ to ⅜ pound (115 to 170 g) feta cheese

2 tablespoons (30 mL/7 g) chopped parsley, for garnish

Preheat oven to 425° F (220° C).

In a skillet, heat 4 tablespoons (60 mL) of the oil. Sauté the onion and garlic until transparent. Add the tomatoes, sugar, salt, and pepper. Simmer until thickened, stirring occasionally to prevent burning. Set aside.

In a large skillet, heat the butter and remaining oil. Sauté the shrimp until just pink. Add the ouzo and brandy. When the liquor is warm, flambé it.

Divide the shrimp among 12 shells to serve as an appetizer or among 6 to 8 ramekins for luncheon.

Spoon the sauce over the shrimp. Top with the feta cheese. Place the shells or ramekins on a foil-covered baking sheet. Bake for 10 minutes.

Garnish with parsley.

Note:
Serve with piping hot crusty bread.

May be prepared ahead and baked just before serving.

Serves 6 to 8 for luncheon; 12 as an appetizer.

R. Jackson Seay

Winslow Homer
(American, 1836-1910)
The Wreck, 1896
Oil on canvas
30 × 48 in. (76.2 × 121.9 cm.)
Museum Purchase, 1896

Sole Almondine

2¼ to 3 pounds (1.02 to 1.36 kg) lemon or Canadian sole, cut into 6 pieces

½ cup (120 mL/73 g) cornmeal

1 teaspoon (5 mL/6 g) salt

Freshly ground pepper to taste

2 cloves garlic, minced

4 cups (960 mL/650 g) tomatoes, cut into ½-inch (1.3 cm) cubes

2 tablespoons (30 mL/7 g) chopped fresh tarragon **or** 1 tablespoon (15 mL/1 g) dried tarragon

4 tablespoons (60 mL/ 57 g) unsalted butter

4 tablespoons (60 mL/ 57 g) unsalted margarine

¾ cup (180 mL/100 g) slivered almonds

3 tablespoons (45 mL) dry white wine

3 tablespoons (45 mL) lemon juice

¼ teaspoon (1.3 mL/0.6 g) white pepper

1 bunch watercress

Rinse the fish in salted water. Pat dry. Combine the cornmeal, ½ teaspoon (2.5 mL/3 g) of the salt, freshly ground pepper, and half the garlic. Coat the fish, and allow it to stand for at least ½ hour.

Sprinkle the tomatoes with the remaining garlic and the tarragon. Mix well, and place in a skillet. Set aside.

Just before serving, in a large skillet, melt 2 tablespoons (30 mL/ 29 g) of the butter and 2 tablespoons (30 mL/ 29 g) of the margarine. Sauté the fish fillets on both sides until they are lightly browned and flake easily with a fork. Remove from the pan, and keep warm.

Add the remaining butter and margarine to the skillet. Scrape to loosen the bits of fish. Add the almonds, and brown lightly. Stir in the wine, lemon juice, remaining salt, and white pepper. Keep the heat very low.

Heat the tomatoes quickly, and drain in a colander. Spoon onto a heated serving platter. Arrange the fish over the tomatoes. Bring the sauce to a quick boil, and pour over the fish. Garnish with the watercress. Serve immediately.

Serves 4 to 6.

R. Jackson Seay

Sole and Broccoli Beurre Blanc

4 medium broccoli florets

2 3-ounce (85 g) fillets of sole

Juice of ½ lemon

1 ounce (30 mL) white wine

1 tablespoon (15 mL/14 g) unsalted butter

Beurre Blanc:
2 ounces (57 g) minced shallots

½ ounce (14 g) black peppercorns, crushed

1 ounce (30 mL) white vinegar

3 ounces (90 mL) white wine

3 ounces (90 mL) heavy cream

1 tablespoon (15 mL/ 14 g) butter

Preheat oven to 300° F (150° C).

Place 2 broccoli florets in the center of each fish fillet. Roll the fillets, and place them in a shallow, ungreased baking dish. Top with the lemon juice, wine, and butter. Bake for 10 minutes.

Beurre Blanc:
Combine the shallots, peppercorns, vinegar, and wine. Cook until the liquid is almost evaporated. Add the cream, and bring to a boil. Remove from the heat, and add the butter in small pieces, shaking the pan until it melts. Strain the sauce.

To serve:
Spoon the sauce onto a plate. Top with the baked sole fillets.

Serves 1 or 2.

M's, Ligonier, Pennsylvania

Turbans of Sole with Shrimp Mousse

1 pound (455 g) raw shrimp, shelled and deveined

3 egg whites

1 cup (240 mL) heavy cream

Salt and pepper to taste

½ teaspoon (2.5 mL/1.2 g) freshly grated nutmeg

1 teaspoon (5 mL/0.3 g) dried dillweed

6 fillets of sole, cut in half

1 cup (240 mL/230 g) hollandaise sauce **or** mayonnaise

Sliced truffle and parsley, for garnish

Preheat oven to 425° F (220° C). Grease 6 ramekins or ovenproof custard cups.

In a processor with a metal blade, process the shrimp and egg whites to a smooth paste. With the processor running, add the cream slowly through the feed tube. Add the salt, pepper, nutmeg, and dill.

Line each ramekin or custard cup with 1 piece of sole. Divide the shrimp mixture among the ramekins. Cover with the remaining pieces of sole.

Place the cups in a baking pan. Add hot water to reach halfway up the sides of the cups. Bake for 15 to 20 minutes.

To serve hot:
Run a knife around the edges of the cups. Invert onto warm serving plates. Cover with hollandaise, and garnish with truffle and parsley.

To serve cold:
Cover with mayonnaise instead of hollandaise sauce.

Serves 6.

R. Jackson Seay

Swordfish Baked in Foil

1½ cups (360 mL/115 g) sliced mushrooms

2 medium onions, sliced

3 tablespoons (45 mL/ 26 g) chopped green pepper **or** parsley

3 tablespoons (45 mL) lemon juice

3 tablespoons (45 mL) olive **or** vegetable oil

1 teaspoon (5 mL/1.1 g) fresh dill **or** ½ teaspoon (2.5 mL/1 g) dillseed

Salt and freshly ground pepper to taste

2 pounds (905 g) swordfish, cut into individual servings

6 thick slices tomato

5 small pieces bay leaf

Preheat oven to 425° F (220° C). Line the bottom of a baking dish with foil, leaving enough foil along one side to fold over the fish.

Combine the mushrooms, onions, and green pepper or parsley with the lemon juice, oil, dill, salt, and pepper. Spread half the marinade in the bottom of the pan. Place the swordfish on top of the marinade. Cover with the tomato, bay leaf, and remaining marinade. Fold the foil over the fish. Bake for 45 minutes.

Serves 4 to 6.

Mrs. Robert O. Read

Barbecued Swordfish

½ cup (120 mL) Japanese soy sauce

¼ cup (60 mL/68 g) ketchup

¼ cup (60 mL/13 g) chopped parsley

½ cup (120 mL) orange juice

2 cloves garlic, crushed

2 tablespoons (30 mL) lemon juice

1 teaspoon (5 mL/2.7 g) pepper

1½ to 2 pounds (680 to 905 g) 1-inch (2.5 cm) -thick swordfish

---

Thoroughly combine the soy sauce, ketchup, parsley, orange juice, garlic, lemon juice, and pepper. Add the swordfish, and marinate for at least 1 hour.

Preheat charcoal grill.

Grill or broil the swordfish about 4 inches (10 cm) from hot coals for 8 minutes. Turn, and grill for 7 minutes on the other side. Brush frequently with the marinade.

Serves 4.

Mrs. Fred I. Sharp

Swordfish with Herbed Butter Sauce

2 pounds (905 g) 1½-inch (3.8 cm) -thick swordfish

1 cup (240 mL) French dressing

½ pound (225 g) unsalted butter

Juice of 1 or 2 limes to taste

1 tablespoon (15 mL/3 g) chopped parsley

1 tablespoon (15 mL/3 g) chopped chives

1 tablespoon (15 mL/3 g) chopped mint

Salt and pepper to taste

Marinate the swordfish in the French dressing in the refrigerator for about 2 hours, turning once. Remove ½ hour before cooking.

Preheat the broiler.

Broil the fish in the marinade about 4 inches (10 cm) from the heat. Turn when golden brown. The other side will broil in half the time.

Melt the butter, and combine with the remaining ingredients.

Serve the fish with the herbed butter sauce.

Note:
If grilling the fish over charcoal, baste frequently with French dressing.

Serves 4.

Mrs. T. D. Mullins

David Smith
(American, 1906-1965)
Cubi XXIV, 1964
Stainless steel

114¼ × 84¼ in.
(290.2 × 214 cm.)
Howard Heinz Endowment
Purchase Fund, 1967

Swordfish Steak with Dill

8 to 10 ounces (225 to 285 g) swordfish steak

¼ cup (60 mL) lime juice

1 cup (240 mL) Chablis

1 tablespoon (15 mL/3 g) chopped fresh dillweed

2 tablespoons Clarified Butter (see page 20)

Preheat oven to 400° F (205° C).

Marinate the swordfish in the lime juice, wine, and dill for 5 minutes. Place it in a shallow, ungreased baking pan. Spoon the butter and 2 ounces (60 mL) of the marinade on top. Bake for 8 to 10 minutes. Serve with the baking liquid.

Serves 2 or 3.

M's, Ligonier, Pennsylvania

Broiled Swordfish with Mustard

Butter, for broiler pan

1 swordfish steak*, cut 1 inch (2.5 cm) thick

Salt and freshly ground pepper to taste

2 teaspoons (10 mL/11 g) Dijon mustard

2 teaspoons (10 mL/8 g) mustard seeds

1 teaspoon (5 mL/4.8 g) unsalted butter, melted (optional)

Lemon wedges

Preheat broiler to high. Brush the broiler pan with butter.

Season the swordfish on both sides with salt and pepper. Brush both sides with the mustard, and sprinkle generously with the mustard seeds. Place the fish in the pan, and broil about 4 inches (10 cm) from the heat for 2 to 3 minutes on each side. Do not overcook.

*Allow ⅓ to ½ pound (150 to 225 grams) per person.

Pour the melted butter on top, if desired. Serve with lemon wedges.

Note:
May be assembled ahead and broiled at the last minute.

Serves 2 or 3.

Audrey and David Alpern

Meissen Factory
(German, 1710-)
Seated Monkey Eating a Pear,
c. 1730-35
Porcelain
H. 16 in. (40.6 cm)
Ailsa Mellon Bruce Collection, 1970

Vegetables

Beets in Caraway Cream

1½ pounds (680 g) baby beets

1 tablespoon (15 mL/8 g) crushed caraway seeds

⅛ teaspoon (0.6 mL/0.3 g) ground cardamom

½ cup (120 mL/125 g) sour cream **or** Crème Fraîche (see page 119)

½ cup (120 mL) heavy cream

Preheat oven to 400° F (205° C).

Cook the beets in boiling water for 10 minutes. Drain, cool, peel, and set aside. Combine the remaining ingredients, and mix well with the beets.

Spoon into a baking dish, and cover. Reduce the oven to 350° F (175° C), and bake for 20 to 25 minutes.

Serves 4.

The Cookbook Committee

Broccoli Purée

1½ pounds (680 g) broccoli, trimmed, peeled, and cut into 1-inch (2.5 cm) sections

1 medium onion, chopped **or** ½ cup (120 mL/58 g) chopped shallots

1 clove garlic, chopped (optional)

1 cup (240 mL/115 g) walnuts, toasted

2 teaspoons (10 mL/2.1 g) fresh basil (optional)

1 tablespoon (15 mL/3 g) chopped parsley

½ teaspoon (2.5 mL/3 g) salt

¼ teaspoon (1.3 mL/0.6 g) white pepper

¼ pound (115 g) unsalted butter

Juice of ½ lemon

Cook the broccoli in just enough water to cover until crisp-tender or softer, if desired. Drain, reserving liquid, and cool.

Cook the onion or shallots, and garlic, if desired, until tender in the reserved liquid. Drain, and cool.

Blend or process the vegetables until thoroughly puréed and creamy. Blend or process the walnuts, basil, if desired, and parsley. Combine all with the remaining ingredients, and heat in the top of a double boiler.

Serves 6.

The Cookbook Committee

Stuffed Cabbage

1 large head cabbage

2 pounds (905 g) ground beef

½ cup (120 mL/100 g) rice

2 large onions

2 tablespoons (30 mL/29 g) unsalted margarine **or** butter

Salt and pepper to taste

1 green pepper

1 28-ounce can (795 g) tomatoes **or** 6 fresh tomatoes

½ cup (120 mL) cold water

Juice of 3 lemons

½ cup (120 mL/115 g) sugar, or to taste

6 to 8 gingersnaps

½ cup (120 mL) boiling water

Boil the cabbage, whole, for about 10 minutes, or until the leaves are pliable. Separate the leaves. Set aside.

Combine the ground beef and rice. Mince 1 of the onions into fine pieces, heat the margarine or butter, and sauté the onions. Add the onion to the ground meat and rice. Season with salt and pepper. Place 1 large tablespoon (25 mL) of this mixture on the bottom third of a cabbage leaf. Roll, tucking in the sides. Fill and roll the leaves until all the ground meat mixture has been used.

Place the cabbage rolls in a very large pot. Chop the remaining onion, green pepper, and any remaining cabbage leaves into coarse pieces. Cover the cabbage rolls with the chopped vegetables. Add the tomatoes and the cold water. Add the lemon juice, sugar, salt, and pepper. Simmer over low heat for about 4 hours.

Preheat oven to 350° F (175° C).

Transfer the cabbage with all vegetables and juices to an ungreased roasting pan. Add the gingersnaps, dissolved in the boiling water. Bake for about 1 hour, or until the cabbage rolls are browned. Do not overcook because the sauce will become too thick.

Serves 6 to 8.

Joan M. Kaplan

Carrots with Port

¼ cup (60 mL) olive oil

2 cloves garlic, mashed

1 yellow onion, cut into ¼-inch (0.6 cm) -thick slices

1½ pounds (680 g) carrots, cut into strips 2 inches (5 cm) long and ¼ inch (0.6 cm) thick

Salt and freshly ground pepper to taste

¼ cup (60 mL) strong beef stock

¾ cup (180 mL) port

Chopped parsley

In a skillet, heat the oil. Add the garlic and onion. Cook over low heat for 5 minutes. Add the carrots, salt, and pepper. Mix well.

In a small saucepan, combine the stock and port. Bring to a boil, and pour over the carrots. Cook, covered, over moderate heat for about 5 minutes, or until the carrots are almost tender.

Remove the cover, and cook over high heat, stirring, until the liquid has evaporated. Sprinkle with the parsley before serving.

Serves 5 or 6.

Moore-Betty
School of Fine Cooking

Savory Carrots

6 to 8 cooked julienne carrots

¼ cup (60 mL) liquid from the carrots

2 tablespoons (30 mL/ 30 g) grated onion

2 tablespoons (30 mL/ 36 g) horseradish

½ cup (120 mL/115 g) mayonnaise

½ teaspoon (2.5 mL/3 g) salt

¼ teaspoon (1.3 mL/0.7 g) pepper

¼ cup (60 mL/19 g) cracker crumbs

1 tablespoon (15 mL/14 g) unsalted butter

Paprika

Parsley, for garnish

Preheat oven to 375° F (190° C).

In a shallow, greased baking dish, arrange the carrots. Combine the carrot liquid, onion, horseradish, mayonnaise, salt, and pepper. Pour over the carrots. Top with the crumbs, butter, and paprika. Bake for 20 minutes. Garnish with parsley.

Serves 4 to 6.

Mary Jane Seamans

Celeriac with Parmesan

2 pounds (905 g) celeriac

Boiling water

2 tablespoons (30 mL) lemon juice

2 cups (480 mL) vegetable oil

4 tablespoons (60 mL/ 31 g) grated Parmesan cheese

3 tablespoons (45 mL/ 10 g) chopped parsley **or** chervil

Peel and trim the celeriac. Cover with boiling water, and cook for 20 to 25 minutes, or until tender. Cool.

Cut the celeriac into ¼-inch (0.6 cm) rounds or slices, and sprinkle lightly with the lemon juice to prevent discoloring.

In a deep fryer, heat the oil to 375° F (190° C). Pat the celeriac dry, and fry until browned and crisp.

Sprinkle with the Parmesan and parsley or chervil. Serve hot.

Serves 4.

The Cookbook Committee

Eggplant Monte Cristo

1¼ pounds (565 g) eggplant, peeled and cut into 12 ¼-inch (0.6 cm) -thick slices

Salt

2 eggs

1 cup (240 mL/120 g) grated sharp Cheddar cheese

1 tablespoon (15 mL) water

1 cup (240 mL/74 g) cracker crumbs

¼ to ½ cup (60 to 120 mL) vegetable oil

Place the eggplant slices on a large platter. Sprinkle them with salt. Let stand for 20 minutes. Pat dry on both sides with paper towels.

Beat 1 of the eggs, and combine it with the cheese. Spoon it onto 6 eggplant slices, and top with the remaining 6 slices.

Combine the remaining egg with the water. Dip each eggplant sandwich into the egg mixture, then into the cracker crumbs.

In a skillet, heat the oil. Fry the eggplant until browned and crisp on both sides. Serve immediately.

Serves 6.

Bede Purner

Hush Puppies

1⅓ cups (320 mL/195 g) white cornmeal

4 tablespoons (60 mL/ 33 g) all-purpose flour

1 teaspoon (5 mL/3.4 g) baking powder

1 teaspoon (5 mL/6 g) salt

6 tablespoons (90 mL/ 43 g) chopped onion

1 egg

2 cups (480 mL) boiling water

Vegetable oil

Combine the dry ingredients, onion, and egg. Add the boiling water, stirring constantly, until the mixture is smooth. Add water if necessary. Drop by the teaspoonful into deep hot (375° F [190° C]) oil. Cook for about 5 to 6 minutes, or until golden brown.

Note:
A perfect accompaniment to any fish chowder or gumbo.

Serves 8 to 10.

Scona Lodge

225

Kohlrabi with Chinese Black Mushrooms

Tiffany and Company
(American, 1853-   )
Demi-Tasse Pot, 1893
Silver, enamel and agate
H. 10 in. (25.4 cm.), wt. 19 oz.
16 dwt.
AODA Purchase Fund, 1983

10 large Chinese black
mushrooms*

1 cup (240 mL) boiling
water

1½ pounds (680 g)
kohlrabi

2 scallions

1 teaspoon (5 mL/2.7 g)
cornstarch

1 tablespoon (15 mL) dry
sherry

¼ teaspoon (1.3 mL/1.5 g)
salt

⅛ teaspoon (0.6 mL/0.3 g)
pepper

¼ teaspoon (1.3 mL/
1.2 g) sugar

1 teaspoon (5 mL)
sesame oil

3 tablespoons (45 mL)
peanut oil

3 1- by 1-inch (2.5 cm by
2.5 cm) slices ginger root,
crushed

*Available in Asian food
stores.

Soak the mushrooms in
the boiling water for 30
minutes. Drain, reserving
the liquid. Discard the
stems, and slice the caps
into ⅛-inch (3 mm) strips.

Trim and peel the
kohlrabi. Cut them into
thin slices and then into
⅛-inch (3 mm) strips.

Trim and cut the scallions
into 2-inch (5 cm)
sections, then lengthwise
into thin strips.

Mix together the
cornstarch, sherry, salt,
pepper, sugar, and sesame
oil with 3 tablespoons
(45 mL) of the reserved
mushroom liquid.
Set aside.

In a wok or heavy skillet,
heat the peanut oil over
medium heat. Add the
ginger and stir for 10
seconds. Add the
vegetables, and stir for
1 minute. Add the
remaining mushroom
liquid, cover and cook
1 minute.

Uncover, and reduce heat.
Add the cornstarch-sherry
mixture. Stir and cover
for 1 minute. Lift cover,
stir, and serve
immediately.

Serves 4 to 6.

The Cookbook Committee

226

Leeks au Gratin

3 leeks, including white part and ¼ inch (0.6 cm) green part

3 tablespoons (45 mL/ 43 g) unsalted butter

⅔ cup (160 mL/43 g) cubed Jarlsberg cheese

¾ cup (180 mL/190 g) sour cream

2 teaspoons (10 mL/11 g) Dijon mustard

¼ cup (60 mL/30 g) crumbled Boucheron **or** other chèvre (goat cheese)

Salt to taste

Preheat oven to 350° F (175° C).

Cut the leeks into julienne strips, 3 inches (8 cm) long. Heat the butter, and sauté the leeks for 5 minutes. Cover the pan, and cook for 15 minutes. Cool. Combine with the remaining ingredients. Spoon the mixture into 4 greased scallop shells. Bake for 15 to 20 minutes, or until heated through.

Serves 4.

The Cookbook Committee

Onion Cups with Artichoke Purée

12 medium onions

1 10-ounce (285 g) package frozen artichoke hearts

1 cup (240 mL) chicken stock

1 tablespoon (15 mL/14 g) unsalted butter

Parsley sprigs, for garnish

Preheat oven to 350° F (175° C).

Peel the onions carefully. Cut off the top quarter of each onion. Cut a thin slice from the bottom so the onion will stand upright. With a melon ball cutter, scoop out enough onion so that the cavity will hold about 2 tablespoons (30 mL) purée. Reserve the scooped-out onion. Place the onion cups on a rack in a steamer, and steam for about 20 minutes, or until tender.

Combine the artichoke hearts, 4 ounces (115 g) of the reserved scooped-out onion, and the stock. Cook for 20 minutes. In a food processor, purée with the butter until very smooth.

Grease a baking dish with nonstick spray. Fill the onion cups with the purée, place them in the baking dish, and bake for 20 minutes. Garnish each cup with a sprig of parsley, and serve immediately.

Serves 12.

Margaret T. Donnelly

Golden Potato Casserole

6 medium potatoes

¼ cup (60 mL/57 g) unsalted butter

2 cups (480 mL/240 g) grated sharp Cheddar cheese

1 pint (480 mL/505 g) sour cream

⅓ cup (80 mL/39 g) chopped scallions

Salt and pepper to taste

Preheat oven to 350° F (175° C). Grease a 10-inch (25 cm) round baking dish.

Boil the potatoes until they are fork-tender. Chill, peel, and grate. Place in a large mixing bowl.

In a saucepan, melt the butter and cheese together over low heat. Remove from the heat. Stir in the sour cream and the scallions, and pour over the potatoes. Mix gently.

Add seasoning. Turn into the baking dish. Bake for 45 to 55 minutes, or until golden brown.

Serves 8.

Reanette Frobouck

Rosti (Swiss Potato Cake)

2 to 2½ pounds (905 g to 1.13 kg) potatoes

6 tablespoons (90 mL/ 86 g) unsalted butter

¾ teaspoon (3.8 mL/4.5 g) salt

2 to 3 tablespoons (30 to 45 mL) hot water

Boil the potatoes in their skins for about 20 minutes, or until fork-tender. Drain, and cool. Chill for several hours. Peel the potatoes. Cut into thin slices or julienne strips, or on a rosti or traditional grater, grate into long shreds.

In a large skillet, heat the butter. Gradually add the potatoes. Sprinkle with the salt. Cook over low heat, turning frequently with a spatula, until the potatoes are soft and yellow.

Press the potatoes into a flat cake. Sprinkle with the hot water. Cover, and cook over low heat for 15 to 20 minutes, or until the potatoes are golden and crusty on the bottom. Shake the skillet frequently to prevent sticking.

Turn onto a warm platter, crusty side up. Serve immediately.

Serves 6.

Mrs. Rolf K. Bungeroth

Snow Peas, Peas, and Cashews

1 pound (455 g) snow peas, ends trimmed

½ pound (225 g) green peas, shelled

4 tablespoons (60 mL/ 57 g) unsalted butter

½ teaspoon (2.5 mL/3 g) salt

¼ teaspoon (1.3 mL/0.7 g) pepper ·

¼ cup (60 mL/13 g) fine-chopped parsley

1 cup (240 mL/145 g) unsalted cashews **or** peanuts

Blanch the snow peas and green peas separately, in just enough water to cover, until tender. While the peas are cooking, melt the butter, and add the salt, pepper, and parsley. Drain the pea pods and peas, and combine in a bowl. Stir in the butter mixture and the cashews, and serve immediately.

Serves 4 to 6.

The Cookbook Committee

Whipped Squash

1 butternut squash

4 tablespoons (60 mL/ 57 g) unsalted margarine **or** butter

1 cup (240 mL) milk

¼ cup (60 mL/57 g) sugar

3 eggs, lightly beaten

½ teaspoon (2.5 mL/1.4 g) cinnamon

¼ teaspoon (1.3 mL/0.6 g) ginger

Salt to taste

Preheat oven to 350° F (175° C). Grease a baking sheet and an 8-inch (20 cm) baking dish.

Cut the squash in half, and place, cut sides down, on the baking sheet. Bake for about 1 hour, or until tender. Scrape out and discard the fiber and seeds. Spoon the pulp into a bowl; there should be about 2 cups (480 mL). Mash with the margarine or butter while still warm. Combine with the remaining ingredients, and turn into the baking dish. Bake for 35 to 40 minutes, or until set. Serve hot.

Note:
Recipe may be prepared to the point of baking and then refrigerated.

Serves 6.

Margot Sutton McConnel

Deep-Dish Sweet Potatoes

8 large sweet potatoes **or** yams

About ½ pound (225 g) unsalted butter

About ¼ cup (60 mL) dark rum

½ cup (120 mL/50 g) pecans

½ cup (120 mL/88 g) brown sugar

Preheat oven to 300° F (150° C). Grease a 2-quart (1.92 L) casserole.

Boil, peel, and mash the potatoes. Stir in the butter and rum to taste. Spoon into the casserole.

In a blender, pulverize the pecans. Combine with the sugar. Spread over the potato mixture at least ½ inch (1.3 cm) thick.

Bake for about 4 hours, or until the top becomes candied. To reheat, place in a 400° F (205° C) oven for approximately ½ hour.

Note:
May be made up to a week in advance. Good with turkey or ham.

Serves 8 to 10.

Lee Hall

Tomato Pie

1 baked pastry shell in a 10-inch (25 cm) quiche pan or piepan (see Pâte Brisée, page 98)

4 to 6 tomatoes, peeled and cut into thick slices

Salt and pepper to taste

1 tablespoon (15 mL/3 g) chopped fresh basil **or** ½ to 1 teaspoon (2.5 mL/ 0.4 g to 5 mL/0.8 g) dried basil

2 tablespoons (30 mL/6 g) chopped chives

½ cup (120 mL/115 g) mayonnaise

1 cup (240 mL/120 g) grated Cheddar cheese

Preheat oven to 400° F (205° C).

Fill the baked pastry with the tomato slices. Sprinkle with salt, pepper, basil, and chives. Combine the cheese and mayonnaise. Spread over the tomatoes. Bake for 30 to 35 minutes. Serve hot.

Serves 6.

Mrs. Robert S. Morton

Tomato Pudding

1 tablespoon (15 mL/8 g) cornstarch

¼ cup (60 mL) hot water

10 ounces (285 g) tomato purée

½ teaspoon (2.5 mL/3 g) salt

1 teaspoon (5 mL/4.7 g) sugar

½ pound (225 g) unsalted butter, melted

3 cups (720 mL/135 g) fresh bread crumbs

Preheat oven to 375° F (190° C).

Mix the cornstarch with the water. Combine with the tomato purée. Add the salt and sugar. Boil for 10 minutes.

Pour the butter over the bread crumbs, add to the tomato mixture, and pour into a 1½-quart (1.44 L) greased casserole. Bake for 30 to 50 minutes.

Note:
Serve with ham or pork or at brunch with scrambled eggs.

Serves 5 or 6.

Mrs. Jack M. Tillman

Glazed Turnips and Chestnuts

2 to 3 pounds (905 g to 1.36 kg) turnips

1½ pounds (680 g) small chestnuts in shell **or** ½ pound (225 g) vacuum-packed roasted whole chestnuts

Boiling water

2 tablespoons (30 mL/ 29 g) unsalted butter

2 tablespoons (30 mL/ 29 g) bacon fat **or** roast drippings

3 tablespoons (45 mL/ 10 g) fine-chopped parsley

1 tablespoon (15 mL/ 3 g) fine-chopped fresh thyme or sage **or** 1 teaspoon (5 mL/1 g) dried thyme or sage

Peel the turnips. With the large scoop of a melon ball cutter, scoop out 1½ pounds (680 g) of perfect balls. Parboil for 15 minutes, or until tender. Drain, and set aside to cool.

If fresh chestnuts are used, cover the chestnuts with boiling water, and simmer for 15 to 25 minutes. Drain, and remove the shells and skins (the yield should be ½ pound [225 g] of tender chestnuts).

In a large skillet, melt the butter and bacon fat or drippings. Add the turnip balls and chestnuts. Glaze slowly over low heat for 20 to 30 minutes, turning a few times so that they brown evenly.

Toss the turnips and chestnuts with the parsley and herbs. Serve immediately.

Serves 6 to 8.

The Cookbook Committee

Stir-Fried Vegetables

½ cup (120 mL) peanut **or** sesame oil

1 clove garlic, chopped

1½ cups (360 mL/180 g) broccoli florets

1½ cups (360 mL/180 g) cauliflower, broken into bite-size pieces

1½ cups (360 mL/115 g) sliced mushrooms

½ cup (120 mL) sherry, vermouth, **or** dry white wine

1 teaspoon (5 mL/2.4 g) ground ginger **or** 1 tablespoon (15 mL/7 g) chopped fresh ginger root

1 tablespoon (15 mL) soy sauce

Pepper to taste

In a heavy skillet or wok, heat the oil over high heat. Add the garlic, and cook for 1 minute. Add the broccoli and cauliflower, and stir-fry for 3 minutes. Add the mushrooms, wine, ginger, and soy sauce. Cook, stirring constantly, for 5 minutes. Add pepper. Serve immediately.

Serves 4.

Mrs. O. Harry Gruner III

Caribbean Yams

2 pounds (905 g) yams, cooked, peeled, and diced into coarse pieces

1 ripe plantain, diced into coarse pieces

2 cups (480 mL/255 g) diced ripe peaches, mangoes, or papayas

½ teaspoon (2.5 mL/1.1 g) allspice

¼ teaspoon (1.3 mL/0.6 g) nutmeg

⅛ teaspoon (0.6 mL/0.3 g) ground cloves

½ teaspoon (2.5 mL/3 g) salt

Juice of two oranges

½ cup (120 mL/88 g) dark brown sugar **or** molasses

¼ cup (60 mL) Southern Comfort, dark rum, **or** bourbon

3 eggs

2 egg yolks

½ cup (120 mL/50 g) broken pecans

2 tablespoons (30 mL/ 22 g) dark brown sugar for topping

About 2 tablespoons (30 mL/29 g) unsalted butter

Preheat oven to 375° F (190° C). Grease a casserole.

Combine the yams, plantain, and other fruit.

Combine the spices, salt, orange juice, ½ cup (120 mL/115 g) sugar or molasses, and liquor, and fold into the vegetables and fruit. Beat the eggs and egg yolks thoroughly, and fold into the mixture. Pour into the casserole. Top with the pecans, and 2 tablespoons (30 mL/22g) dark brown sugar, and dot with butter. Bake for 45 minutes to 1 hour.

Serves 6.

The Cookbook Committee

Zucchini Blossoms with Brazil Nut Stuffing

Beer Batter:

1 12-ounce can (360 mL) beer

1¼ cups (300 mL/165 g) all-purpose flour

1 tablespoon (15 mL/ 18 g) salt

1 tablespoon (15 mL/ 8 g) sweet paprika

Brazil Nut Stuffing:

3 tablespoons (45 mL/ 43 g) unsalted butter

2 tablespoons (30 mL/ 14 g) chopped onion

2 tablespoons (30 mL/ 6 g) chopped fresh basil

1 cup (240 mL/150 g) chopped Brazil nuts

3 slices fresh bread, crumbled

½ teaspoon (2.5 mL/3 g) salt

⅛ teaspoon (0.6 mL/ 0.3 g) pepper

1 tablespoon (15 mL) lemon juice

24 male zucchini blossoms*

Vegetable oil, for frying

Beer Batter:
In a bowl, combine all the ingredients, whisking until smooth. (May stand, covered, for several hours. Whisk again, before using.)

Brazil Nut Stuffing:
Heat the butter, and sauté the onions until transparent. Place in a food processor, and add the remaining ingredients, one at a time, processing briefly after each addition.

*To preserve a zucchini crop, select fresh male blossoms late in the day after the flowers have closed. Male blossoms are found at the end of thin stems, not the thick ones on which the zucchini form. Any squash blossom may be substituted. Blossoms are often available at local farmers' markets.

Assembly:
Gently spread the blossom petals open under cool running water, being careful to wash away any small insects. Shake out the water, and roll the blossoms gently on a towel to dry.

Fill the stem end of each blossom with about 1 tablespoon (15 mL) of the stuffing. Squeeze and lightly twist the petals to close them. Dip the blossoms, one at a time, in the beer batter to coat. Using a deep fryer set at 350° F (175° C) or a wok with 3 inches (8 cm) of hot oil in it, fry the blossoms for about 3 minutes, or until golden brown. Drain, and serve at once.

Note:
Blossoms may be stuffed a day ahead if they are very fresh. Cover, and refrigerate them until serving time. Then coat them with the batter, and fry. Blossoms may also be lightly fried early on the day they are to be served; just before serving, reheat them on an ungreased baking sheet in a 375° F (190° C) oven, for about 10 minutes, or until crisp.

Serve with sliced fresh tomatoes and grilled fish, chicken, or steak.

Serves 10 to 12.

Eva Lu Damianos

Millview Zucchini

Cream Sauce:

2 tablespoons (30 mL/ 29 g) unsalted butter

1½ to 2 tablespoons (23 mL/12 g to 30 mL/ 17 g) all-purpose flour

1 cup (240 mL) milk

1 small onion, studded with 2 or 3 whole cloves

½ bay leaf

5 medium zucchini, cut into ½-inch (1.3 cm) cubes

6 ounces (170 g) seasoned (not cheese- or garlic-flavored) croutons

1 pound (455 g) sharp Cheddar cheese, grated

Chopped parsley (optional)

Preheat oven to 350° F (175° C). Grease a baking dish.

Cream Sauce:
Melt the butter over low heat. Blend in the flour. Add the milk slowly, stirring. Add the onion and bay leaf. Cook, stirring with a wire whisk or wooden spoon, until thickened and smooth. Remove the onion and bay leaf.

In a baking dish, combine the zucchini and croutons. Add the cheese to the cream sauce. Pour over the zucchini. Bake for 30 minutes. Sprinkle with parsley, if desired.

Serves 10.

Wallace W. Smith, Jr.

Attributed to David Roentgen (German, 1743-1807)
Medals Cabinet, c. 1790
Mahogany, mahogany veneer and ormolu
65¼ × 56¼ × 25¼ in.
(165.7 × 142.9 × 64.1 cm.)
Museum Purchase: Sarah Scaife Foundation, 1975

Salads

Artichoke Rice Salad

1½ cups (360 mL/300 g)
white rice

3¼ cups (780 mL) chicken
stock

4 green onions,
cut into thin slices

½ green pepper, chopped

12 pimiento-stuffed olives,
sliced

1 12-ounce (340 g) jar
marinated artichoke
hearts, quartered (reserve
marinade)

¾ teaspoon (3.8 mL/1.7 g)
curry powder

⅓ cup (80 mL/77 g)
mayonnaise

Cook the rice in the stock
until tender. Combine
with the onions, green
pepper, olives, and
artichokes.

Combine the reserved
marinade with the
curry powder and
mayonnaise. Add to the
rice mixture. Toss and
chill.

Note:
Ideal for picnics as an
accompaniment to grilled
meat.

Serves 6 to 8.

Margaret Reese Hoffman

Crispy Chicken Salad

Vegetable oil for frying

2 ounces (57 g) rice sticks*

3 chicken breasts, halved, skinned, and boned

Boiling water

1 cucumber, cut into thin slices

3 cups (720 mL/145 g) shredded iceberg lettuce

Dressing:
2 tablespoons (30 mL/ 34 g) hot Chinese mustard

¼ cup (60 mL) chicken stock

3 tablespoons (45 mL) soy sauce

2 tablespoons (30 mL/ 33 g) peanut butter

2 tablespoons (30 mL/ 15 g) minced scallions

2 tablespoons (30 mL) red wine vinegar

1 tablespoon (15 mL) sesame oil

2 cloves garlic, crushed

2 teaspoons (10 mL/ 9 g) sugar

2 teaspoons (10 mL/ 6 g) minced ginger

1 teaspoon (5 mL/6 g) salt

2 tablespoons (30 mL/ 17 g) sesame seeds

In a wok, heat the oil. Break up the rice sticks, and deep fry a handful at a time for 2 seconds, or until they puff up. Remove immediately to paper towels.

Place the chicken in a pot. Cover with boiling water. Simmer for about 15 minutes, or until just tender. Shred the chicken by hand. Combine with the cucumber and lettuce.

Dressing:
In a bowl, combine all the ingredients. Set aside.

Just before serving, either mix the fried rice sticks with the chicken mixture, and toss lightly with the dressing, or place the rice sticks on top. Serve immediately before the rice sticks become soggy.

Serves 6.

Singer Euwer

Cucumber Ring Mold

1 envelope (¼ ounce/7 g) unflavored gelatin

¼ cup (60 mL) cold water

9 ounces (255 g) cream cheese, softened

2 cups (480 mL/260 g) pared, grated, and drained cucumbers

1 cup (240 mL/230 g) mayonnaise

¼ cup (60 mL/29 g) minced onion

¼ cup (60 mL/13 g) minced parsley

¼ teaspoon (1.3 mL/1.5 g) salt

Watercress, for garnish

In the top of a double boiler, soften the gelatin in the cold water. Dissolve over hot water.

*Available in Asian food stores.

In a bowl, combine the cream cheese, cucumber, mayonnaise, onion, parsley, and salt. Mix well. Stir the gelatin into the cheese mixture. Pour into a 5-cup (1.2 L) mold, and chill until firm.

Garnish with watercress.

Serves 8.

Kathleen E. Lee

Salad Dieppoise (Spinach, Shrimp, and Enoki Mushrooms in Lemon and Mustard Seed Dressing)

---

1 pound (455 g) medium shrimp

1 tablespoon (15 mL/14 g) honey

4 tablespoons (60 mL) lemon juice

1 tablespoon (15 mL/11 g) mustard seeds

¼ teaspoon (1.3 mL/1.5 g) salt

⅔ cup (160 mL) vegetable oil

1 egg yolk

2 teaspoons (10 mL/11 g) Dijon mustard

1 pound (455 g) spinach

12 ounces (340 g) fresh enoki mushrooms*

In a pot, cover the shrimp with cold water. Bring to a boil. Cover. Remove from the heat, and let stand for about 2 minutes, or until the shrimp turn pink. Drain. Rinse with cold water. Peel and devein. Refrigerate until ready to use.

In a jar with a lid, combine the honey, lemon juice, mustard seeds, salt, vegetable oil, egg yolk, and Dijon mustard. Shake together until blended. Let stand for 1 hour to allow the mustard seeds to soften and the flavors to blend.

Wash the spinach, and remove the stems. Wipe the mushrooms. Combine the shrimp, spinach, and mushrooms. Toss well with the dressing.

Serves 4.

Eva Lu Damianos

*Enoki mushrooms are very small; they are to be used whole. If large mushrooms are substituted, they should be sliced.

Belgian Endive and Chicken Salad with Curried Russian Dressing

Salad:

4 heads Belgian endive

1 bunch watercress

Juice and grated rind of ½ lemon

3 tablespoons (45 mL/ 30 g) golden raisins

3 tablespoons (45 mL/ 26 g) coarse-chopped and toasted cashews, peanuts, pistachios, **or** pumpkin seeds

⅓ cup (80 mL/41 g) chopped celery

1½ cups (360 mL/160 g) diced cooked chicken breast

Dressing:

1½ teaspoons (8 mL) dry vermouth

1 teaspoon (5 mL/2.3 g) curry powder

⅓ cup (80 mL/91 g) ketchup

½ teaspoon (2.5 mL) hot pepper sauce

Juice and grated rind of ½ lemon

⅔ cup (160 mL/155 g) mayonnaise

Freshly ground pepper

Salad:
Remove the large endive leaves, and reserve for lining the salad plates. Dice the endive hearts. Clean the watercress, removing the hard, thick stems; reserve several small stems for a garnish.

In a bowl, combine the diced endives, watercress, lemon juice and rind, raisins, 2 tablespoons (30 mL/17 g) of the nuts or seeds, celery, and chicken. Cover, and chill for 1 to 2 hours.

Dressing:
In a saucepan, combine the vermouth and curry powder, and heat to the boiling point. Remove from the heat, and cool. Blend with the remaining ingredients, and chill.

Assembly:
Ten minutes before serving, toss the salad with enough dressing to coat. Divide among the endive-lined salad plates. Garnish with the reserved watercress and remaining nuts.

Serve with freshly ground pepper and additional dressing on the side.

Serves 4.

The Cookbook Committee

Gourmet Salad

2 ounces (57 g) salad greens (mixture of any four, such as Boston, Bibb, oakleaf, Batavia, Belgian endive, field lettuce, watercress, radicchio)

½ teaspoon (2.5 mL) sherry vinegar

½ teaspoon (2.5 mL) red wine vinegar

1 tablespoon (15 mL) olive oil

A pinch of salt

A pinch of sugar

1 teaspoon (5 mL/1.1 g) chopped fresh dill

1 medium-size artichoke bottom, boiled, choke removed, and cut into pieces

1 ounce (28 g) parboiled fresh asparagus tips

1 ounce (28 g) parboiled fresh green beans

2 ounces (57 g) peeled tomato, cut into small wedges

1 ounce (28 g) fresh mushrooms, cut into thin slices

2 ounces (57 g) boiled lobster tail, cut into pieces

1 thin slice of freshly fried goose liver **or** 1 thin slice of country pâté, fried 1 minute per side.

Spread a mixture of the greens on a plate. Combine the vinegars, oil, salt, and sugar, and sprinkle half on the greens. Sprinkle with the dill. Arrange the artichoke, asparagus, beans, tomato, mushrooms, and lobster pieces in and around the greens. Add the remaining dressing, and top with a slice of warm goose liver or pâté.

Note:
Artichoke leaves may be reserved for other use.

Serves 1 for luncheon; 2 as a first course.

Hotel Krone
Assmannshausen am Rhein

Ham and Cheese Salad

¾ pound (340 g) cooked ham, sliced ½ inch (1.3 cm) thick

¼ pound (115 g) Gruyère cheese, sliced ¼ inch (0.6 cm) thick

4 to 6 celery stalks, sliced

24 small stuffed green olives, halved

2 cups (480 mL/325 g) peeled, seeded, and chopped ripe tomatoes

1 cup (240 mL/155 g) cooked fresh corn, cut from the cob

¾ cup (180 mL/40 g) chopped parsley

1 cup (240 mL/115 g) chopped onions

Mustard Vinaigrette:
2 teaspoons (10 mL/ 11 g) Dijon mustard

1 tablespoon (15 mL) wine vinegar

Salt and freshly ground pepper to taste

¾ cup (180 mL) olive oil

1 teaspoon (5 mL/2.8 g) fine-minced garlic

Cut the ham into ½-inch (1.3 cm) cubes. Cut the cheese into ¼-inch (0.6 cm) cubes. In a large bowl, combine the ham and cheese with the celery, olives, tomatoes, corn, parsley, and onions.

Mustard Vinaigrette:
In a bowl, combine the mustard, vinegar, salt, and pepper. Blend with a wire whisk, gradually adding the oil and stirring vigorously. Add the garlic, and stir.

Toss the salad well with the vinaigrette dressing.

Serves 6 to 8.

Mrs. Fred I. Sharp

Mushroom Salad

1 pound (455 g) mushrooms

1 bunch Pascal celery

2 tablespoons (30 mL/6 g) minced chives

3 tablespoons (45 mL) olive oil

1 tablespoon (15 mL) tarragon vinegar

Salt and pepper to taste

Bibb **or** romaine lettuce leaves

Freshly ground black pepper

Cut the mushrooms into thin slices. Cut the inner celery stalks into cubes. Combine the chives with the oil, vinegar, salt, and pepper. Add the mushrooms and celery. Chill for 30 minutes.

Before serving, remove the vegetables from the oil marinade, and spoon them onto lettuce leaves. Dust with freshly ground pepper.

Serves 6.

Mrs. Paul B. Steele, Jr.

Mushroom Endive Salad

1 pound (455 g) large mushrooms

Juice of 2 lemons

4 Belgian endives

1 teaspoon (5 mL/6 g) salt

½ teaspoon (2.5 mL/1.4 g) freshly ground pepper

¼ teaspoon (1.3 mL/0.4 g) savory

1 tablespoon (15 mL/3 g) chopped chives

½ cup (120 mL/60 g) fine-chopped celery

3 tablespoons (45 g) olive oil

Wipe the mushrooms, and remove the stems. Cut into very thin slices. Pour the lemon juice over the mushrooms, coating them thoroughly.

Cut the endives lengthwise into thin slices. Add to the mushrooms, along with the salt, pepper, savory, chives, and celery. Toss. Add the oil, and toss again. Chill. Mix again before serving.

Serves 4 to 6.

Mrs. Anthony J. A. Bryan

Pasta Salad with Tuna

1 large clove garlic, peeled and crushed

¾ cup (180 mL) olive oil

3 tablespoons (45 mL) lemon juice

4 ounces (115 g) small ruffled egg noodles

Vegetable oil

2 7-ounce (200 g) cans solid white tuna in oil, drained and flaked

1 cup (240 mL/110 g) pitted black olives, halved

1 large sweet red pepper, seeded and cut into narrow strips

¼ cup (60 mL/41 g) capers, drained

½ cup (120 mL/27 g) minced parsley

Salt to taste (optional)

Freshly ground pepper to taste

Combine the garlic, olive oil, and lemon juice into a dressing.

Cook the noodles according to package directions, adding a little vegetable oil to the cooking water. Drain the noodles. Toss with the dressing.

Add the tuna, olives, red pepper, capers, and parsley. Season with salt, if desired, and plenty of freshly ground pepper. Toss to combine.

Serve at room temperature or slightly chilled.

Serves 4.

Mrs. Fred I. Sharp

Shrimp Salad

16 large spinach leaves

1 head Bibb lettuce

1 head Boston lettuce, cut into bite-size pieces

1 red onion, cut into thin slices

¾ cup (180 mL/170 g) olive oil

1¼ pounds (565 g) shrimp, peeled and deveined

Salt and freshly ground pepper to taste

½ cup (120 mL/58 g) snow peas

¼ teaspoon (1.3 mL/0.4 g) dried red pepper flakes

¼ cup (60 mL) red wine vinegar

2 tablespoons (30 mL/6 g) chopped chives

2 tablespoons (30 mL/7 g) chopped dill, parsley, **or** mint

On each of 4 salad plates, arrange 4 spinach leaves alternately with Bibb lettuce. In the center place the Boston lettuce. Top with the onion rings.

In a skillet, heat the oil, and add the shrimp, salt, and pepper. Cook, stirring, until the shrimp turn pink. Add the snow peas and pepper flakes. Cook for 2 minutes. Remove from the heat.

Add the vinegar and herbs. Toss. Spoon the shrimp mixture onto the center of the salad plates.

Serves 4.

Singer Euwer

Snow Peas and Corn Salad

1 pound (455 g) snow peas, strings removed, cut into ¼-inch (0.6 cm) strips; reserve a few whole snow peas for garnish

6 small ears of corn

1 shallot, chopped

2 tablespoons (30 mL/ 34 g) moutarde de Meaux **or** other mild mustard

2 tablespoons (30 mL) cider vinegar

9 fresh tarragon leaves **or** ⅛ teaspoon (0.6 mL/0.1 g) dried tarragon

5 fresh mint leaves

2 fresh basil leaves **or** ½ teaspoon (2.5 mL/0.4 g) dried basil

A pinch of sugar

6 tablespoons (90 mL) peanut oil

Salt and pepper to taste

Pour boiling water over the snow peas in a colander. Drain well, and immediately plunge them into ice water. Drain again. Transfer them to a serving bowl. Remove the kernels from the ears of corn, and blanch. Combine with the snow peas, and set aside.

In a blender or processor, combine the shallot, mustard, vinegar, tarragon, mint, basil, and sugar. Process until smooth. With the motor running, add the oil in a slow stream. Process until creamy. Season with salt and pepper. Pour over the vegetables, and mix gently. Cover, and refrigerate for 4 hours or overnight.

Garnish with whole snow peas.

Note:
A nice accompaniment to cold salmon.

Serves 6.

Mrs. George R. McCullough

Dilled Snow Pea Salad

2 pounds (905 g) snow peas

2 cups (480 mL/230 g) fresh peas **or** 2 20-ounce (565 g) packages frozen peas, defrosted

½ cup (120 mL/125 g) sour cream

Fresh chopped dill **and/or** chives

Salt and pepper to taste

Boston lettuce

Parboil the snow peas for 1 to 2 minutes. Refresh with cold water. Combine with the other peas, sour cream, and seasonings to taste. Chill, and serve on Boston lettuce.

Note:
Serve with chicken or fish.

Serves 6.

Mrs. William T. Tobin

Steak Salad

Dressing:
1 cup (240 mL) vegetable oil

¼ cup (60 mL) red wine vinegar

2 teaspoons (10 mL/ 0.8 g) tarragon

½ teaspoon (2.5 mL) Worcestershire sauce

1 teaspoon (5 mL/2.3 g) dry mustard

1 teaspoon (5 mL/6 g) salt

1 teaspoon (5 mL/1 g) minced chives

1 teaspoon (5 mL/1.1 g) minced parsley

1 teaspoon (5 mL) lemon juice

¼ teaspoon (1.3 mL/ 0.7 g) black pepper

¼ teaspoon (1.3 mL/ 0.4 g) thyme

2 pounds (905 g) lean sirloin steak

¼ pound (115 g) mushrooms, sliced

1 dill pickle, cut into julienne strips

1 green pepper, cut into julienne strips

1 Bermuda onion, cut into thin rings

1 celery stalk, sliced diagonally

Lettuce and cherry tomatoes

The day before, in a blender, combine the dressing ingredients, and blend thoroughly. Set aside.

Broil the steak to medium rare, at most. Let cool; then cut into julienne strips, eliminating all fat and gristle.

In a container with a tight-fitting lid, combine the steak, mushrooms, pickle, green pepper, onion, and celery. Pour the dressing over the steak mixture, and toss to mix. Cover, and refrigerate for 24 hours. Stir or invert several times while refrigerated.

Drain. Serve in a bowl lined with lettuce. Garnish with cherry tomatoes.

Serves 8.

Beth Smith

Tabouleh

1 cup (240 mL/170 g) bulgur wheat

1½ cups (360 mL) boiling water

2 cups (480 mL/105 g) chopped parsley

1 cup (240 mL/116 g) chopped scallion bulbs

1 cup (240 mL/165 g) chopped tomatoes

2 tablespoons (30 mL/ 7 g) chopped fresh mint

6 tablespoons (90 mL) lemon juice

2 to 3 tablespoons (30 to 45 mL) olive oil

Salt to taste

In a large bowl, soak the bulgur wheat in the boiling water until all the water is absorbed and the wheat has cooled. Add the parsley, scallions, tomatoes, and mint. Mix together. Add the lemon juice, oil, and salt. Mix, and refrigerate.

Note:
For variety, vary the proportions, or add garlic, cucumber, or other vegetables to taste.

Serve with pita bread as a salad or a vegetable.

Makes approximately 1 quart (960 milliliters).

Paula S. Atlas

Tomato Aspic

12 ounces (360 mL) V-8 juice **or** tomato juice

Juice of 1 lemon

¼ to ½ teaspoon (1.3 to 2.5 mL) Tabasco sauce

1 tablespoon (15 mL) Worcestershire sauce

3 ounces (85 g) lemon gelatin

1 tablespoon (15 mL) cider vinegar

1 avocado, diced (optional)

In a saucepan, bring to a boil the V-8 or tomato juice, lemon juice, Tabasco, and Worcestershire. Remove from the heat, and stir in the gelatin until it is dissolved. Stir in the vinegar.

Pour into a ring mold. Chill for at least 6 hours. If adding the avocado, allow the aspic to thicken slightly first.

Note:
Fill the center of the mold with cottage cheese, or tuna or chicken salad.

Serves 4.

Mrs. George R. McCullough

Tomatoes Lutèce

8 ½-inch (1.3 cm) -thick slices beefsteak tomato

¼ cup (60 mL/13 g) chopped parsley

1 clove garlic, crushed

1 teaspoon (5 mL/6 g) salt

1 teaspoon (5 mL/4.8 g) sugar

¼ teaspoon (1.3 mL/0.7 g) freshly ground pepper

¼ cup (60 mL) olive oil **or** vegetable oil

2 tablespoons (30 mL) cider vinegar

2 teaspoons (10 mL/11 g) light mustard

Arrange the tomato slices on a platter.

Combine the remaining ingredients in a jar, and shake well. Let stand at room temperature for at least ½ hour. Remove the garlic (the garlic flavor will become stronger if it remains in the dressing).

Pour the dressing over the tomatoes just before serving.

Serves 4 to 6.

Mrs. W. Bruce McConnel, Jr.

Curried Tuna Salad

1 7-ounce (200 g) can tuna in water, drained

½ cup (120 mL/54 g) cubed, unpeeled apple

¼ cup (60 mL/31 g) diced celery

1 tablespoon (15 mL/9 g) currants

¾ cup (180 mL/85 g) thin-sliced scallions

1 tablespoon (15 mL/7 g) minced onion

2 tablespoons (30 mL/ 13 g) chopped pecans

1½ cups (360 mL/350 g) mayonnaise

1½ tablespoons (23 mL/ 28 g) chutney

3 tablespoons (45 mL/ 20 g) curry powder

Combine the tuna, apple, celery, currants, scallions, onion, and pecans.

Combine the mayonnaise, chutney, and curry powder. Stir into the tuna mixture.

Serves 10.

Mrs. Robert O. Read

Utagawa Hiroshige I
(Japanese, 1797-1858)
Japan Bridge in the Rain, c. 1835
Color woodcut
14¼ × 9¾ in. (36.2 × 24.8 cm.)
Gift of Dr. and Mrs. James B. Austin, 1927

Sauces and Garnishes

Recipes in Menu Section

Caper Cream Sauce

2 tablespoons (30 mL/ 29 g) unsalted butter

¼ to ½ cup (60 mL/41 g to 120 mL/82 g) capers to taste

1 tablespoon (15 mL/4 g) grated lemon rind

1 tablespoon (15 mL/3 g) chopped parsley

½ cup (120 mL) white wine

½ cup (120 mL) heavy cream

Heat the butter, and sauté the capers, lemon rind, and parsley for 1 minute. Add the wine, and cook for 2 minutes. Slowly pour in the cream. Cook, stirring, until the sauce thickens.

Note:
Pour over poached or baked monkfish, halibut, or other firm-fleshed fish. Serve with rice or barley pilaf.

May be prepared a day ahead and reheated.

Serves 4.

Linda Youtzy

245

Red Pepper Chutney

12 red peppers, seeded

1 tablespoon (15 mL/18 g) salt

1 pint (480 mL) cider vinegar

2¾ cups (660 mL/625 g) sugar

In a meat grinder or food processor, grind the peppers. Add the salt, and let stand for 3 hours. Drain, and rinse with boiling water.

In a large saucepan, heat the vinegar and sugar. Add the peppers, and cook for at least 1 hour, or until the mixture is thick. Place in sterilized jars. Cover with paraffin wax and lids.

Makes 3 pints (1.44 liters).

Sibby McCrady

Hollandaise Sauce

4 egg yolks

1 teaspoon (5 mL/6 g) salt

A dash of pepper

1 tablespoon (15 mL) lemon juice

¼ pound (115 g) unsalted butter

In the top of a double boiler, beat the egg yolks with a wire whisk. Add the salt, pepper, and lemon juice. Add the butter. Place over (not in) boiling water. Cook, stirring continuously. The sauce will turn watery before it thickens. Cook to desired consistency.

Note:
May be stored in the refrigerator for 2 or 3 weeks. Reheat over hot or boiling water. If the sauce begins to curdle, add 1 to 3 teaspoons (5 mL to 15 mL) cold water. Beat vigorously.

Serves 4.

Mrs. James D. Williams

Maltaise Mayonnaise

2 teaspoons (10 mL/4.9 g) orange zest

1⅔ tablespoons (25 mL/28 g) frozen orange juice concentrate

1 teaspoon (5 mL) fresh lemon juice

1 large egg

1 teaspoon (5 mL/2.3 g) dry mustard

½ teaspoon (2.5 mL/3 g) salt

1¼ cups (300 mL) vegetable oil

In a food processor or blender, place the orange zest, orange juice concentrate, lemon juice, egg, mustard, salt, and 2 tablespoons (30 mL) of the oil. Process for 8 to 10 seconds, or until thickened.

With the processor or blender running, drizzle the remaining oil in a fine stream into the mixture.

This will take several minutes. Allow the mayonnaise to rest for about 1 hour before using.

Makes 1⅔ cups (400 milliliters).

Marlene Parrish

246

Dill Mustard Sauce

1½ to 2 cups (360 mL/ 340 g to 480 mL/455 g) sugar

4 cups (960 mL/210 g) fresh dill

3 cups (720 mL/815 g) Dijon mustard

1 cup (240 mL) white wine vinegar

2 cups (480 mL/465 g) mayonnaise

½ cup (120 mL/45 g) wilted watercress

½ cup (120 mL/85 g) wilted spinach

¼ cup (60 mL) vegetable oil

In a food processor, combine all the ingredients except the oil. Blend until smooth. Continue to process while adding the oil slowly. Cover, and store in the refrigerator (this will keep indefinitely).

Note:
Serve as an accompaniment to fish or chicken, or spread on top of fish or chicken before broiling.

Makes 3¼ quarts (3.12 liters).

Ellen Lehman

Sweet and Sour Mustard

6 ounces (170 g) dry mustard

½ teaspoon (2.5 mL/1.4 g) freshly ground black pepper

¼ teaspoon (1.3 mL/0.6 g) white pepper

¼ teaspoon (1.3 mL/0.6 g) red pepper

1 to 1½ cups (240 to 360 mL) white wine

2 cups (480 mL/455 g) sugar

½ cup (120 mL) vinegar

1 tablespoon (15 mL/18 g) salt

4 tablespoons (60 mL/ 57 g) unsalted butter

3 eggs, beaten well

In a heavy saucepan, combine the mustard and the peppers. Add the wine to make a paste. Add the sugar, vinegar, and salt. Bring to a boil, stirring constantly; be careful not to burn. Add the butter and eggs, and bring to a boil, stirring constantly. Strain. Spoon into jars, and store in the refrigerator.

Note:
Flavor will vary with type of mustard or vinegar.

Superb for sandwiches or hors d'oeuvres.

Makes 4 cups.

Ann and David Wilkins

Pesto

1 cup (240 mL/50 g) fresh
basil leaves

2 cloves garlic

¼ cup (60 mL/34 g) pine
nuts (pignoli)

1 cup (240 mL/110 g)
grated Parmesan cheese

⅔ cup (160 mL)
(Portuguese, if available)
olive oil

In a food processor,
process the basil, garlic,
and pine nuts. Add the
Parmesan cheese, and
blend to form a thick
purée. Slowly add the
oil, and blend until it has
the consistency of butter.
Pour into a jar. Film with
a thin layer of olive oil.
Cover, and refrigerate
until ready to use.

Makes 2½ cups (600
milliliters).

Judith M. Davenport

Spinach Pecan Pesto

2 ounces (57 g) grated
Parmesan cheese

2 cups (5 ounces)
(480 mL/140 g) washed
fresh spinach leaves

½ cup (120 mL/52 g)
pecans

1½ tablespoons (23 mL/
5 g) minced parsley

3 large cloves garlic

1 teaspoon (5 mL/0.8 g)
dried basil

¾ cup (180 mL) or less
olive oil

Place the cheese, spinach,
pecans, parsley, garlic, and
basil in a food processor.
Blend. Add the oil
gradually, and process
until smooth.

May be served hot or at
room temperature. If
served hot, stir while
heating.

Note:
An alternative to the
traditional pesto sauce.
Serve hot on pasta,
broiled fish, or vegetables;
at room temperature on
thick tomato slices or
unsalted crackers.

Makes 1½ cups (360
milliliters).

Mrs. Robert O. Read

Quince Preserves

3 cups (720 mL/680 g)
sugar

2 quarts (1.92 L) water

7 cups (1.68 L/1.06 kg)
quinces, peeled and sliced

In a large kettle, boil the
sugar and water for 5
minutes. Add the fruit,
and cook for about 1
hour, or until the liquid is
clear red. Stir frequently.

Note:
A deliciously different
accompaniment for pork,
chicken, or lamb.

Makes 8 to 12 cups
(1.92 to 2.88 liters).

Duella S. Stranahan

Roquefort Dressing

1 quart (960 mL/930 g) mayonnaise

2 cups (480 mL/240 g) Roquefort cheese, softened

1 tablespoon (15 mL/8 g) freshly ground pepper

2 teaspoons (10 mL/9 g) garlic salt

1 tablespoon (15 mL/2 g) oregano

½ teaspoon (2.5 mL/0.7 g) thyme

½ teaspoon (2.5 mL/0.2 g) dill

½ teaspoon (2.5 mL/0.4 g) basil

2 tablespoons (30 mL) Worcestershire sauce

¼ cup (60 mL) kosher dill pickle juice

¼ cup (60 mL) Spanish olive juice

½ cup (120 mL) cider vinegar

In an electric mixer or food processor, combine all the ingredients except the vinegar. Gradually add the vinegar, beating continuously until smooth and creamy.

Note:
Serve with crumbled Roquefort cheese on top. The dressing thickens as it chills. It will keep in the refrigerator for several weeks.

Makes 7 cups (1.68 liters).

Anonymous

Adelaide Alsop Robineau
(American, 1865-1929)
Urn of Dreams, 1921
Porcelain
H. 10⅜ in. (26.4 cm.)
Gift of Dana Robineau Kelley,
Grandson of the Artist, and
Family, 1982

249

Breads

Applesauce Honey Bread

1 cup (240 mL/130 g) whole wheat flour

½ cup (120 mL/36 g) wheat germ

½ cup (120 mL/18 g) bran flakes

1 teaspoon (5 mL/3.4 g) baking powder

½ teaspoon (2.5 mL/2.2 g) baking soda

½ teaspoon (2.5 mL/3 g) salt

¼ cup (60 mL/29 g) cocoa

½ cup (120 mL/80 g) raisins

½ cup (120 mL/58 g) chopped walnuts

2 eggs

¾ cup (180 mL/190 g) sweetened or unsweetened applesauce

¼ cup (60 mL/57 g) unsulfured molasses

¼ cup (60 mL/57 g) honey

Preheat oven to 350° F (175° C). Grease a 5- by 9-inch (13 cm by 23 cm) loaf pan.

Combine the flour, wheat germ, bran flakes, baking powder, baking soda, salt, cocoa, raisins, and walnuts.

In a separate bowl, combine the eggs, applesauce, molasses, and honey. Pour the egg mixture into the dry mixture. Mix quickly but thoroughly. Turn immediately into the loaf pan. Bake for 40 to 50 minutes.

Makes 1 loaf.

Marilyn McDevitt Rubin

Apricot Bread

1 cup (240 mL/140 g) coarse-chopped dried apricots

1 cup (240 mL/160 g) seedless golden raisins

1⅓ cups (320 mL) water

¼ pound (115 g) unsalted butter

½ cup (120 mL/115 g) sugar

1 egg

1½ cups (360 mL/200 g) all-purpose flour

½ teaspoon (2.5 mL/2.2 g) baking soda

¼ teaspoon (1.3 mL/1.5 g) salt

Milk, as required

The day before, preheat oven to 300° F (150° C). Line a 4½- by 9-inch (11 cm by 23 cm) loaf pan or two smaller pans with brown paper. Grease well.

In a saucepan, combine the apricots, raisins, and water. Bring to a boil. Simmer for 10 minutes. Cool to room temperature.

Cream together the butter, sugar, and egg. Combine the flour, baking soda, and salt. Stir into the creamed mixture. Blend in the fruit mixture. If the batter is too stiff, add a little milk.

Pour the batter into the loaf pan. Bake for about 1¼ hours. Test with a toothpick for doneness. Leave in the pan overnight to cool.

Remove from the pan the following day, and wrap in foil. Refrigerate until ready to use.

Note:
Apricot bread may be stored for several weeks. It will remain quite moist.

Makes 1 large loaf or 2 small loaves.

Mrs. Roger D. Phelps

BLT Bread

1 envelope (¼ ounce/7 g) dry yeast

1⅓ cups (320 mL) warm water

3 tablespoons (45 mL/ 43 g) sugar

3½ to 4 cups (840 mL/ 460 g to 960 mL/530 g) unsifted all-purpose flour

1½ cups (360 mL/180 g) grated Cheddar cheese

1½ teaspoons (8 mL/ 9 g) salt

3 tablespoons (45 mL/ 16 g) nonfat dry milk

1 egg, beaten with 1½ teaspoons (8 mL) water

In a large bowl, sprinkle the yeast over the warm water, and let stand for 3 minutes. Stir in the sugar. Add 3 cups (720 mL/ 395 g) of the flour, the cheese, salt, and dry milk. Turn out on a lightly floured board, and knead for about 10 minutes, or until smooth and satiny, adding ½ to 1 cup (120 mL/66 g to 240 mL/ 130 g) of flour to produce a dough that is barely sticky.

Return the dough to the bowl, cover lightly with plastic wrap, and let rise for about 1 hour, or until doubled in volume. Punch down. Roll or pat the dough into a 9- by 14-inch (23 by 36 cm) rectangle; then roll to form a 9-inch (23 cm) -long cylinder. Place in a well-greased 9- by 5-inch (23 by 13 cm) loaf pan. Brush with the beaten egg glaze, taking care that the glaze does not drip down the sides of the loaf. Cover lightly with plastic wrap, and let rise for about 1 hour, or until doubled.

Fifteen minutes before baking, preheat the oven to 400° F (205° C).

Bake for 20 minutes. Cover with foil or brown paper to prevent excess browning, and bake for 15 to 25 minutes, or until tapping the bottom crust produces a hollow sound. Cool on a rack.

Note:
This bread, toasted, is wonderful for bacon, lettuce, and tomato sandwiches. Also very good on its own. Recipe may be doubled or tripled.

Makes 1 loaf.

Susan Hershenson

Boston Brown Bread

2 cups (480 mL)
buttermilk

6 ounces (180 mL) dark
molasses

6 ounces (170 g) raisins

1 cup (240 mL/130 g)
rye flour

1 cup (240 mL/130 g)
whole wheat flour

1 cup (240 mL/145 g)
cornmeal

¾ teaspoon (3.8 mL/
3.3 g) baking soda

1 teaspoon (5 mL/6 g) salt

1 tablespoon (15 mL/14 g)
softened unsalted butter

In a deep bowl, beat the
buttermilk and molasses
vigorously. Stir in the
raisins. Combine the rye
flour, whole wheat flour,
cornmeal, baking soda,
and salt, and sift them
into the buttermilk
mixture, 1 cup (240 mL)
at a time, stirring well
after each addition.

Thoroughly wash and dry
two empty 2½-cup
(600 mL) No. 2 size cans.
Brush the softened butter
over the bottoms and
sides of the cans. Pour the
batter into the cans,
dividing it evenly. The
batter should reach within
1 inch (2.5 cm) of the top.
Cover each can loosely
with a circle of greased
wax paper. On top of the
wax paper, place a large
circle of foil. Raise the foil
above the can, press the
edge against the can, and
secure it with string or
tape. The foil will puff
out, resembling a chef's
hat. Set the cans on a
rack in a pot. Add
enough boiling water to
reach about three-fourths
of the way up the sides of
the cans. Return the water
to a boil over high heat.
Cover the pot tightly, and
reduce the heat to low.
Steam the bread for 2
hours and 15 minutes.

Immediately remove the
foil and paper from the
cans, and turn the bread
out onto a heated platter.

Note:
Bread may be kept
covered in the cans, or
wrapped in foil, in the
refrigerator for about
10 days.

Makes 2 loaves.

Nicholas Colletti
Duquesne Club

Carrot Nut Muffins

2 cups (480 mL/265 g)
all-purpose flour

1 cup (240 mL/225 g)
sugar

2 teaspoons (10 mL/9 g)
baking soda

2 teaspoons (10 mL/6 g)
cinnamon

½ teaspoon (2.5 mL/
3 g) salt

2 cups (480 mL/265 g)
grated carrots

½ cup (120 mL/80 g)
raisins

½ cup (120 mL/52 g)
chopped pecans

½ cup (120 mL/46 g)
shredded sweetened
coconut

1 apple, peeled and grated

3 large eggs

1 cup (240 mL)
vegetable oil

2 teaspoons (10 mL)
vanilla

Preheat oven to 350° F
(175° C). Grease 15
muffin cups well.

Sift together the flour, sugar, baking soda, cinnamon, and salt. Stir in the carrots, raisins, pecans, coconut, and apple.

Beat the eggs with the oil and vanilla, and stir into the flour mixture until just combined. Spoon the batter into the muffin cups, filling them to the top. Bake for about 35 minutes, or until springy to the touch.

Let the muffins cool on a rack for 5 minutes. Turn out onto the rack, and let cool completely.

Makes 15.

Marilyn McDevitt Rubin

Cheddar Raisin Muffins

2 cups (480 mL/265 g) all-purpose flour

3½ teaspoons (18 mL/ 12 g) baking powder

¾ teaspoon (3.8 mL/4.5 g) salt

6 tablespoons (90 mL/ 86 g) unsalted butter **or** margarine

1 cup (240 mL/120 g) grated sharp Cheddar cheese

1 egg, beaten

1 cup (240 mL) milk

¾ cup (180 mL/120 g) raisins

Preheat oven to 400° F (205° C). Grease 2 6-cup muffin tins.

Sift the flour with the baking powder and salt. Add the butter or margarine, and with a pastry blender or knives, combine until small particles form. Stir in the cheese.

Combine the egg and milk. Add to the dry mixture, stirring until all the flour is moistened. Fold in the raisins.

Spoon the batter into the muffin cups. Fill about two-thirds full. Bake for about 25 minutes, or until nicely browned. Remove from the tins, and serve hot.

Makes 12.

Marilyn McDevitt Rubin

Cornmeal Bread

1⅔ cups (400 mL/240 g) yellow or white, preferably water-ground, cornmeal

⅔ cup (160 mL/88 g) all-purpose flour

2 teaspoons (10 mL/7 g) baking powder

½ teaspoon (2.5 mL/3 g) salt

1 teaspoon (5 mL/4.7 g) sugar

½ teaspoon (2.5 mL/2.2 g) baking soda

1½ cups (360 mL) milk

3 tablespoons (45 mL/ 43 g) lard **or** unsalted butter, melted

2 eggs, beaten

Have all ingredients at room temperature.

Preheat oven to 425° F (220° C). Oil a 10-inch heavy iron skillet, and place it in the oven.

Sift together all the dry ingredients, and set aside. In a bowl, combine the milk, and lard or butter.

Add the eggs. Whisk the mixture into the dry ingredients. Pour the mixture into the hot skillet, and bake for about 30 minutes. Test by inserting a knife into the center; the knife should come out clean.

Makes 1 round loaf.

Mrs. Dorothy R. Hughes

Date and Nut Bread

1½ cups (360 mL) boiling water

1 pound (455 g) dates, pitted and chopped

1 tablespoon (15 mL/14 g) melted unsalted butter

1½ cups (360 mL/340 g) sugar

1 egg

2 teaspoons (10 mL/9 g) baking soda

2¾ cups (660 mL/365 g) all-purpose flour

1 cup (240 mL/115 g) chopped walnuts

Preheat oven to 325° F (165° C). Grease 2 loaf pans.

Pour the boiling water over the chopped dates.

Cream the butter with the sugar and egg. Add the baking soda, flour, dates, and nuts. Stir until mixed. Pour into pans. Bake for 1 hour. Cool before removing from pans.

Makes 2 loaves.

Mrs. Walter E. Reineman, Jr.

Pecan Muffins

1 cup (240 mL/120 g) all-purpose flour, sifted

⅓ cup (80 mL/76 g) sugar

A pinch of salt

2 teaspoons (10 mL/7 g) baking powder

¼ cup (60 mL) vegetable oil

½ cup (120 mL) milk

1 egg

1 teaspoon (5 mL) vanilla

½ cup (120 mL/52 g) chopped pecans

Preheat oven to 400° F (205° C). Grease a 6-cup muffin tin.

Combine the flour, sugar, salt, and baking powder. Add the oil, milk, egg, vanilla, and pecans to the dry ingredients. Mix until incorporated.

Pour into the muffin cups until they are half filled. Bake for 20 minutes.

Note:
Other nuts or blueberries may be substituted for the pecans.

Makes 6.

The Cookbook Committee

Rosemary Rolls

1 envelope (¼ ounce/7 g) dry yeast

¾ cup (180 mL) warm water

3 tablespoons (45 mL/ 43 g) sugar

¼ cup (60 mL/43 g) mashed, instant **or** boiled potatoes

3 to 3¼ cups (720 mL/ 395 g to 780 mL/430 g) unsifted all-purpose flour

1½ teaspoons (8 mL/9 g) salt

1 egg

4 tablespoons (60 mL/ 57 g) unsalted butter, at room temperature

Olive oil

Fresh rosemary

Sprinkle the yeast over the warm water. Let stand for 3 minutes. Stir in the sugar and potatoes. Stir in 2 cups (480 mL/265 g) of the flour, the salt, egg, and butter. Turn out onto a lightly floured work surface, and knead for about 10 minutes, or until smooth and elastic. If the dough is sticky, add the remaining flour a little at a time.

Place the dough in a large, greased bowl. Cover it with plastic wrap, and refrigerate for 2 hours. Remove from the refrigerator, and punch down. Return it to the refrigerator for at least 4 hours or up to 2 days.

Remove the dough from the refrigerator 2 hours before baking. Divide it into 18 pieces. Roll each piece into a ball, and place the balls 2 inches (5 cm) apart on a greased baking sheet. Cover them lightly with plastic wrap, and let them rise in a warm place for 1 to 1½ hours, or until doubled in volume.

Preheat oven fifteen minutes before baking to 400° F (205° C).

Brush the rolls gently with olive oil, and sprinkle generously with rosemary. Bake for 12 to 15 minutes. Cool on a rack.

Note:
Pepper rolls may be made by substituting freshly ground black pepper for the rosemary.

Makes 18.

Susan Hershenson

Three Grain Muffins

⅓ cup (80 mL/48 g), preferably stone-ground, cornmeal

⅓ cup (80 mL/76 g) sugar

⅓ cup (80 mL/44 g) soy flour

1 cup (240 mL/130 g) whole wheat flour

¾ teaspoon (3.8 mL/4.5 g) salt

1 teaspoon (5 mL/4.4 g) baking soda

1 large egg

1 cup (240 mL/260 g) plain yogurt

⅓ cup (80 mL/76 g) melted unsalted butter

Preheat oven to 350° F (175° C). Grease 2 6-cup muffin tins.

Combine the cornmeal, sugar, soy flour, whole wheat flour, salt, and baking soda. Lightly combine the egg and yogurt. Add to the dry ingredients. Stir in the butter. Fill the muffin cups two-thirds full. Bake for about 25 minutes.

Makes 12.

Marlene Parrish

American, New York, New York, 18th century
Side Chair, c. 1740-50
Walnut, walnut veneer and poplar

38½ × 21½ × 22 in. (97.8 × 54.6 × 55.9 cm)
Gift of the Women's Committee of the Museum of Art in memory of Mrs. John Berdan, 1983

256

Desserts

Almond Soufflé

8 tablespoons (120 mL/ 115 g) sugar

3 tablespoons (45 mL) water

1 cup (240 mL) heavy cream

3 tablespoons (45 mL/ 25 g) cornstarch

2 to 3 tablespoons (30 mL/29 g to 45 mL/43 g) unsalted butter

⅔ cup (160 mL/100 g) marzipan, cut into small pieces

1 tablespoon (15 mL) kirsch **or** amaretto

1 tablespoon (15 mL) rum

3 eggs, separated

2 tablespoons (30 mL/ 17 g) toasted slivered almonds

Combine 6 tablespoons (90 mL/85 g) of the sugar and the water. Simmer until the sugar is dissolved. Set aside.

Preheat oven to 400° F (205° C). Lightly grease a 1-quart (960 mL) soufflé dish or 4 individual soufflé dishes. Sprinkle the sides lightly with sugar.

In a thick-bottomed saucepan, combine the cream, cornstarch, butter, and marzipan. Cook over low heat until the liquid thickens, stirring occasionally to dissolve the marzipan. Add the kirsch or amaretto and rum. Simmer slowly until the mixture returns to its previous consistency. Remove from the heat. Pour into a mixing bowl. Add the egg yolks, one at a time, mixing after each addition. Set aside.

Beat the egg whites until stiff but not dry. Quickly and thoroughly fold them into the batter a third at a time (this may be done up to 1 hour before baking).

Place the almonds and the syrup in the soufflé dish or dishes. Pour the soufflé mixture over the nuts and syrup. Fill to the rim, and smooth the top. Bake in the lower third of the oven, 12 to 20 minutes for individual soufflés and 25 to 30 minutes for the 1-quart (960 mL) soufflé.

Serves 4 to 6.

Mrs. Anthony J. A. Bryan

Scandinavian Apple Cake

3 or 4 medium-size apples

1 cup plus 2 tablespoons (270 mL/255 g) sugar

1 teaspoon (5 mL/2.8 g) cinnamon

2 cups (480 mL/245 g) all-purpose flour, sifted

1½ teaspoons (8 mL/5 g) baking powder

¼ teaspoon (1.3 mL/1.5 g) salt

6 ounces (170 g) unsalted butter **or** margarine, softened

3 eggs

1 teaspoon (5 mL) vanilla

½ cup (120 mL/125 g) sour cream **or** plain yogurt

¼ cup (60 mL/77 g) melted apple jelly

2 tablespoons (30 mL/ 17 g) toasted sliced almonds

Preheat oven to 350° F (175° C). Grease a 9-inch (23 cm) springform pan.

Pare the apples, and cut each into 6 wedges.

Remove the cores. Toss with 2 tablespoons (30 mL/ 28 g) of the sugar and the cinnamon. Set aside. Sift together the flour, baking powder, and salt.

Combine the butter or margarine, sugar, eggs, and vanilla. Beat until very light and fluffy. With a wooden spoon, stir in half the flour mixture until blended. Stir in the sour cream or yogurt. Add the remaining flour, and mix well. Pour into the springform pan. Arrange the apples on top, pushing the pieces partly into the batter.

Bake for 1 hour and 15 minutes. Cool on a wire rack for 10 minutes. Loosen the cake around the edge with a knife. Carefully remove the rim of the pan. Brush the top with the melted jelly. Sprinkle with the nuts. Serve warm or cold.

Note:
May be frozen. Good for dessert or for breakfast.

Serves 10 to 12.

Judi Bobenage

Blueberry Orange Shells

6 oranges

1 pint (480 mL/310 g) orange sherbet

1 cup (240 mL/115 g) fresh blueberries

6 tablespoons (90 mL) Grand Marnier, or to taste

3 tablespoons (45 mL/ 43 g) sugar

2 teaspoons (10 mL/6 g) cinnamon

Cut off the tops of the oranges. Scoop out the fruit, and reserve for another use. Place the orange shells in plastic bags, and freeze.

To serve:
Fill each shell with the orange sherbet. Top each with the blueberries. Add 1 tablespoon (15 mL) of the Grand Marnier to each. Mix the sugar and cinnamon; sprinkle over the berries.

Serves 6.

Velma Ferrari

View of the Sculpture
Courtyard

Brandied Fruit Cream

1 pint (480 mL/230 g)
raspberries, strawberries,
or peaches, slightly
crushed

6 tablespoons (90 mL)
brandy **or** kirsch

8 ounces (225 g) cream
cheese, softened

2 eggs, separated

¼ cup (60 mL/29 g)
confectioners' sugar

Soak the fruit in
4 tablespoons (60 mL) of
the brandy or kirsch. Beat
the cheese, egg yolks, and
sugar until fluffy. Beat the
egg whites until stiff. Fold
into the cheese mixture.
Fold in the remaining
brandy or kirsch.

Pile the mixture lightly
into sherbet glasses. Top
with the fruit.

Note:
Serve at room temperature
with cookies or biscuits.
May also be used as a
topping for sponge or
angel food cake.

May be made ahead and
refrigerated.

Serves 4.

Shirley Bonello

Brown Sugar Cookies Supreme

1 pound (455 g) unsalted
butter, at room
temperature

1¼ cups (300 mL/220 g)
light brown sugar, packed
firm

4 cups (960 mL/530 g)
all-purpose flour

Preheat oven to 350° F
(175° C).

In a food processor or
with your fingers, combine
all the ingredients. Divide
the dough into 2 or 3
portions, shaping each
into a log about 2 inches
(5 cm) in diameter. Wrap
in wax paper or plastic.
Chill thoroughly.

When ready to bake, let
the dough stand at room
temperature for about 1
minute. Slice into ¼-inch
(0.6 cm) -thick slices. Bake
on ungreased baking
sheets for 8 to 10 minutes.
Watch closely—the cookies
burn quickly!

After baking, allow to rest
for 1 minute on the
baking sheets before
removing to a cooling
rack. Store in tightly
closed containers.

Makes 8 dozen.

Beth Adams

Frozen Cappuccino

1 quart (960 mL/505 g) coffee ice cream

¼ cup (60 mL) light rum

¼ cup (60 mL) dark rum

¼ cup (60 mL) coffee liqueur

1 ounce (28 g) semisweet chocolate, shaved

Chill a food processor bowl and metal cutting blade. In the processor bowl, combine the ice cream, rums, and liqueur. Process until blended. Pour into wine or pony glasses, and freeze. Garnish with the chocolate shavings.

Serves 4 to 6.

Mrs. James S. Beckwith III

Cheesecake Deluxe

½ pound (225 g) graham cracker crumbs

4 tablespoons (60 mL/ 57 g) unsalted butter, softened or melted

3 8-ounce (225 g) packages cream cheese

5 eggs

1½ cups (360 mL/340 g) sugar

Juice of 1 lemon

1 pint (480 mL/505 g) sour cream

1½ teaspoons (8 mL) vanilla

Preheat oven to 350° F (175° C). Grease a 9-inch (23 cm) springform pan.

Combine the crumbs with the butter. Press them against the sides and bottom of the pan. Set aside.

Soften the cream cheese. Combine with the eggs and sugar. With an electric mixer, beat for 30 minutes. Add the lemon juice, sour cream, and vanilla. Beat the entire mixture for 15 minutes. Pour into the prepared pan. Bake for 55 minutes. Turn off the heat. Leave in the oven with the door open for 1 hour longer. Remove from the oven. Cool to room temperature, and refrigerate.

Serves 12.

Silvia C. Speyer

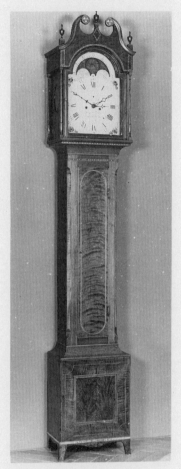

John Johnston and Samuel Davis (American, Pittsburgh, working 1804-06)
Tall Clock, c. 1805
Walnut, walnut and cherry veneer, and pine
95¾ × 18⅛ × 10⅝ in.
(243.2 × 46.0 × 27.0 cm.)
Gift of Mr. and Mrs. James A. Drain, 1973

Moist Chocolate Cake

2 cups (480 mL/455 g) sugar

1 cup (240 mL) oil

2 eggs

1 cup (240 mL) milk

1 cup (240 mL) hot coffee

1 teaspoon (5 mL) vanilla

¾ cup (180 mL/86 g) cocoa

2 cups (480 mL/265 g) flour

1 teaspoon (5 mL/6 g) salt

1 teaspoon (5 mL/3.4 g) baking powder

2 teaspoons (10 mL/9 g) baking soda

Confectioners' sugar **or** whipped cream, for garnish

Preheat oven to 325° F (165° C). Grease and flour a 9- by 13-inch (23- by 33-cm) pan.

Combine the ingredients in order, 1 at a time, mixing well after each addition. Pour into the pan. Bake about 40 minutes, or until a toothpick inserted comes out clean.

Serve with confectioners' sugar or whipped cream. For best results, bake one day before serving.

Serves 8 to 10.

Judith M. Davenport

Chocolate Mousse Pie

Crust:
¾ cup (180 mL/99 g) all-purpose flour

6 tablespoons (90 mL/86 g) unsalted butter

½ cup (120 mL/68 g) minced almonds

3 tablespoons (45 mL/33 g) brown sugar

2 teaspoons (10 mL/4.8 g) cocoa

Filling:
6 ounces (170 g) semisweet chocolate chips

4 eggs, separated

3⅓ tablespoons (50 mL) Kahlúa **or** other coffee liqueur

1 teaspoon (5 mL/1.5 g) instant coffee

½ cup (120 mL/115 g) granulated sugar

A pinch of salt

½ cup (120 mL) heavy cream, whipped

Preheat oven to 375° F (190° C). Grease an 8-inch (20 cm) quiche pan or piepan with a nonstick spray.

Crust:
Combine all the ingredients. Mix until crumbly. Press firmly into the pan. Bake for 10 minutes. Cool.

Filling:
In the top of a double boiler, melt the chocolate chips. Cool for a few seconds, stirring. Add the egg yolks, one at a time, beating with a wooden spoon after each addition. Add 3 tablespoons (45 mL) of the liqueur and the instant coffee.

Beat the egg whites with the granulated sugar and salt until stiff. Stir a small amount of the egg whites into the chocolate. Fold in the remaining egg whites. Pour into the cooled shell, and refrigerate for at least 1 hour.

Serve with whipped cream flavored with the remaining liqueur.

Serves 6 to 8.

Mrs. Liza M. Gossett

Chocolate Supreme

3 ounces (85 g) sweet chocolate

1 ounce (28 g) unsweetened chocolate

4 tablespoons (60 mL/ 57 g) sugar

4 eggs, separated

3½ ounces (99 g) unsalted butter, softened

Vanilla Cream:
  1 pint (480 mL) milk

  4 tablespoons (60 mL/ 55 g) sugar

  1-inch (2.5 cm) vanilla bean

  3 egg yolks, beaten

Melt the chocolates. With a fork, stir in the sugar and egg yolks, one at a time. Stir in the butter. Beat well for 20 minutes.

Beat the egg whites until very stiff. Fold into the chocolate mixture. Pour into an oiled mold, or heap onto a serving dish. Let stand for several hours.

Vanilla Cream:
Simmer the milk, sugar, and vanilla bean for 5 minutes. Remove the bean. Stir the egg yolks gradually into the milk. Place in the top of a double boiler. Cook over hot water until thick, stirring constantly. Serve with the chocolate.

Serves 6.

Mrs. Robert Wardrop II

Crème Caramel

1½ cups (360 mL/340 g) sugar

2 to 3 tablespoons (30 to 45 mL) water

2 cups (480 mL) whole milk **or** evaporated whole milk

4 eggs **or** 2 eggs and 4 egg yolks

1½ teaspoons (8 mL) vanilla

Preheat oven to 350° F (175° C).

In a small saucepan, combine 1 cup (240 mL/ 225 g) of the sugar with just enough water to moisten. Cover, and cook over moderate heat, without stirring, until the syrup turns light brown or honey-colored. Pour the syrup quickly into 6 custard cups or a 6-cup (1.44 L) mold, tipping to coat the sides. Set aside.

Scald the milk.

In a large mixing bowl, beat the eggs, and lightly stir in the remaining sugar. Add the milk slowly, stirring constantly. Add the vanilla. Blend well. Strain, and pour into the cups or mold.

Place the cups or mold in a shallow baking pan. Fill the pan with boiling water to a depth of 1¼ inches (3.2 cm). Set on the middle rack of the oven. Bake for about 35 minutes for the cups, 45 minutes for the mold, or until the custard center feels firm when pressed. Remove from the water immediately. Cool. Chill in the refrigerator before serving.

Note:
May be prepared a day ahead.

Serves 6.

James J. White

Date and Nut Cheesecake

Crust:

1½ cups (360 mL/110 g) (20 graham crackers) graham cracker crumbs

¼ cup (60 mL/57 g) sugar

4 tablespoons (60 mL/ 57 g) unsalted butter

¼ cup (60 mL/29 g) chopped walnuts

½ teaspoon (2.5 mL/ 1.4 g) cinnamon

Filling:

3 8-ounce (225 g) packages cream cheese, softened

1 cup (240 mL/225 g) sugar

4 eggs

½ teaspoon (2.5 mL) vanilla

½ cup (120 mL/58 g) chopped walnuts

½ cup (120 mL/130 g) chopped dates

Topping:

1 pint (480 mL/505 g) sour cream

2 tablespoons (30 mL/ 28 g) sugar

½ teaspoon (2.5 mL) vanilla

Preheat oven to 375° F (190° C). Grease a 9-inch (23 cm) springform pan.

Crust:
Combine all the ingredients. Pour into the pan. Press against the bottom and sides.

Filling:
Combine all the ingredients. Mix well. Pour into the crust. Bake for 1 hour. Cool in the oven with the door open.

Topping:
Combine all the ingredients. Pour on top of the cooled cake. Bake at 475° F (245° C) for 5 minutes.

Serves 12.

Carl D. Lobell

Forgotten Cookies

2 egg whites

½ cup (120 mL/115 g) sugar

1 teaspoon (5 mL) vanilla

1 cup (240 mL/115 g) fine-chopped walnuts **or** pecans

6 ounces (170 g) chocolate chips **or** 1 cup (240 mL/ 160 g) raisins or sliced dates

Preheat the oven to 400° F (205° C). Grease a baking sheet.

Beat the egg whites until stiff. Add the sugar, vanilla, nuts, and chocolate chips or raisins or dates. Drop 1 teaspoonful (5 mL) of dough at a time, 1 inch (2.5 cm) apart on the baking sheet. Place in the oven, and immediately reduce the heat to 275° F (135° C). Bake for 10 minutes; turn the heat off.

Leave the cookies in the oven for 4 to 5 hours or overnight. Do not open the oven door.

Makes 36 to 40.

Bella Heppenheimer

Austrian Fruit Kuchen with Vanilla Cream

2 cups (480 mL/265 g) all-purpose flour, sifted

1 to 1¼ cups (240 mL/ 225 g to 300 mL/285 g) sugar

10 tablespoons (150 mL/ 145 g) unsalted butter

1 teaspoon (5 mL/1.3 g) lemon rind, grated

2 egg yolks

1 to 2 tablespoons (15 to 30 mL) water

7 or 8 apples, peeled and cored

A dash of cinnamon

½ teaspoon (2.5 mL/1.2 g) nutmeg (optional)

¼ cup (60 mL) heavy cream

2 teaspoons (10 mL) vanilla

1 egg

Sauce:
   ¼ cup (60 mL) heavy cream

   1 egg

   1 teaspoon (5 mL) vanilla

Preheat oven to 375° F (190° C).

In a food processor, process the flour, ½ to ¾ cup (120 mL/115 g to 180 mL/170 g) of the sugar, and the butter until they have the consistency of cornmeal. Add the lemon rind and egg yolks. Process until the mixture forms a ball. If the dough is too stiff, add water by the tablespoon (15 mL). Chill for 1 hour. Roll out the dough to fit a 9-inch (23 cm) springform or fluted tart pan.

In the processor, slice the apples. Arrange the slices on the pastry in an overlapping pattern from the outside to the center. Combine the cinnamon, the remaining sugar, and nutmeg, if desired. Sprinkle over the apples. Beat together the cream, vanilla, and egg. Pour over the tart. Bake for 40 minutes, or until lightly browned.

Cool. Remove sides of pan.

Sauce:
In the top of a double boiler, heat the cream. Add the egg. Cook, stirring, until the mixture coats a spoon. Add the vanilla. Remove from the heat, and cool.

To serve:
Spoon the sauce over the kuchen.

Serves 6 or more.

Evie Bippart

Fresh Fruit Sorbet

1½ cups (360 mL/175 g) seasonal fresh fruits (blueberries, raspberries, kiwis, grapefruits, pineapples, and others)

¾ cup (180 mL/170 g) sugar

½ cup (120 mL) lemon juice

½ cup (120 mL) orange **or** grapefruit juice

In a processor or blender, combine 1 cup (240 mL/ 115 g) of the whole fruit, sugar, and juices. Purée. Strain the fruit into an ice cream maker. Freeze according to directions, without straining, if desired.

Scoop the sorbet into individual serving dishes. Garnish with the remaining whole fruit.

Serves 4.

Linda Youtzy

265

Ginger Ice Cream

2 inches (5 cm) fresh
ginger root, peeled

4 tablespoons (60 mL/
57 g) sugar

1 quart (960 mL/505 g)
vanilla ice cream,
preferably homemade,
softened

In a food processor,
combine the ginger with
the sugar until grated fine.
Fold into softened ice
cream, or if making
homemade, add to the ice
cream maker at the end of
the process.

Note:
If a less spicy taste is
preferred, use less of the
ginger-sugar mixture.

Makes 1 quart
(960 milliliters/505 grams).

The Cookbook Committee

Gin Sorbet

1 16-ounce (455 g) can
grapefruit sections in syrup

½ cup (120 mL/115 g)
sugar

½ to ¾ cup (120 to
180 mL) gin

Drain the grapefruit,
reserving the syrup. Add
water to the syrup to
make 1½ cups (360 mL)
liquid. In a saucepan,
combine the liquid and
sugar. Cook for about 5
minutes, or until syrupy.
Cool.

In a blender, blend the
grapefruit, gin, and syrup
well. Pour into ice
cube trays or a plastic
container, and freeze for
1 hour. Remove from the
freezer. Stir thoroughly.
Cover, and return to the
freezer to solidify (sorbet
never becomes completely
solid). Keep in the freezer
until ready to use (it will
keep indefinitely). Stir
before serving.

Note:
Serve between courses to
clear the palate or with
cookies as a dessert.

Makes about 3 cups
(720 milliliters/600 grams).

Serves 6 to 8.

Larry Adams

Grand Marnier Parfait

¾ cup (180 mL) cold water

2½ cups (600 mL/570 g)
sugar

14 egg yolks*

6 tablespoons (90 mL)
Grand Marnier

Juice and grated rind of
2 oranges

3 cups (720 mL) heavy
cream

2 oranges, peeled and
sectioned

Cook the water and sugar
together for 5 minutes.
Cool.

In a large saucepan, beat
the egg yolks until thick
and lemon-colored. Place
the saucepan over very
low heat. Add 2 cups
(480 mL) of the cooled
syrup, beating constantly
until thick and smooth.
Remove from the heat.
Set the saucepan in a
bowl of ice water. Beat
until the mixture is cold.

*Egg whites may be frozen
in portions for later use.

Stir in the Grand Marnier, orange rind, and orange juice.

Whip 2 cups (480 mL) of the cream, and fold into the egg yolk mixture. Pour into a 3-quart (2.88 L) mold. Cover with foil. Freeze for at least 6 hours, or until solid.

Just before serving, whip the remaining cream. Unmold the parfait onto a platter. Decorate it with orange sections and swirls of whipped cream.

Serves 12.

Mrs. Rolf K. Bungeroth

Hazelnut Cookies

4 egg whites, at room temperature

¼ teaspoon (1.3 mL/0.5 g) cream of tartar

1 cup (240 mL/225 g) granulated sugar

2½ cups (600 mL/415 g) ground hazelnuts with skin

1 tablespoon (15 mL/7 g) fine bread crumbs

Filling:

4 ounces (115 g) semisweet chocolate

2 tablespoons (30 mL) strong coffee

2 tablespoons (30 mL) cognac

4 tablespoons (60 mL/ 57 g) unsalted butter

1 cup (240 mL/115 g) confectioners' sugar

2 egg yolks

Preheat oven to 325° F (165° C). Lightly grease and flour 2 large baking sheets. Line with wax paper.

In a large bowl, beat the egg whites until frothy. Add the cream of tartar. Add the granulated sugar gradually, beating constantly. Fold in the hazelnuts and bread crumbs. Form into ½-inch (1.3 cm) balls. Place on the baking sheets. Bake for 15 to 18 minutes, depending on size. Do not overbake.

Filling:
In the top of a double boiler, melt the chocolate and coffee. Add the cognac. In a bowl, cream the butter. Add the confectioners' sugar and egg yolks. Fold in the melted chocolate. Mix well.

When the cookies are cool, spread a generous amount of filling on one cookie, and cover with a second.

Note:
This recipe is from the donor's Swiss great-grandmother. The cookies are excellent after luncheon, for afternoon tea, or with coffee after dinner.

Makes 7½ dozen.

Mrs. Rolf K. Bungeroth

Honey Mousse

Mousse:

¾ cup (180 mL/ 170 g) honey

6 egg yolks, lightly beaten

2 cups (480 mL) heavy cream

Fruit Purée:

2 pints (960 mL/460 g) strawberries **or** raspberries

A pinch of salt

2 tablespoons (30 mL) kirsch

or

Unsweetened chocolate curls, for garnish

Mousse:
In the top of a double boiler, combine the honey and eggs. Cook for about 5 minutes, or until the mixture coats a spoon. Place the pan in a bowl of cracked ice, and stir until cool.

Whip the cream until peaks form. Fold into the honey mixture. Spoon the mousse into a 2-quart (1.92 L) container, or to avoid unmolding, freeze in a serving bowl. Freeze for 3 to 4 hours.

Fruit Purée:
Purée the fruit. Stir in the salt and kirsch. Cover, and chill.

To serve:
Top the mousse with the fruit purée or unsweetened chocolate curls.

Serves 8 to 12.

Sybil P. Veeder

Ruth Washburn's Lace Cookies

½ cup (120 mL/115 g) unsalted butter

½ cup (120 mL/115 g) granulated sugar

½ cup (120 mL/88 g) brown sugar

1 egg

½ cup (120 mL/66 g) all-purpose flour

½ teaspoon (2.5 mL/2.2 g) baking soda

A pinch of salt

1 cup (240 mL/78 g) rolled oats

Preheat oven to 325° F (165° C). Grease 2 baking sheets.

Mix together the butter, sugars, and egg. Combine the flour, baking soda, and salt. Add the flour mixture to the butter mixture. Add the rolled oats, and mix.

Drop by half teaspoonfuls onto baking sheets. Bake until lightly browned. Allow to cool slightly and harden. With a thin spatula, remove while still warm. Cookies will be very thin and lacelike.

Makes 4 dozen.

American, Portsmouth, New Hampshire, 18th century
Tea Table, c. 1765-80
Mahogany and pine
28⅝ × 36 × 22⅜ in.
(72.7 × 91.4 × 56.8 cm.)
Museum Purchase: Richard King Mellon Foundation, 1972

Frozen Lemon Cream

1¾ cups (420 mL/195 g) crushed vanilla wafers

1½ cups (360 mL/340 g) sugar

9 tablespoons (135 mL) (3 lemons) lemon juice

3 cups (720 mL) heavy cream

6 eggs, separated

¼ teaspoon (1.3 mL/1.5 g) salt

The day before, line the bottom of an ungreased 9-inch (23 cm) pan with 1 cup (240 mL/110 g) of the wafer crumbs.

In a large mixing bowl, dissolve the sugar in the lemon juice. Stir thoroughly. Whip the cream, and set aside. Beat the egg yolks lightly with the salt. Add them to the lemon mixture, and beat until thick and creamy. Fold in the whipped cream.

Beat the egg whites until stiff, and fold them into the lemon-cream mixture. Pour into the pan. Top with the remaining crumbs. Wrap and freeze overnight.

On the morning of the serving day, unmold onto a platter, and place in the freezer. Transfer it to the refrigerator 2½ to 3 hours before serving.

Note:
Serve by itself, or top with strawberry or Melba sauce.

Serves 10 to 12.

Mrs. William P. Moyles

Lemon Custard Tart

1 recipe of Pâte Sucrée (Sweet Pastry Dough) (see next page)

4 large eggs

1½ cups (360 mL/340 g) sugar

Zest of ½ large orange

½ cup (120 mL) fresh lemon juice

½ cup (120 mL) fresh orange juice

¼ cup (60 mL) heavy cream

1½ tablespoons (23 mL/ 11 g) confectioners' sugar

1 lemon, cut into segments, rind and membrane removed

Preheat oven to 375° F (190° C). Grease an 11-inch (28 cm) quiche pan.

Line the pan with the pastry. Prick the pastry, and bake for 12 minutes.

Beat together the eggs, sugar, and orange zest until they are light and fluffy. Add the juices and cream. Pour into the partially baked crust. Bake for 10 minutes. Reduce the heat to 350° F (175° C). Bake for about 15 minutes, or until the filling is browned and moves slightly when the pan is shaken. Remove from the oven.

Preheat broiler. Set the rack 4 inches (10 cm) from the heat.

Sprinkle the confectioners' sugar through a sieve over the tart. Arrange the lemon segments in a circle on the tart. Place under the broiler, rotating every few seconds to brown evenly. Remove to a wire rack, and cool. Serve at room temperature.

Serves 8 to 10.

Phyllis Beeson Susen

Pâte Sucrée
(Sweet Pastry Dough):

1½ cups (360 mL/200 g) all-purpose flour

9 tablespoons (135 mL/ 130 g) frozen unsalted butter, cut into 6 pieces

3 tablespoons (45 mL/ 43 g) sugar

1½ egg yolks

1½ tablespoons (23 mL) cold water

¼ teaspoon (1.3 mL/1.5 g) salt

In a food processor with a metal blade, process all the ingredients, turning the switch on and off, for 5 seconds. Continue to process until the dough almost forms a ball. Remove the dough, and wrap it in wax paper. Refrigerate for 2 hours.

Makes enough dough for one 11-inch (28 cm) pastry shell.

The Cookbook Committee

Macaroon Cake with Oranges

1 11-ounce (310 g) can mandarin oranges with syrup

⅓ cup (80 mL) Grand Marnier or to taste

6 eggs, separated, at room temperature

¾ cup (180 mL) vegetable oil

4 ounces (115 g) margarine, at room temperature

3 cups (720 mL/680 g) sugar

1 teaspoon (5 mL) almond extract

1 teaspoon (5 mL) vanilla

3 cups (720 mL/290 g) cake flour, sifted

1 cup (240 mL) milk

1 7-ounce (200 g) package grated coconut

Combine the mandarin oranges, syrup, and Grand Marnier. Cover, and let rest, stirring occasionally.

Preheat oven to 300° F (150° C). Grease and flour a 10-inch (25 cm) tube pan.

Beat the egg yolks, oil, and margarine at high speed. Gradually add the sugar, and continue beating until light and fluffy. Add the extracts, and blend.

Add the flour slowly, one-fourth at a time, alternately with the milk, beginning and ending with the flour. Mix in the coconut.

In a separate bowl, beat the egg whites until stiff but not dry. Fold into the cake batter. Turn the batter into the prepared pan, and bake for about 2 hours, or until a cake tester comes out clean. Cool the cake on a rack for 20 to 30 minutes. Remove from the pan, and cool completely.

Serve the cake with the mandarin orange topping.

Serves 12 to 16.

Mrs. Steven N. Hutchinson

Mango Sorbet with Lime

2 cups (480 mL) water

1 cup (240 mL/225 g) sugar

6 mangoes

Juice of 2 lemons

2 limes, cut into wedges, for garnish

In a heavy pot, bring to a boil the water and sugar, stirring until the sugar dissolves.

Peel and halve the mangoes, and coat them with the lemon juice to prevent discoloration. Remove the pits, and add them to the syrup. Cook for 10 minutes. Remove the pits, and chill the syrup.

In a food processor with the metal blade, process the mango flesh to a fine purée. Freeze. Remove the purée from the freezer before it is totally firm. Add 1 cup (240 mL) of the chilled syrup, and process until fluffy. Spoon into 6 cups, and garnish with the lime wedges.

Serves 6.

Dana Kline

Molotov Meringue

Custard Sauce:

2 cups (480 mL) milk

3 egg yolks

¼ cup (60 mL/57 g) sugar

⅛ teaspoon (0.6 mL/ 0.8 g) salt

1 teaspoon (5 mL) vanilla

12 egg whites

1 teaspoon (5 mL/2.2 g) cream of tartar

A pinch of salt

1¼ cups (300 mL/285 g) sugar

Custard Sauce:
In the top of a double boiler, scald the milk over hot water. Beat the egg yolks slightly, and add the sugar and salt. Add the mixture to the scalded milk, and cook, stirring constantly, until the custard begins to thicken. Cool, add the vanilla, and chill.

Preheat oven to 375° F (190° C).

In a large bowl, beat the egg whites until almost stiff. Add the cream of tartar and salt. Continue beating for about 5 minutes, or until the whites are very stiff.

In a skillet, slowly melt ¾ cup (180 mL/170 g) of the sugar until it forms a brown syrup. Use very low heat. Fold the hot syrup into the egg whites. Blend until the mixture turns uniformly brown. Pour the mixture into an ungreased 10-cup (2.4 L) heavy, decorative ring mold. Bake for 20 minutes. Mixture should be golden brown and should reach 2 to 3 inches (5 to 8 cm) above the edge of the mold. Turn the heat off, and leave the meringue in the oven for 15 minutes with the door closed.

Remove the meringue from the oven. Let it rest for approximately 5 minutes. Invert on a cake rack. The meringue mixture will fall to about the height of the mold.

To serve:
Place the meringue on a rimmed dish. Pour the chilled custard on top and into the center. Melt the remaining sugar, as directed above. Pour the hot syrup on the custard to give a crystallized effect.

Serves 8 to 10.

Mrs. Simoes-Ferreira

Nut Bar Wafers

2 cups (480 mL/265 g) all-purpose flour

½ cup (120 mL/115 g) granulated sugar

A pinch of salt

½ pound (225 g) unsalted butter

Filling:
  ½ cup (120 mL/66 g) shelled, skinned pistachios

  1 cup (240 mL/305 g) almond paste

  5 to 8 tablespoons (75 mL to 120 mL) light corn syrup

  1½ tablespoons (23 mL) amaretto

  2 teaspoons (10 mL) lemon juice

  ½ teaspoon (2.5 mL/ 0.7 g) lemon rind

Topping:
  3 large eggs

  1½ cups (360 mL/265 g) brown sugar

  1 teaspoon (5 mL) vanilla

  1½ cups (360 mL/205 g) chopped almonds **or** pistachios

¾ cup (180 mL/68 g) flaked coconut

4½ tablespoons (68 mL/ 37 g) all-purpose flour

¾ teaspoon (3.8 mL/ 2.5 g) baking powder

A pinch of salt

Preheat oven to 350° F (175° C).

With a pastry blender or knives, cut the flour, granulated sugar, and salt into the butter until the mixture becomes coarse crumbs. Knead lightly. Pat the dough into a 15½- by 10-inch (39 by 25 cm) greased jelly roll pan. Bake for about 15 minutes, or until lightly browned. Remove from the oven, and cool on a rack for 15 minutes.

Filling:
Pulverize the pistachios. Cut the almond paste into small pieces. Combine 5 tablespoons (75 mL) of the corn syrup with the remaining ingredients. Knead to a smooth paste, adding syrup if needed.

Spread the filling over the crust.

Topping:
Beat the eggs, brown sugar, and vanilla until light and fluffy. Add the nuts and coconut, and fold in the flour, baking powder, and salt.

Spread over the filling.

Bake for 35 to 45 minutes, or until browned. Cool on a rack. Cut into bars while still warm.

Note:
Strained peach, plum, or raspberry preserves or jelly may be used in place of the almond-pistachio filling.

Makes 2½ to 4 dozen.

Maria Soloknovic

Caramelized Oranges with Grand Marnier

12 large oranges

1 pound (455 g) sugar

2¼ cups (540 mL) white wine

4 to 6 ounces (120 to 180 mL) Grand Marnier

The day before, cut very thin slices from the ends of the oranges so the oranges will stand upright. Carefully remove the skin in long strips, and set aside; a zesting knife is helpful, if available. Be sure all the white membrane is removed from both the skin and the oranges. The result should be whole oranges with all flesh exposed and strips of orange zest.

In a serving bowl, arrange the oranges. Pour the sugar into a thick-bottomed, medium-size saucepan. Place over low heat, and with a wooden spoon, stir constantly until the sugar has completely dissolved and become amber-colored.

Quickly and carefully pour the wine into the sugar; the sugar may pop or spurt. Add the orange zest. Boil until the sugar is completely dissolved. Remove from the heat. Add the Grand Marnier. Pour over the oranges. Cool overnight at room temperature. Then place in the refrigerator until 1 hour before serving.

Serves 12.

Vincent Cimatti
The Mill, Bath, England

Orange Flambée

4 large oranges, peeled, sectioned, and cut into bite-size pieces

2 tablespoons (30 mL/ 29 g) unsalted butter

⅓ cup (80 mL/76 g) sugar

2 tablespoons (30 mL/ 34 g) frozen orange juice concentrate

2 tablespoons (30 mL) Grand Marnier **or** other orange liqueur

Ice cream

Chopped walnuts or pecans

In a small skillet, heat the orange sections gently. In a small saucepan, mix the butter, sugar, and orange juice. Bring to a boil. Simmer for 5 minutes. Pour the syrup over the hot orange sections.

In a small saucepan, heat the liqueur, and pour it over the oranges. Ignite it at the table. Serve over ice cream. Top with nuts.

Note:
Orange flambée may be prepared ahead of time. After the syrup has been poured over the orange sections, cool, then refrigerate the mixture. When ready to serve, reheat the mixture before proceeding to flambée.

Serves 8.

Ann Soske

Baked Pears au Gratin

2 pounds (905 g) ripe Anjou pears, peeled, cored, and quartered

5 tablespoons (75 mL/ 71 g) unsalted butter

½ cup (120 mL) dry vermouth

¼ cup (60 mL/81 g) apricot preserves

1 cup (240 mL/110 g) fine-crumbled macaroons

Whipped cream, slightly sweetened

Preheat oven to 400° F (205° C).

Grease an 8-inch-square (20 cm) baking dish with 2 tablespoons (30 mL/29 g) of the butter, and arrange the pears, overlapping each piece.

Thoroughly combine the vermouth and preserves, and pour over the pears. Top with the macaroon crumbs, and dot with the remaining butter. Bake for 25 minutes. Serve hot or cold with whipped cream.

Serves 4 to 6.

R. Jackson Seay

Poires Ninette

6 large or 8 small, firm pears

About 1½ cups (360 mL/ 340 g) sugar

4 tablespoons (60 mL/ 57 g) unsalted butter

1 cup (240 mL) heavy cream

Whipped cream (optional)

Preheat oven to 450° F (230° C).

Peel, quarter, and core the pears. In a greased baking dish, place the pears very close together in one layer. Sprinkle them liberally with the sugar. Dot them with the butter.

Bake for about 10 to 15 minutes, or until the sugar caramelizes. Watch closely. Remove from the oven, and spoon the cream on top.

Serve warm or cold. Top with whipped cream, if desired.

Serves 4 to 6.

Mrs. O. Harry Gruner III

Pear Tart with Crème Patissière

Crème Patissière:
½ cup (120 mL/115 g) sugar

3 egg yolks

⅓ cup (80 mL/44 g) all-purpose flour

1 cup (240 mL) milk

½ tablespoon (8 mL/7 g) unsalted butter

½ tablespoon (8 mL) Grand Marnier **or** other orange liqueur

Pastry Tart:
¾ pound (340 g) homemade Puff Pastry (see page 147)

1 tablespoon (15 mL/ 10 g) Fruit-Fresh

¼ cup (60 mL) cold water

6 to 10 pears

3 tablespoons (45 mL/ 43 g) unsalted butter, cut into bits

4 tablespoons (60 mL/ 57 g) sugar

2 tablespoons (30 mL/ 41 g) marmalade **or** apricot jam, dissolved in 1 tablespoon (15 mL) water

Crème Patissière:
In a mixer bowl, beat together the sugar, egg yolks, and flour.

In a heavy saucepan, bring the milk to a boil, and add it slowly in a thin stream to the egg yolk mixture. Pour the mixture into a heavy saucepan, and cook it over medium heat, stirring constantly with a wooden spoon, until it begins to thicken. Bring the mixture to a boil, stirring constantly, until it is thick and slightly lumpy. Remove from the heat, add the butter, and stir. Add the Grand Marnier. Chill until ready to use.

Pastry Tart:
Roll the pastry ⅛ inch (0.3 cm) thick, and prick all over with a fork. Carefully press the pastry into an 11-inch (28 cm) greased tart pan with a removable bottom. Do not stretch the dough. Chill thoroughly.

Preheat oven to 450° F (230° C).

In a stainless steel or glass container, mix the Fruit-Fresh and the water. Peel the pears. Place them in the Fruit-Fresh mixture. Add enough water to cover.

Core and quarter the pears. Slice them into long crescents, approximately ¼ inch (0.6 cm) thick. Return them to the Fruit-Fresh mixture until ready to assemble the tart.

Remove the chilled pastry from the refrigerator. Spread the crème patissière ¼ inch (0.6 cm) thick over the pastry. Place the pears in overlapping concentric circles, working from the outside edge to the center. Dot with the butter, and sprinkle with the sugar.

Place in the oven immediately (puff pastry should be cold when placed in the oven). Bake for about 1 hour, or until the pastry is crisp and golden and pears are slightly browned. If the tart is browning too quickly, reduce the heat to 350° F (175° C) for the last ½ hour.

While the tart is baking, make a glaze by heating the dissolved jam. Brush the baked tart with the glaze.

Serves 8.

Dana Kline

Southern Comfort Pecan Pie

4 eggs

½ cup (120 mL) light corn syrup

1 cup (240 mL/175 g) brown sugar

2 tablespoons (30 mL/ 29 g) melted unsalted butter

2 tablespoons (30 mL) bourbon

1 cup (240 mL/105 g) pecan halves

1 unbaked 9-inch (23 cm) pie shell (see Pâte Brisée, page 98)

Whipped cream (optional)

Preheat oven to 375° F (190° C).

Beat the eggs until light. Slowly beat in the syrup, sugar, butter, and bourbon. Stir in the pecans. Pour into the pie shell, and bake for 40 minutes.

Serve warm or cold, with whipped cream, if desired.

Serves 6 to 8.

Mimi Cadman

Pistachio Honey Cream with Raspberries

¼ pound (115 g) pistachio nuts in the shell*

6 egg yolks

⅓ cup (80 mL/76 g) honey

A dash of salt

1 cup (240 mL) milk, scalded

1 cup (240 mL) cream, scalded

2 drops green vegetable coloring (optional)

1 quart (960 mL/460 g) red raspberries **or** other berries in season

Preheat oven to 325° F (165° C).

Shell the pistachios, and blanch in boiling water for 30 seconds. Drain. Rub off the skins with a towel. Spread in a piepan, and dry in the oven for 10 minutes. Cool. Chop fine.

In a mixing bowl, combine the egg yolks, honey, and salt. Beat until thick and lemon-colored. Transfer the mixture to a double boiler. Add the scalded milk and cream in a steady stream, beating constantly. Cook, stirring, over simmering (not boiling) water for about 8 minutes, or until the mixture thickens and coats a metal spoon. Watch carefully. Add coloring, if desired.

Strain into a metal bowl. Cool, stirring several times. Chill. Stir in the pistachios. Pour into chilled glass serving dishes or wineglasses. Top with the berries.

Serves 6.

Eva Lu Damianos

*Pistachios should equal ⅓ cup (80 mL/44 g) shelled nuts.

Pots de Crème Javanais

½ cup (120 mL/115 g) sugar

2 tablespoons (30 mL) water

1⅔ cups (400 mL) light cream, heated

1 ounce (28 g) semisweet chocolate, cut into bits

2 tablespoons (30 mL/9 g) instant espresso, dissolved in ¼ cup (60 mL) hot water

1 teaspoon (5 mL) vanilla

5 egg yolks

1 egg

Sweetened whipped cream, flavored with vanilla **or** rum

Preheat oven to 325° F (165° C).

In a saucepan, dissolve ¼ cup (60 mL/57 g) of the sugar in 2 tablespoons (30 mL) of water over low heat. When it is dissolved, increase the heat to medium-high, and cook until the sugar is light caramel. Add the hot cream, the remaining sugar, chocolate, espresso, and vanilla. Bring the mixture to a boil, stirring until mixed.

In a bowl, lightly whisk together the egg yolks and whole egg. Pour in a stream into the cream mixture. Skim off the froth. Pour the custard mixture into 6 pots de crème or ramekins. Skim off any remaining froth. Cover with lids or foil, and set in a baking pan. Add hot water to the pan to reach two-thirds up the sides of the pots.

Bake for 25 minutes. Remove from the water. Cool, uncovered. Cover again, and chill for 4 hours before serving. Garnish with whipped cream.

Serves 6.

Mrs. Anthony J. A. Bryan

Old-Fashioned Pound Cake

1 cup (240 mL/230 g) vegetable shortening

¼ pound (115 g) unsalted margarine **or** butter

3 cups (720 mL/680 g) sugar

1½ teaspoons (8 mL) vanilla **or** other flavoring such as lemon extract

3 cups (720 mL/395 g) all-purpose flour

A pinch of salt

1 teaspoon (5 mL/3.4 g) baking powder

6 eggs

1 cup (240 mL) milk

Preheat oven to 300° to 325° F (150° to 165° C). Grease a 10-inch (25 cm) tube pan or 2 9-by-5-by-2½-inch (23-by-13-by-6-cm) bread pans.

Cream the shortening and margarine or butter. Add the sugar and vanilla, and mix well.

Sift together twice the flour, salt, and baking powder.

Add the eggs, one at a time, to the shortening mixture, beating well with each addition.

Combine the milk and egg mixtures. Fold in the flour mixture. Bake for 1 to 1½ hours, or until a straw or toothpick comes out dry.

Note:
All ingredients must be at room temperature.

Serves 12 to 16.

Mrs. Dorothy R. Hughes

Praline Cookies

4 tablespoons (60 mL/ 57 g) unsalted butter **or** margarine

1¼ cups (300 mL/220 g) light brown sugar, packed firm

⅓ cup (80 mL/44 g) all-purpose flour

1 teaspoon (5 mL) maple extract

¼ teaspoon (1.3 mL/ 1.5 g) salt

1 egg

6 ounces (170 g) chopped pecans

Preheat oven to 350° F (175° C). Line a baking sheet with foil.

In a saucepan, melt the butter over low heat. Remove from the heat, and add the brown sugar, flour, maple extract, salt, and egg. Blend well. Stir in the pecans.

Drop the mixture, by tablespoonfuls, 3 inches (8 cm) apart onto the baking sheet. Bake for 12 to 15 minutes. If the cookies are not baked long enough, the foil will be difficult to remove. Slide the foil with the cookies onto a wire rack. Cool completely. Reline the baking sheet with foil, and repeat with the remaining mixture.

Gently peel the foil from the cookies. Store in a tightly covered container.

Makes 2 to 2½ dozen.

Rita P. Coney

Texas Pralines

1 teaspoon (5 mL/4.4 g) baking soda

3 cups (720 mL/680 g) sugar

1 cup (240 mL) buttermilk

3 tablespoons (45 mL) light corn syrup

6 tablespoons (90 mL/ 86 g) unsalted butter

1 teaspoon (5 mL) vanilla

1½ to 2 cups (360 mL/ 155g to 480 mL/205 g) chopped pecans

In a saucepan, mix the baking soda with the sugar. Add the buttermilk and syrup. Cook, stirring constantly, until the mixture is dark brown and registers 236° F (115° C) on a candy thermometer or reaches the hardball stage. Remove from the heat. Add the butter and vanilla. Stir. Place the pan in a bowl of cold water for 3 to 5 minutes, or until the candy begins to thicken.

Remove from the water, and with a wooden spoon, beat until the candy changes color. Add the pecans, and stir quickly. Working fast, with two spoons, drop mounds on wax paper. The candy may also be poured into a greased pan and cut when cool. When the pralines cool, store in a tightly covered container.

Note:
Wait a day before serving. These keep well.

Makes 12 large patties.

Kathleen E. Lee

277

Praline Pumpkin Pie

Praline Layer:
3 tablespoons (45 mL/ 43 g) unsalted butter

⅓ cup (80 mL/59 g) brown sugar, packed firm

⅓ cup (80 mL/34 g) chopped pecans

1 9-inch (23 cm) unbaked pie shell (see Pâte Brisée, page 98)

Custard Layer:
1 cup (240 mL) evaporated milk

½ cup (120 mL) water

3 eggs, lightly beaten

1½ cups (360 mL/340 g) cooked pumpkin

½ cup (120 mL/115 g) granulated sugar

½ cup (120 mL/88 g) brown sugar, packed firm

2 teaspoons (10 mL/ 6 g) pumpkin pie spice

1 teaspoon (5 mL/6 g) salt

Praline Lace Cones:
¼ cup (60 mL/57 g) unsalted butter, softened

½ cup (120 mL/88 g) brown sugar, packed firm

1 egg

¼ cup (60 mL/26 g) fine-chopped pecans

2 tablespoons (30 mL/ 17 g) all-purpose flour

¼ teaspoon (1.3 mL/ 1.5 g) salt

½ cup (120 mL) heavy cream

Praline Layer:
Preheat oven to 450° F (230° C). Lightly grease a baking sheet.

In a medium-size bowl, cream the butter and brown sugar. Stir in the chopped pecans. Press evenly over the bottom of the pie shell. Bake for 10 minutes. Cool on a wire rack for 10 minutes.

Custard Layer:
Lower the oven to 350° F (175° C). Combine the milk and water. In a large bowl, combine the remaining ingredients. Beat in the milk mixture. Pour into the cooked shell. Bake for 50 minutes. Cool.

Praline Lace Cones:
Lower the oven to 300° F (150° C). Lightly grease a baking sheet.

In a medium bowl, cream the butter and brown sugar. Beat in the egg until fluffy. Stir in the pecans, flour, and salt.

Drop the batter by half teaspoonfuls, about 5 inches (13 cm) apart, on the prepared baking sheet. Spread each into a very thin 2½-inch (6 cm) round. Bake for about 10 minutes, or until golden brown.

Cool on the baking sheet for about 1 minute, or until just firm enough to hold a shape. Cut each in half; then loosen with a spatula. Quickly roll each half into a tiny cone shape. Place on a wire rack to cool and crisp. If the cookies become too brittle to shape, return them to the oven for 30 seconds to soften. For variety, some cookies may be left flat.

Just before serving, whip the cream, and spread it over the pie. Decorate the top with praline lace cones arranged in a pinwheel pattern.

Serves 8.

Susan C. Johnson

Rum Balls

12 ounces (340 g) bittersweet chocolate

3 tablespoons (45 mL/ 43 g) unsalted butter

¼ cup (60 mL) dark rum

¼ cup (60 mL/29 g) confectioners' sugar

1½ cups (360 mL/110 g) wheat germ

Ground almonds **or** coconut flakes

In the top of a double boiler, melt the chocolate with the butter. Add the rum and confectioners' sugar. Mix until smooth. Stir in the wheat germ. Form the mixture into a ball. While it is still warm, divide into smaller balls, and roll in ground almonds or coconut flakes. Refrigerate.

Makes 2 dozen.

Julia N. Williamson

Seventeen-Year-Old Cookies

6 egg whites

1 pound (455 g) dark brown sugar

1 teaspoon (5 mL) vanilla

2 scant cups (480 mL/ 265 g) all-purpose flour

Salt to taste

1 pound (455 g) shelled pecans

Preheat oven to 350° F (175° C). Cover a baking sheet with wax paper, and lightly oil the paper.

Beat the egg whites until stiff but not dry. Fold in the sugar. Add the vanilla. Combine the flour and salt, and fold into the egg whites. Fold in the pecans. Drop the meringue, by the teaspoonful, 1½ to 2 inches (3.8 cm to 5 cm) apart, onto the baking sheet. Bake for 15 to 20 minutes. Remove from the paper while still hot.

Makes 5 dozen.

Mrs. Robert Wardrop II

Belgian, Brussels, 16th century
The Triumph of Hope, c. 1530
Wool and silk
176 × 216 in.
(447.0 × 548.6 cm.)
Gift of the Hearst Foundation, Inc., 1954

Cold Strawberry Soufflé

3 pints (1.44 L/690 g) fresh strawberries

1½ cups (360 mL/340 g) sugar

3 tablespoons (45 mL/ 30 g) unflavored gelatin

2 tablespoons (30 mL) lemon juice

8 egg whites

¼ teaspoon (1.3 mL/ 1.5 g) salt

1 pint (480 mL) heavy cream

1 tablespoon (15 mL) light corn syrup

¼ cup (60 mL/29 g) fine-chopped walnuts

Whole strawberries, for garnish

Make a collar for a 1½ quart (1.44 L) soufflé dish. Use a 30-inch (76 cm) strip of foil, folded in half lengthwise. Fasten it tightly to the outside of the dish with tape. The collar should extend 3 inches (8 cm) above the rim. Lightly oil the inside of the foil.

In a processor or blender, purée the strawberries, 1 pint (480 mL/230 g) at a time. There will be about 3½ cups (840 mL) of purée.

In a saucepan, combine 1 cup (240 mL/225 g) of the sugar, the gelatin, and 1¾ cups (420 mL) purée. Cook over medium heat, stirring constantly, until the gelatin is completely dissolved. Cool. Add the lemon juice and the remaining purée. Chill over ice, stirring, until the mixture is syrupy.

In a large bowl, beat the egg whites with the salt until foamy. Continue to beat, gradually adding the remaining sugar. Beat until the egg whites hold soft peaks.

Whip the cream. With a rubber spatula, carefully fold the whipped cream and chilled purée into the egg whites. Pour into the soufflé dish. Refrigerate for at least 2 hours, or until set.

To serve:
Carefully remove foil. Delicately brush the exposed soufflé with the corn syrup. Gently pat on the chopped nuts. As an optional garnish, slice strawberries, and arrange in a floral pattern on top.

Serves 10 to 12.

Mrs. Robert Wardrop II

White Chocolate Mousse

¼ cup (60 mL/57 g) sugar

⅓ cup (80 mL) water

1½ cups (360 mL) heavy cream

6 ounces (170 g) white chocolate, broken into small pieces

3 tablespoons (45 mL) amaretto **or** Triple Sec

3 eggs, separated

½ cup (120 mL/68 g) almonds, slivered and toasted

Dark chocolate **or** toasted almonds, for garnish

In a small saucepan, combine the sugar and water. Boil for 3 minutes.

In a food processor, whip the cream for about 1 minute. Transfer to a large bowl.

Place the chocolate in the processor, and process for 15 to 20 seconds, turning the motor on and off.

With the motor running, gradually add the hot syrup, liqueur, and egg yolks. Add the almonds, and process into coarse pieces. Fold the mixture into the whipped cream.

Beat the egg whites until stiff, and fold into the cream mixture. Spoon into stemmed goblets, and chill thoroughly or freeze. (If the goblets are frozen, remove them from the freezer at least ½ hour before serving.) Garnish with long curls of dark chocolate or toasted almonds.

Serves 6.

Bettie Studer

White Chocolate Mousse with Raspberry Sauce

¼ pound (115 g) sugar cubes

¼ cup (60 mL) water

½ cup (120 mL) (about 4 large eggs) egg whites, at room temperature

12½ ounces (355 g) imported first-quality white chocolate, cut into very fine pieces

2 cups (480 mL) heavy cream, chilled

Raspberry Sauce:
  2 pints (960 mL/460 g) fresh raspberries or 4 10-ounce (285 g) packages frozen raspberries

  2 tablespoons (30 mL) Framboise or kirsch

  1 tablespoon (15 mL/ 14 g) sugar*

  A pinch of salt

6 mint leaves, for garnish

*Do not use sugar with frozen raspberries.

In a saucepan, bring the sugar cubes and water to a boil, stirring or shaking the pan occasionally until the sugar melts. Cook without stirring until the syrup reaches the hardball stage, 255° F (125° C), on a candy thermometer.

Whip the egg whites until soft peaks form. Add the syrup slowly, and beat in the chocolate (the chocolate must be cut into very fine pieces so that it will be partially melted by the hot syrup). Cool to lukewarm.

Whip the cream until stiff, and fold it into the mousse. Chill for at least 4 hours.

Raspberry Sauce:
Purée the raspberries. Stir in the remaining ingredients. Cover, and chill thoroughly.

To serve:
Place some raspberry sauce in 6 chilled dessert plates. Top with mousse, and garnish each with a mint leaf. Pass the remaining sauce.

Note:
The mousse and sauce may be prepared 2 or 3 days ahead and refrigerated until serving time.

Serves 6.

Alexander C. Speyer III

Acknowledgments

The Women's Committee of the Museum of Art, Carnegie Institute, wishes to express special gratitude to these individuals and organizations for their contributions to this cookbook.

Henry Adams
Leon A. Arkus
Matthew J. Bulvony
(photograph, page 110)
Gloria Chantry
John Cheek
Sue B. Eastland
James A. Fisher
Marlin K. Frihart
Michael Garrity
Joan G. Hill
Bette L. Hughes
Phillip M. Johnston
Kabuki Incorporated
J. Edward Kolter
Garth E. Massingill
Edward T. Parrack
Barbara L. Phillips
Phipps Conservatory
Florence Rosner
Martine Sheon
James B. Stevenson
Virginia G. Tenney
The Flower Barn
Edward M. Vasilcik
Lorene Vinski
Ways and Means
David D. Wilson
Martha A. Wood

Cookbook Committee

Mrs. Leon A. Arkus
Mrs. Myles P. Berkman
Mrs. William Boyd, Jr.
Mrs. Dixon R. Brown
Mrs. Clinton L. Childs, Jr.
Mrs. Frederic L. Cook
Mrs. Paul Euwer, Jr.,
  Co-Chairman
Mrs. Danforth P. Fales
Mrs. John T. Galey
Mrs. W. H. Krome
  George
Mrs. John M. Gilmore
Mrs. A. Emerson
  Johnson III
Mrs. James E. Lee
Mrs. Brittan C. MacIsaac
Mrs. David McCargo
Mrs. George R.
  McCullough
Mrs. James A. McGowan
Mrs. Charles P. Orr
Mrs. S. Raymond Rackoff
Mrs. Richard M. Scaife
Mrs. Augustus O.
  Schroeder
Mrs. Arthur M. Scully, Jr.
Mrs. Fred I. Sharp
Mrs. Richard S. Smith
Mrs. Holly W. Sphar, Jr.
Mrs. A. James Starr
Mrs. William N. Steitz
Mrs. William T. Tobin
Mrs. Robert Wardrop II
Mrs. James D. Williams
Mrs. James M. Walton,
  Co-Chairman
Mrs. James A. Fisher,
  Chairman

Testing Committee

Mrs. William C. Bickel
Mrs. Anthony J. A. Bryan
Mrs. Rolf K. Bungeroth
Mrs. Sylvester Damianos
Mrs. Ronald R.
  Davenport
Mrs. Danforth P. Fales
Mrs. James A. Fisher
Mrs. John T. Galey
Mrs. O. Harry Gruner III
William P. Hackney
Mrs. Bayard T. Kiliani
Mrs. J. Craig Kuhn, Jr.
Mrs. John R. Lane
Mrs. W. Duff McCrady
Mrs. George R.
  McCullough
Charles P. Orr
Mrs. William H. Rea
Mrs. Robert O. Read
R. Jackson Seay
Mrs. Fred I. Sharp
Mrs. J. Todd Simonds
Mrs. Holly W. Sphar, Jr.
Mrs. William T. Tobin
Mrs. Peter G. Veeder
Mrs. Paul Euwer, Jr.,
  Chairman
Mrs. Brittan C. MacIsaac,
  Co-Chairman
John Cheek and Dana
  Kline, Advisers
Alexander C. Speyer III,
  Adviser on wines

Index

Cheesecake
  date and nut, 264
  deluxe, 261
  hazelnut, 139

Chestnuts, glazed turnips
and, 231

Chèvre (cheese), 25

Chicken
  Abiquiu, 104–5
  breasts
    rollatini of, 202
    saltimbocca, 198
    suprêmes, with fresh figs
    in gin, 203
    suprêmes, stuffed, 202–3
  Coronation, 199
  curried, 200
  Danica, 200
  ginger, with broccoli, 201
  ivory noodles with, 90
  liver
    pâté, with apple
    slices, 54
    on sautéed toast, 204
  minted, 201
  du Roi René, 131
  salad
    and Belgian endive, 238
    Coronation, 199
    crispy, 236
  tortilla casserole, 204
  wings, teriyaki grilled, 49

Chili
  corn and cheese pie, 187
  red hot, 190

Chilies
  cornbread with cheese
  and, 118

green chili sorbet, 107
  preparation of, 107
  stuffed, 105

Chinese black mushrooms
with kohlrabi, 226

Chinese dinner, 87–93

Chinese spinach soup, 171

Chocolate
  cake
    moist, 262
    roll (Torta da
    Alice), 113
  mousse
    pie, 262
    soufflé, 63
    white, 280-81
  supreme, 263
  truffles, 15

Chowder
  creamy corn, 165
  hunt, 168

Chutney, red pepper, 246

Clarified butter, 20

Coffee-roasted lamb, 145

Cognac dressing, 34

Cookie(s)
  baskets, with lemon
  mousse, 35
  brown sugar supreme, 260
  Forgotten, 264
  hazelnut, 267
  nut bar wafers, 272
  praline, 277
  rum balls, 279
  Ruth Washburn's lace, 268
  Seventeen-year-old, 279

Coriander, 111

Corn
  cheese and chili pie, 187
  chowder, creamy, 165
  and snow peas salad, 241

Corn bread, with cheese and
chilies, 118

Corned beef quiche, 186

Cornish game hens. See Rock
Cornish game hens

Cornmeal bread, 254

Coronation chicken, 199

Country herb soup, 167

Crab, crabmeat
  baked, 57
  mousse, 154
  and tomato soup, 166
  -zucchini tidbits, 155

Cream
  brandied fruit, 260
  caraway, beets in, 221
  crème Anglaise, 148
  crème fraîche, 119
  pistachio honey, with
  raspberries, 275
  pots de crème
    Javanais, 276
    mocha rum, 125
  sauce, 234
    caper, 245
  soups
    carrot, 165
    corn chowder, 165
    eggplant, 166–67
    spinach, chilled, 40
  vanilla, 263, 265

Coriander, 111 — Crème Anglaise, 148
Crème caramel, 263

Crème fraîche, 119

Crème patissière, 274

Crudités, with bleu cheese
mousse, 55

Cucumber ring mold, 236–37

Curried chicken, 200

Curried mussel and broccoli
soup, 80

Curried Russian dressing, 238

Curried tuna salad, 244

Custard
  lemon tart, 269–70
  pumpkin, 278
  sauce, 271

D

Date
  and nut bread, 254
  and nut cheesecake, 264

Desserts, 257–81
  almond float, 93
  Champagne zabaglione, 83
  chocolate supreme, 263
  chocolate truffles, 15
  crème caramel, 263
  mint meringue mushrooms,
  14–15
  pots de crème
    Javanais, 276
    mocha rum, 125
  See also Cakes; Cookies;
  Frozen desserts; Fruit
  desserts; Mousse, dessert;
  Pies and tarts, dessert;
  Soufflé, dessert

G

Game
  Moravian rabbit stew, 206-7
  pheasant stew with wild rice, 62
  Rock Cornish game hen
    with apricot sauce, 207
    marinated, 12-13
  squab with apricots and macadamia nuts, 112-13

Garlic
  and rosemary with lamb, 191
  shrimp in wine and, 214

Gin
  figs in, 203
  sorbet, 266

Ginger
  chicken with broccoli, 201
  ice cream, 266
  sauce, 211

Glaze, apricot, 27

Gorgonzola risotto, 124

Gougère, 34

Grand Marnier
  caramelized oranges with, 272-73
  parfait, 266-67

Greek shrimp, 215

Green beans vinaigrette, 132-33

Green chili sorbet, 107

Green chili sauce, 105

Green pepper. See Peppers, green and red

Grilled steak, 74

Grits soufflé, 187

Guacamole, 104

Gumbo, party seafood, 213

H

Ham
  and cheese salad, 239
  Smithfield, old-fashioned biscuits with, 57

Hard sauce, 99

Hazelnut
  cheesecake, 139
  cookies, 267

Herb(s)
  butter sauce, 219
  dressing, 181
  soup, country, 167
  See also specific names

Herbed Shrimp, 48

Hollandaise sauce, 246

Honey
  applesauce bread, 250
  mousse, 268
  sopaipillas with, 106

Hors d'oeuvres. See Appetizers

Huevos Rancheros, 188

Hush Puppies, 225

I

Ice cream
  brown bread, 69
  ginger, 266

K

Kiwis, 31
  mousseline, 32

Kohlrabi with Chinese black mushrooms, 226

Kung Pao shrimp, 89

L

Lamb
  chops supreme, 191
  coffee-roasted, 145
  with garlic and rosemary, 191
  leg of, steamed, with pesto stuffing, 192
  rack of, 68

Leeks au gratin, 227

Lemon
  cream, frozen, 269
  custard tart, 269-70
  mousse in cookie baskets, 35
  and mustard seed dressing, 237
  popovers, 14

Lentil and sausage soup, 170

Lettuce
  and carrots, braised, 99
  romaine soufflé, 12

Lima bean purée, 68

Lime, mango sorbet with, 270-71

Liver(s)
  chicken, on sautéed toast, 204
  pâté, with apple slices, 54

Lobster

Lobster
  salad, with avocados, mangoes and oranges, 40-41
  spread, 156

M

Macadamia nuts and apricots with squab, 112-13

Macaroon cake with oranges, 270

Mallard duck pie, 98

Maltaise mayonnaise, 246

Mango(s)
  avocados and oranges, lobster salad with, 40-41
  sorbet with lime, 270-71

Maple bourbon sauce, 206

Marinade
  for mushrooms, 49
  for Rock Cornish game hen, 12-13
  for scallops, 212

Marmalade, orange soufflé, 21

Mayonnaise, 40
  Maltaise, 246
  tarragon, 208

Meat. See specific type

Meat bombe, 193

Meat pie, 192-93

Meringue(s)
  mint mushrooms, 14-15
  Molotov, 271
  shells, 75

spaghetti carbonara, 184

summer, 182

See also Noodle(s)

Pastry cheese triangles, 154

Pastry dough

for meat pie, 192, 193

pâte brisée, 98

pâte à chou, 132

puff, 147

sweet (pâte sucrée), 270

Pâté, liver, 54

Pâte brisée, 98

Pâte à chou, 132

Pâte sucrée, 270

Peanuts

Sechuan pork with, 194

spicy, 49

Pear(s)

au gratin, baked, 273

poached, 148

poires Ninette, 274

tart with crème patissière, 274–75

Peas

and salmon with pasta, 180–81

snow peas and cashews, 229

See also Snow peas

Pecan(s)

muffins, 254–55

pie, Southern Comfort, 275

seasoned, 132, 133

spinach pesto, 248

Peixe "Avo Maria" (grilled stuffed fish), 211

Peking duck with Mandarin pancakes, 92–93

Pepper rolls, 255

Peppers, green and red

green pepper steak, 196

red pepper chutney, 246

tomato and onion stew (Friggione), 75

See also Chilies

Persimmon pudding with hard sauce, 99

Pesto, 78, 80, 81, 248

capellini and scallops, 175

spinach pecan, 248

stuffing, 192

Pheasant stew with wild rice, 62

Pickled mushrooms, 49

Piecrust. *See* Pastry dough

Pies and tarts, dessert

Austrian fruit kuchen with vanilla cream, 265

chocolate mousse pie, 262

lemon custard tart, 269–70

nectarine tarts, 27

pear tart with crème patissière, 274–75

praline pumpkin, 278

Southern Comfort pecan, 275

See also Fruit desserts

Pies and tarts, main dish

corn, cheese and chili, 187

corned beef quiche, 186

Mallard duck, 98

meat, 192–93

tomato, 230

Pistachio honey cream with raspberries, 275

Plum soup, 112

Poires Ninette, 274

Popcorn soup, 74

Popovers, lemon, 14

Pork

butterflied with mustard sauce, 138

with peanuts, Sechuan, 194

ribs, barbecued, 195

sausage

frittata, 188

and lentil soup, 170

and wild rice casserole, 195

Port, carrots with, 223

Potato(s)

cake, parsleyed, 20

Dauphine, 132

frybakers, 74

golden casserole, 228

new, 33

with sour cream and caviar, 56

Rosti (Swiss potato cake), 228

Pots de crème

Javanais, 276

mocha rum, 125

Poultry. *See specific type*

Pound cake, old-fashioned, 276

Praline(s)

candy, Texas, 277

cookies, 277

pumpkin pie, 278

Preserves, quince, 248

Pudding

persimmon with hard sauce, 99

tomato, 230–31

Puff pastry, 147

Pumpkin pie, praline, 278

Q

Quiche, corned beef, 186

Quince preserves, 248

R

Rabbit stew, Moravian, 206–7

Raisin Cheddar muffins, 253

Raspberries

with pistachio honey cream, 275

Among Roses, 43

Raspberry sauce, 206, 281

Red pepper. *See* Peppers, green and red

Rice, 182–84

ring, 182–83

risotta Gorgonzola, 124

salad

artichoke, 235

vegetable, 139

scallion, 183

Valencian, 183

wild. *See* Wild rice

Ricotta torte, dilled, 158–59

Risotta Gorgonzola, 124